Career
Intelligence

Career Intelligence

THE 12 NEW RULES FOR WORK AND LIFE SUCCESS

BARBARA MOSES PH.D.

Berrett-Koehler Publishers, Inc.
San Francisco

Berrett-Koehler Publishers, Inc.
450 Sansome Street, Suite 1200
San Francisco, CA 94111-3320
Tel.: (415) 288-0260   Fax: (415) 362-2512   Website: www.bkpub.com

ORDERING INFORMATION

Individual sales. Berrett-Koehler publications are available through most bookstores. They can also be ordered direct from Berrett-Koehler at the address above.

Quantity sales. Special discounts are available on quantity purchases by corporations, associations, and others. For details, contact the "Special Sales Department" at the Berrett-Koehler address above.

Orders for college textbook/course adoption use. Please contact Berrett-Koehler Publishers at the address above.

Orders by U.S. trade bookstores and wholesalers. Please contact Publishers Group West, 1700 Fourth Street, Berkeley, CA 94710; Tel.: (510) 528-1444; Fax: (510) 528-3444.

Printed in the United States of America.

Printed on acid-free and recycled paper that is composed of 50% recovered fiber, including 10% postconsumer waste.

Career Intelligence was published in hardcover in 1997 by Stoddart Publishing Co. Limited. This paperback printing contains the complete text of the original hardcover edition.

Library of Congress Cataloging-in-Publication Data

Moses, Barbara.
    Career intelligence : the new rules for work and life success /
Barbara Moses.
        p.   cm.
    Includes bibliographical references and index.
      ISBN 1-57675-048-5 (alk. paper)
      1. Vocational guidance.   2. Success.   I. Title.
    HF5381.M7378   1998
    650.1–dc21   98-21727
                                                                                CIP

First Paperback printing: July 1998

2001 00 99 98   10 9 8 7 6 5 4 3 2 1

In loving memory of Nat Moses (1913–74) and Sylvia Stober Moses (1915–96), who would have been proud.

To Andrew, Nathaniel, and Tamara, who are proud and relieved.

Contents

Acknowledgments   IX

Introduction   XIII

PART ONE: MELTDOWN

ONE   The New Landscape   *3*

TWO   Facing the Fallout: The Unprotected Self   *21*

THREE   Talking About Your Generation: Pre-Boomers and Early Boomers   *37*

FOUR   Late for the Feast: Late Boomers and Post-Boomers   *57*

FIVE   Squished, Squashed, Sliced, and Diced   *75*

SIX   Singing the New Career Blues   *91*

PART TWO: RENEWAL

SEVEN   Welcome to TempWorld   *109*

EIGHT   Become a Career Activist   *137*

NINE   Twelve New Rules for Career Success   *169*

TEN   Career Intelligence for Managers and Organizations   *201*

ELEVEN   Preparing the Next Generation: Career-Proofing Your Kids   *235*

References   *267*

Index   *273*

About the Author   *281*

Acknowledgments

I am privileged to count as my friends, colleagues, and clients some of the most extraordinary people who have been a constant source of support and emotional and intellectual generosity. This book is full of their stories. I hope I have done them justice.

I have worked with many people in many organizations, and I have learned from all of them. Space does not permit me to thank each and every one of them. I single out those who were particularly instrumental to my thinking in this book, recognizing that they do not work alone but were part of a much larger team. I am sure I am forgetting some people, and I apologize in advance for any oversights.

I would like to thank the people at Stentor, whose work environment is an inspiration for all, and who provided me with wonderful learning experiences, in particular Marie Ierfino, who made it happen; Sandra Dummett, Steve Lashbrook, Nancy Semkin, and Sharon Wingfelder at the Royal Bank of Canada for their commitment to helping employees manage the new work realities; Jeff Davidson at CIBC for a ten-year conversation about, and tremendous insight into, people, organizations, and careers; Marsha Bidloff

Acknowledgments

for her groundbreaking work at CIBC, along with Heather Taylor for interpreting career management in a project environment; the designers and implementers of the Bank of Montreal Possibilities Centre – Joan Mesic, George Salley, and Nadia Valerio; Fernando Vescio at Ontario Hydro for his insights and consistent support over the past ten years; Jonathan Hamovitch at Wal-Mart for his wry insights; John Young at Four Seasons Hotels and Resorts who has taught me so much about people and work and creating work environments that reflect a genuine commitment to staff development; Susannah Kelly at NCR, a role model for all managers in her unwavering commitment to employees; Pam MacIntyre at Crown Life for her wit and insight, another role model; Margo Gordon at Dylex, and Dan Gordon, for their thoughtful comments on the new work realities; Gaetan Ranger of CSIS and Louise Leveille of Industry, Science and Technology Canada, leaders in career management in the public sector; Bill Pallett at Delta Hotels and Resorts for his appreciation for, and long-term commitment to, career management; Karen Lambo at Dofasco for her sensitivity to important work issues; Carolyn Clark at CP Hotels and Resorts for sharing her appreciation of work and family issues; my clients at the public accounting firms, in particular, Wayne McFarlane and the partners at Coopers & Lybrand, and Lori Pearson and the partners at Ernst & Young, for their sophisticated approaches in responding to the career issues of professionals; Leslee Wilson at Canada Trust, Helen Bozinovski at the Bank of Montreal, Keith Southey at CIBC, John Lynch of Prologue Health and Barbara Steinberg at the United Nations, consistent sources of wry, informed commentary; Jean Harris at LOMA for giving me an opportunity to test out my ideas across North America.

I owe a particular debt of gratitude to Dr. Michael Godkewitsch of MG Productivity Partners for his early support and mentoring; Kathleen Conway of Camdem Communications for her invaluable advice and support at the dawn of my career as an independent consultant; Irene Taylor of Corporate

Sculpture and Terrie Russell of Russell-Hille Associates for their longtime support; Dr. John Bryan of Bryan Weir-Bryan Consultants, always a wry observer of the human condition; my printer, George Singer of Copygraph, conscientious to a fault; and my associates Laurie Hillis and Ann Toombs in Calgary, JoAnn Maurer in Vancouver, Frank Rambeau in Ottawa, Roslyn Slawner and Denise Lapointe in Montreal, B. J. and Ken Chakiris in Chicago, Joan Caruso in New York, Elaine Christie in Auckland, New Zealand, and Ken Saltrese in London, England.

I would like to offer special thanks to Tamara Weir-Bryan, friend, teacher and mentor, my twenty-year partner in dialogue about careers, work, and life; to my longtime colleague Joan Hill, a constant source of ideas, stories, encouragement, and enthusiasm; to Jane Hutcheson of Hay Management, a font of stimulating ideas and amusing stories about people and organizations; and to Charles Green, a continual source of new and interesting perspectives.

This book would not have come to fruition without my longtime friend and literary agent Bruce Westwood, who quite literally called it forth into existence; Harvey Schachter for his help in the early stages of this project; Susan Moses and Lynn Moses for their help with the manuscript; John Brewer for his assistance with research; Karen O'Reilly and Nick Steed for their many suggestions both thoughtful and practical; my fine and very smart editor, Don Bastian, and my most thorough copy editor, Lynne Missen.

Last, and most important, I thank my son Nathaniel, my extraordinarily meticulous and diligent reference-checker – if this book accomplishes what I intended, he will inherit a better work world – and my husband and partner, Andrew Weiner, my toughest editor, who lived every word in this book.

Introduction

Some years ago I came across a quote by Penn State political scientist Larry Spence, describing what he labeled "the soul of a corporation":

"I have become ruthless in order to survive. Change is the only constant in my life. I have learned to have no personal or political loyalties . . . I'm lean, I'm mean, I beat the hell out of whatever challenges my survival."

These sentiments resonated with what I was seeing and hearing in my workshops and speeches with managers and professionals across corporate North America. Everywhere, people seemed more and more disaffected from their employers and critical of how business was being conducted. They complained about how their organizations were becoming "cold," "ruthless," and "soulless."

Still, it was with some trepidation that I used the quote as a springboard for discussion at a conference for senior managers and professionals in the banking industry. I was concerned it might seem like I was mocking them – an independent consultant making a joke at the expense of the business world. Worse, might it not be "biting the hand that feeds me"?

Anxiously I threw the quote on the overhead projector, giving participants just enough time to read it before I withdrew it.

Their response amazed me. Rather than challenging me, they wanted to copy it, to show it to their bosses and colleagues.

Something significant was happening in the business world. Not only were senior managers and professionals having difficulty coping with the shifting new work realities, but more surprisingly, they were prepared to acknowledge it publicly. Indeed, it seemed many were deeply troubled by what was going on in the corporate corridors.

For the past five years, in speeches and workshops with people from all organizational levels across North America, I have routinely asked the following questions:

"How do you feel about the changes going on around you in the workplace?"

"Do you feel confident about your future?"

"Do you feel confident about your children's future?"

I believe that the responses to these questions can be considered a measure of people's general satisfaction with their work and their optimism about the future. Sadly, I am finding that less than one-third of respondents are happy with the changes taking place in the workplace and their lives.

Indeed, most people describe themselves as overworked and underappreciated. They are worried about their own future and that of their children. They can't rely on any traditional yardsticks or rules of thumb to explain what is happening around them, or to make any meaningful predictions about their future. At best, they feel only nominally in control of their lives.

Our economic, social, and cultural environment has changed dramatically in the last few years, causing tremendous confusion and calling for adaptive responses different from those we used in the past.

This book is about the extraordinary sea change that has taken place in the workplace and in our lives and the impact of these changes on:

- How people are feeling about themselves, their work lives, and their future.
- The new expectations on the part of individuals and organizations.
- The psychological contract between individuals and organizations.
- How individuals and organizations can best position themselves to thrive, or at least survive, as we make the transition to a workplace governed by a completely new set of rules.

This book will help you respond effectively to these changes, and equip you with the information and skills you need to navigate successfully in a transformed workplace. It will give you insight into the new work realities and the new rules for career success. In short, it will enhance your *career intelligence*.

When I talk about "career intelligence," I am not talking about "working smarter" – harder, faster, more effectively. People are already doing quite enough of that. Nor am I referring only to having "career smarts" or "career savvy," such as knowing how to position yourself for a promotion. Sharpening your career instincts is indeed a part of career intelligence, but it is only one element of it.

Career intelligence is both a way of *understanding* yourself and the world, and a way of *acting* upon the world, because you can't act effectively on the world without first comprehending it properly.

That means understanding the *external* economic and social landscape, educating yourself about new work and career realities; developing practical wisdom about the new workplace that will allow you to take advantage of opportunities available to you; and knowing what you need to do to ensure your continued marketability.

But equally, it means being attuned to your internal, *personal world*: what engages you, what you care about, what gives your life meaning. Only by knowing yourself will you be able to make the *right* decisions about your career – decisions that reflect your most important personal values and concerns, rather than being driven by external measures of success such as status or income.

Once you have this understanding, you will think about yourself and your career differently. You will reappraise who you are and what you do. You will be able to rise above the frenetic busyness of everyday working life to make choices in terms of your own agenda, and pursue your own goals. You will learn to trust yourself – your own ideas, instincts, and perceptions. You will become a *career activist*.

Above all, career intelligence is about developing a broader vision of yourself in the world, one that expresses who you are and what you want to accomplish in your life. It's about being an *intelligent actor in your own life*. It's about becoming a more *engaged and committed human being*.

Improving your career intelligence will give you the competencies to craft your own future and to ensure a career that is personally meaningful and satisfying. But more than that:

- If you are a manager, you will be better able to support your staff by providing them with the skills and resources to secure their long-term marketability.
- If you are a parent, you will be able to provide your children with the guidance to help ensure that they can navigate and thrive in a new work world.

Everyone – individual contributors, managers, independent contractors, entrepreneurs – can play a role, indeed will *have* to play a role, in promoting career intelligence and making the work world a more human environment.

Not only will you be shaping your own career, you will have the opportunity to shape a work world that is more life-friendly, and one that you will be happy to leave for future generations.

PART ONE

Meltdown

ONE

The New Landscape

"We are looking for someone who finds working less than six days a week a real disadvantage, who routinely works through vacations and who lives to advance the interests of customers and of employees . . . we are not interested in someone who likes to work hard and is interested in the business, rather we are interested in an executive who has to be prevented from working seven days a week and is passionate about business." — CAREER AD SEEKING A CORPORATE VICE PRESIDENT FOR A WELL-KNOWN FOOD SERVICES COMPANY

*E*lizabeth K. is a vice president of human resources in the telecommunications industry. Five downsizings in as many years have left Elizabeth working sixty- to seventy-hour weeks, routinely coming into the office on weekends. She describes the pace of her work as "frenzied . . . ruthless . . . maniacal." Her boss has no sympathy for her complaints. "Life is tough out there," he tells her. "Get used to it." The never-let-up pace combined with impossible expectations for deliverables have moved her close to the breaking point. And she is also worried about the impact of these frenetic work demands on her family, feeling, as she says, "squeezed on all fronts."

△

David P., formerly a general manager in the petrochemicals industry, has lost his job four times in the past ten years — each time as the result of a downsizing or merger. Now in his early fifties, he is "between jobs": he has been unemployed for almost two years, despite a vigorous job search. David really would like to be part of an organization, helping it grow. But he has now resigned himself to making a transition into self-employment as an independent consultant, despite the fact that, as he says, "I don't feel that I have either the skills, temperament, or habits of mind for it."

△

Howard G. is a financial professional in his late thirties. His wife, Sharon C., is a social worker. When Howard and Sharon got married ten years ago, they were full of optimism. "We thought we could have it all," Howard says. "A big house, nice cars, expensive vacations, private school for our kids." Howard and Sharon have a combined income of over $100,000 a year, but it has not brought them the lifestyle they expected. They live in a modest house worth less than the heavy mortgage they still carry on it. Ten years of spending more than they earned have put them even further into debt, to the tune of over $100,000 on their various loans, credit cards, and lines of credit. And now Sharon is facing a layoff. "Like all parents, I wanted my children to have more than I did," Howard says. "Now I'd be happy if they could just have the same."

△

Kathy W. has her B.A. in sociology: she describes her degree as standing for "bugger-all . . . that's what it's worth in today's job market." Since graduation she has held a succession of unrewarding, low-skilled "McJobs," punctuated by periods of unemployment. Kathy's parents are both successful professionals, but she is pretty well resigned to the fact that her own standard of living will not come close to theirs. "What do I need to do," she asks, "to get my foot in the door of a job that will be more intellectually demanding, pay at least half decently, and lead to a real career?"

△

The people described here differ widely in age, seniority, and professional specialties. But each is grappling with the same challenges: pervasive and profound changes in their work, careers, and lives. These extraordinary changes in the workplace, taking place in a bare handful of years, have transformed the way we work, the way we think about our work and our careers, and the relationship between the individual and their employers.

The result has been nothing less than a meltdown in:

- **Our trust in the goodness of organizations:** "I can remember a kinder, gentler workplace," says Elizabeth K., "when organizations looked out for their people instead of seeing every employee as a potential drain on the bottom line."

  Once, no matter how competitive the marketplace, no matter how intense the drive for profits, organizations nurtured their people — developed their capabilities, provided them with elaborate benefit plans and retirement schemes, and gave them a sense of protection from the vagaries of the marketplace. But more than that, organizations offered people a sense of *belonging* to something larger than themselves.

Now that sense of protection has been completely stripped away. To satisfy shareholders, and maximize performance in today's brutally competitive economy, organizations have become as ruthless and profit-driven in dealing with their own people as with their toughest competitors. Our concept of what constitutes a reasonable workplace and what constitutes reasonable behaviors and expectations in that workplace has been turned upside down.

Some individuals, like David P., have been simply tossed onto the scrap heap. Others, like Elizabeth K., have survived, only to face extraordinary new demands in the service of a compulsive preoccupation with productivity and overhead reduction.

— **Our loss of a sense of protection:** People who worked for organizations used to give their loyalty and commitment in exchange for job security. Today, as David P. has discovered, we have been thrust into a cold, hard world in which there is no loyalty and no security — a world in which, ultimately, we are all of us temporary workers, all "free agents."

— **Our expectations about the world, and what we have to do to earn a living:** Most of us, like Howard G. and Sharon C., grew up believing we could have limitless access to all the accoutrements of the good life. Our superior education would translate into an ever-improving standard of living, and the freedom to pick and choose among a variety of challenging work options. Instead, many people now find themselves struggling for economic survival.

— **Our confidence in our children's future:** If thirty- and forty-something professionals are experiencing some hard times, the situation is even tougher for the twenty-something "Generation X-ers" like Kathy W. now trying to make their way into the workplace. And as we look ahead, we wonder what kind of future will confront the generation after that. How can parents best advise their children, when they are so unsure about how to manage their own careers? According to a recent Gallup poll, only 24 percent of North Americans are optimistic that their children will have a better standard of living than they do.

— **Our sense of community:** As a small percentage of the population – CEOs, the rich, the elite of "knowledge workers" – gain an ever-larger share of the economic rewards, everyone else falls back. At the same time, the safety net of public sector social programs is stripped away. Our society has become "mean and crabbed," warns MIT's Robert Solow, winner of a Nobel Prize in Economics, "limited in what it can do, worried about the future."

There is a widespread sense that something has gone profoundly wrong in our society, that we are headed toward a *Blade Runner* world, fractured along ethnic, regional, and economic fault lines, in which the wealthy take refuge behind the walls of "gated communities," while everyone outside those walls suffers the consequences.

The fabric of our society, the opportunities to get ahead for ourselves and our children, and the comforts of family and community life have been shredded, leaving only a residue of uncertainty and cynicism.

CHANGING THE RULES

What has melted down here? In every instance, it is our old *assumptions* about the world. Much of what we once thought was true is no longer true. And many people are feeling profoundly lost as a result.

We grew up believing in a series of rules that guided our behavior, and we thought we could make certain hypotheses about the future based on these rules. For example, "If I work sixty hours a week, I will get a salary increase, or a promotion, or at least someone will say 'well done.'"

Now none of these rules applies. What has replaced them? For the most part, only an *absence* of rules to guide our lives and our careers. We now see only a series of uncertainties on all fronts.

The Old Rules No Longer Apply

What rules did you grow up believing in? It's a question I have often posed to people when delivering speeches and workshops. Here are some of the most common answers.

- A university education is a good guarantee of being able to secure good work.
- If you stay on top of your profession, you should be able to pick and choose the work you want to do.
- Certain professions such as law, accounting, and medicine will always be in demand.
- Buying a house is the best investment you can make.
- If your company is profitable, your job is secure.
- If you receive outstanding performance ratings, you should be confident of a rosy future in your organization.
- If you're really good at what you do, your work will be noticed: you should not have to toot your own horn.
- If you make it to senior management, you have more choices and more job security.
- If you're trained in a high-tech profession, you will always be in demand.
- By the time you're sixty you should be able to retire with the same standard of living.
- If you get the best possible education and stay in touch with your field of expertise, you can ensure that your skills stay current.

CAREER CRUNCH

"My son is twenty-one," a forty-something acquaintance told me recently. "He'll be graduating next year, and he's very worried about his job prospects. I told him how, when I graduated, all the major employers came on campus, vying with each other to recruit us, telling us what great opportunities they were offering. He didn't believe me. He thought I was making it up."

My first major consulting assignment, fifteen years ago, was with a leading multinational energy company that prided itself on its foresight and its state-of-the-art human resource management programs. Looking down the road, this company was concerned that the bulge of baby boomers now moving through the workforce — like the proverbial mouse in the stomach of the python — would lead to a situation of too many people chasing too few promotions. Indeed, some people might have to spend as much as *two years* in the same job before being promoted.

In those days, careers were predictable and well-structured. Like most well-run organizations, this energy company had clear "career paths" for managers and professionals. People believed that if they performed well, they would move up along these career paths. They *expected* regular promotions, regarding rapid advancement through the corporate hierarchy almost as a birthright, and became impatient when they stayed too long at the same level.

As part of my research, I asked the early career professionals there what their aspirations were. Routinely they said they wanted to be vice president in a few years. When they considered career planning, they thought about how to get from Job A to Job B to Job C, and about the developmental experiences and assignments they would need to help them along the way. Training, for them, meant a five-day personal growth experience at a pastoral retreat.

The company worried about the impact of slower career advancement on the morale and performance of these managers and professionals. What would happen if they "plateaued," if they were stuck at the same level with no prospect of further promotion? What could the company do to keep these people motivated and productive?

At the time, these seemed important questions. They have since been rendered moot. Recurrent bouts of downsizing and restructuring have reduced this company from 25,000 people to 5,000, with no end in sight. Driving past their still well-manicured, but eerily empty, corporate head office building, I sometimes wonder how long it will be before they shift their operations to the variety store across the street.

After years of ferocious downsizing, most of the "survivors" in this company, as in so many others, no longer think about long-term career prospects in terms of rapid promotion or the "next move." Instead, they wonder whether or not they will have a job. As for training, it now consists of basic technical training or supervisory skills, preferably done in a half day, or on a self-study basis at home.

So we no longer have definable career paths. Indeed, as we will shortly see, many of us no longer have definable "jobs" – not in the old sense of a job as a stable and unchanging collection of tasks (for more on the end of the job, see Chapter 7).

THE RUTHLESS ECONOMY

A number of powerful social and economic trends have converged to bring us to this state of affairs.

Technology is transforming the nature of our work, bringing a shift from an economy based on production to one based on information. Like the Industrial Revolution of the nineteenth century, this new transformation is displacing millions of workers from their jobs.

There is, however, a fundamental difference. Most of the craft workers swept aside by the Industrial Revolution eventually found new jobs in the new factories. But there is little chance that the current shift will create enough new good jobs to replace those that are being lost.

Technology makes it possible for organizations to do more with less. A small elite of professional and technical workers can now work more intensively, aided by e-mail, voice mail, modems, faxes, spreadsheets, and word processors. But most other jobs are changed by technology to require *less* skill, and command lower wages. So while a few people work longer and harder than ever, many more work less, slipping, as we will see below, either into permanent unemployment or else into part-time, temporary, and low-skilled, home-based work.

At the same time, new technology has accelerated the emergence of a true *global* economy. Capital and information now move ceaselessly across time zones, transmitted by satellite downlinks and fiber optic cables. The markets never close. And the pressures on organizations to produce results for their shareholders become ever more intensive. Work moves ineluctably, like water down a hill, to the lowest-cost producer.

As British industrialist Sir James Goldsmith observes in *The Trap*, "47 Vietnamese or 47 Filipinos can be employed for the cost of one person in a developed country." And it is not just factory jobs that are being exported. Everything from the drawing of TV cartoons to the coding of software programs is now routinely handled by highly trained, but lower-paid, overseas workers.

Forced to operate in a ruthless economy, organizations have become increasingly ruthless themselves. They have cut costs and staff, in wave upon wave of "re-engineering" and downsizing — with each wave of cuts being conducted with even less compassion than the one before.

A study by Harvard business school professor Nitin Nohria of the one hundred largest U.S. public companies found that they averaged fifteen downsizings each between 1978 and 1993, or one per year. Each cutback averaged 2,000 people. So collectively, over this period, these one hundred companies fired some 3 million people!

Economist Robert Topel has estimated that 12.2 million white-collar workers lost their jobs in the U.S. recession of 1989–92, and another 3 million since then. Only 6.3 million of these people have found new jobs, earning on average 30 percent less than before. Meanwhile, U.S. corporate profits soared by 13 percent in 1993 and another 10 percent in 1994.

THE END OF JOB SECURITY

Given the barrage of news stories about layoffs and downsizings over the past decade, and the growing political debate on the subject, it seems almost redundant to talk about the almost complete erosion in job security in today's workplace. Still, the speed and extent of the change have been breathtaking.

Only a few years ago, people could look forward to relatively predictable and secure employment. As author and consultant Richard Pascale has observed, corporations were once "like ocean liners. Anyone fortunate enough to have a berth cruised through a career and disembarked at retirement age." Today, as Pascale says, those "ocean liners have started heaving their crew overboard."

Organizations in every sector have become both leaner and flatter, cutting out entire layers of management and reducing workforces to compete more effectively. They now offer fewer jobs overall, fewer opportunities for advancement, and no guarantees of continuing employment.

As well as creating massive insecurity, this has had some devastating psychological consequences for the individual who once found a sense of belonging at work, consequences that we will explore further in Chapter 2.

CHANGING EMPLOYMENT PATTERNS

The legacy of a decade of downsizing is record unemployment among such groups as young workers and middle-aged males. During the last recession, for the first time since the Depression of the 1930s, middle-aged, college-educated men suffered a decline in their standard of living and prospects for future employment. The ranks of those classified as permanently unemployed have swelled, making this, as Harvard economist James Medoff has put it, the era of the "permanently-unemployed middle-aged male." At the same time, an epidemic of involuntary early retirements has forced many managers and professionals into retirement before they were ready, whether psychologically or financially.

Our best educated and most technically savvy young people have also been deeply hurt by record levels of unemployment and underemployment. Competition is so fierce, and good jobs so scarce, that a university graduate now earns only slightly more, in adjusted dollars, than a 1979 high school graduate.

In part, these high levels of youth unemployment are due to a failure of our colleges and universities to meet job market demands. Jobs for 20,000 new computer programmers went unfilled in Canada in 1996 because universities couldn't meet the demand, according to the Software Research Council. Chapter 4 will look at the impact of these new work realities on today's "Generation X."

Enter the Contingent Workforce

It is not just job security that has disappeared. Conventional full-time permanent jobs are also vanishing, taken over by a "contingent" workforce made up of part-time and temporary employees.

The number of temporary workers in the United States nearly doubled between 1990 and 1995, from 1.2 million to 2 million. Most are filling low-wage clerical and blue-collar jobs. But the fastest growing segment is for *professional* and *technical* jobs, which now make up 20 percent of the total temporary payroll.

Indeed, "outsourcing" of jobs by corporations has become a boom industry, with the number of temporary agencies in the United States doubling over the past ten years. The Canadian Council on Social Development reports that temporary jobs rose 21 percent from 1989 to 1994. One in ten employed

Canadians is a temporary worker, according to Statistics Canada (1996). If we look at all forms of "nonstandard employment," including part-time, free-lance, and contract work, and job sharing, by some forecasts, by the year 2000, less than 50 percent of the workforce will be employed in conventional full-time jobs. The majority will be part-time, temporary, or contract workers.

It all adds up to a complete meltdown in the traditional idea and ideal of a "regular job." In the future, almost all jobs will be in some way or degree *irregular* (as we will see in more detail in Chapter 7).

Growing Inequality

Temporary jobs are by definition short-term jobs. Temporary staff for the most part have limited opportunities to build up skills, earn higher wages, and access opportunities for advancement. Companies increasingly prefer temporary staff because they are cheaper and more flexible – in comparison to permanent staff who require higher salaries and benefits, and are more expensive to lay off.

If these trends continue, the future may see a growing divide in our society between a few people with relatively secure and well-paid jobs and everyone else holding poorly paid temporary positions with poor or nonexistent benefits.

The new technology-intensive "knowledge economy" is helping foster the creation of a two-tiered society, made up of what Peter Drucker has called "knowledge workers" (former U.S. labor secretary Robert Reich prefers the term "symbolic analysts") and everyone else. Drucker fears that a society dominated by knowledge workers will be threatened by "a new class conflict between the large minority of knowledge workers and the majority of people who will make their living traditionally either by manual work . . . or by work in services, whether skilled or unskilled."

Jeremy Rifkin worries in *The End of Work* that in a world where sophisti-cated technologies will be able to replace more and more of the global workforce, "it is unlikely that more than a fortunate few will be retrained for the relatively scarce high tech scientific, professional, and managerial jobs made available in the emerging knowledge sector."

The future of our society may resemble a jumbo jet with a highly skilled flight crew in front, and a less skilled cabin crew in the back, whose job it is to provide food and entertainment for the great masses in the middle "who are no longer able to find satisfying work or any kind of job at all." Or so communications consultant T. Ran Ide and Industry Canada economist Arthur Cordell suggest, in their paper, "The New Tools: Implications for the Future of Work." They write: "Will we have to provide games, movies, food, alcohol and drugs to the unemployed masses of the population to keep them amused through the journey of life?"

Already, the concentration of technological skills and capital in fewer and fewer hands is leading to growing distortions in the distribution of wealth in our society – with a smaller, richer upper class, a shrinking middle class, and a poorer, increasingly larger, marginalized working class.

Between 1979 and 1993, the average annual earnings of the top 5 percent of U.S. households climbed 29 percent, to $178,000, according to U.S. Census Bureau figures. In the same fifteen-year period, the median U.S. income declined almost 5 percent.

People in the top 20 percent now control half of the wealth in the United States. Over the last twenty years, they are the only group who have experienced a net gain in wealth. By the early 1990s, the share of wealth held by the top 1 percent was back to where it was in the late 1920s (at more than 40 percent) before the introduction of progressive taxation (see Lester Thurow's article, "Why Their World Might Crumble").

The median wage of all U.S. working men has fallen by 11 percent since 1973, even though the earnings of the top 20 percent have grown steadily. Only the entry of women into the workforce in growing numbers kept household incomes slowly rising until 1989, when real median wages for women also began to fall. Since 1989 median household incomes, after adjusting for inflation and family size, have fallen more than 7 percent.

Which Side of the Line Are You On?

Recently, I was a guest on a TV show on the new work realities, and the host asked the audience how they felt about their income. "Slipping," one woman yelled out. "Every year," she continued, "I tell myself this is the year I'm finally going to get ahead. I cut back on more and more, and instead of getting ahead, I'm farther and farther behind the eight ball." The television audience, mostly professionals, nodded their heads in vigorous agreement.

The nervous middle class. The besieged middle class. The tenuous middle class. The anxiety class. The reconfiguring of the job market and the decline of income have eroded the firm middle-class belief that if you play by the rules you will thrive.

The middle class is scared, trying to hold on to what is becoming an increasingly fragile lifestyle. It is as if people see a real line being drawn between the 30 percent or so of knowledge workers, and the rest. Everywhere I go, people are talking about this line as if it has the physical properties of a wall – which side will they end up on, and how can they ensure their children are on the right side of the line?

The race is on to private schools, despite the drain on income that their fees represent. As one financially strapped middle manager father commented, "We did a lot of soul searching – I believe in the idea of public education. And I know that if every middle-class parent takes their kid out of the public system, we're just contributing to the problems in the schools. But all that said, we don't want our kid to be an ideological sacrifice. There's so much uncertainty out there, so much competition. You've got to give your kid a leg up."

An even more visible indicator of this great divide is the growth in walled and gated communities. Some 28 million Americans now live in such communities, including privately guarded apartment houses, and that number is expected to double in the next decade. Meanwhile, Americans are currently paying out of their pockets for an additional 1.5 million private security guards to provide, at least in part, protection lacking from the police.

PERVASIVE ANXIETY

Change has made uncertainty the basic characteristic of the workplace, resulting in a pervasive anxiety. This anxiety affects people in the workforce at all levels, as they deal with what they perceive to be tenuous careers and a precarious financial situation.

"The competition comes at you from every side," reports one middle manager. "Colleagues, subordinates, independent contractors. The performance bar has been raised so high you can barely touch it . . ."

Fear of downsizing has become so pervasive, suggests a recent article in *The Family Therapy Networker*, that it could legitimately be given its own name – "Downsizing Terror Disorder" – and its own listing in the next edition of the *Diagnostic and Statistical Manual of Mental Disorders*.

Inevitably, people's anxieties about their future have an impact on their on-the-job behavior. "Everyone is running scared," reports one once-outspoken senior manager. "You can smell the fear. If your boss pushes a dumb idea, you keep your mouth shut. You don't speak out, you don't take risks, you don't do anything to draw attention to yourself."

DEMANDS, DEMANDS, DEMANDS

Do more. Do it better. Do it with less. And do it with no promise of rewards. These are the new imperatives that now characterize people's working lives. As workforces are downsized, the survivors are asked to take up more and more of the slack.

But people are not just being asked to do more. They are also being asked to do it *faster*. In a rapidly changing economy, speed has become a competitive advantage. Companies that can come to market first with new or improved products or processes stand to reap huge gains for their shareholders. People are expected to work as long and as hard as necessary to meet those demanding deadlines.

This cult of speed and stamina has long been true of companies in the computer and software industries, where people on project development teams are routinely expected to work long, intense hours, sacrificing any claim to having a life of their own. But a similar emphasis is now increasingly found even in more traditional industries. (It is no coincidence that one slick new business magazine, a would-be rival to *Fortune* and *Forbes*, chose to call itself *Fast Company*.)

Economically squeezed, and beleaguered at work, individuals must maintain a super-metabolic pace that leaves them with little time or energy for partners, children, friends, or themselves. Expectations about what constitutes reasonable working hours have been radically revised. People in the workforce today work on average one month more a year now than twenty-five years ago.

"I certainly hope Plato was wrong," wrote Pierre Home-Douglas in the *Globe and Mail*, in talking about the relentless demands on a dual-career family raising children. "If the unexamined life is really not worth living, then there must be a lot of worthless lives among the middle class these days."

An Erosion of Boundaries

On a recent short-hop plane ride I sat beside a well-dressed woman in her mid-thirties. She was engaged in an animated conversation with a man across the aisle from her — also well-dressed, somewhere in his late forties — giving him his performance appraisal.

Their conversation continued at a very high pace and at a tone audible to all the neighboring passengers throughout the flight. One example after another was given of the man's poor time management. As the woman talked she carefully annotated a twelve-page bill for her cell phone. What bothered me was that the employee receiving this feedback wasn't the least bit concerned by its timing or "publicness."

For me, it was one more example of the collapse in the boundaries between public and private domains, and between work and personal life. What began as a grim necessity, brought on by the relentless pressure to produce, is now celebrated as chic and fashionable. Work is establishing a beachhead in the home, with business magazines glamorizing the home office. Mobile computing and communications devices ensure that you can be reached anytime and anywhere and expected to perform.

Take the case of a consultant friend of mine who started working from home. In the past he had been available at home only by phone or fax. Now, to enhance his effectiveness, he added to his artillery a laptop computer with modem, a cell phone, a car fax, and a pager. Now his clients could call, e-mail, or fax him at any time of the day or night. "I am my workplace," he complains.

It's a statement many managers and professionals would echo. Although they may still work at an office, they routinely take work home for evenings and weekends, and their bosses often think nothing of calling them there.

Indeed, I hear stories of bosses who get annoyed when people take the full vacation to which they are entitled; of bosses who publicly vilify people who won't come in on Saturdays. Not all bosses, of course, are like this. But as Columbia University psychologist Harley Hornstein observes in *Brutal Bosses and Their Prey*, the incidence of abuse is on the rise — a direct result, Hornstein suggests, of today's productivity pressures.

Endless Complexity

"It's much harder to raise a child today. My parents would deny that it was easy to raise me and my brother. But they didn't have to worry that when we went to school we wouldn't learn anything, or that someone would be selling drugs in

the school yard, or that someone would pull a knife on us on the subway. Today, it's a lot more work being a parent." — FORTY-SOMETHING PARENT

It's not just at work that today's managers and professionals are under pressure. You not only have to be a good manager, a continuous learner, a good team player. You are also expected to take responsibility for everything from your career to your personal finances to your children's education to your health — to stay active in the community, to stay physically fit, to choose the right school for your children.

Never before has it been necessary to be responsive in so many domains of our life. But as both governments and corporations downsize their obligations, more and more responsibility falls upon the individual. And all this is happening at a time when people have less time, energy, and stamina to handle this multiplicity of demands. The result is that people are too busy managing the day-to-day minutiae to derive any pleasure from their lives.

TWO

Facing the Fallout: The Unprotected Self

"The misery of the world of 'eat or be eaten' is not to be measured in income statistics. It is a moral disaster . . . We do not go to work only to earn an income, but to find meaning in our lives. What we do is a large part of who we are. To see ourselves as nothing more than a means to profit reaped by others is a blow to our self-respect." — PRINCETON PROFESSOR ALAN RYAN, THE NEW YORK REVIEW OF BOOKS

A friend of mine was talking about a mutual colleague, someone, she said, who would not be able to make it under the "new program" in her organization — an expression I had been hearing a lot lately. I asked her what she meant by the new program. She said, "Lean and mean. Actually, just plain mean."

Organizations used to offer employees more than simply a steady job in exchange for their hard work and loyalty. They offered people a sense of *psychological* security as well: a feeling of belonging to something bigger than themselves; of connection with like-minded others working together toward a common purpose; perhaps, above all else, a source of pride and identity.

Today, under the new employment contract at work, the whole emotional tenor of organizational life has changed, leaving many people profoundly disturbed and anxious. William Whyte, writing in the mid-1980s – some twenty-odd years after the publication of his classic book, *The Organizational Man* – was among the first of many contemporary observers to suggest that "the American corporation has gone awry . . . Beneficence has gone out the window."

THE NEW EMPLOYMENT CONTRACT

The terms of this new employment contract have been widely discussed in contemporary business books and magazine articles. I use a series of overheads to illustrate this contract in my speeches and workshops. The response shows widespread recognition of the enormous gulf between what organizations say and what people understand it to mean.

My first overhead shows how the organization defines the new employment contract.

What the Organization Says . . .

"You are responsible for your own employability. We will provide you with meaningful, challenging, and skill-building work which will be good for your resume, as long as you continue to add value."

People nod. They have all heard this litany.

My second overhead shows what people really hear when their organizations talk the good talk about "employability."

What the Individual Hears . . .

"We offer no job security. We will fire you when we have no more need for you. We will work you to the bone. We don't pay particularly well. And we will tell you that you are our most important resource."

This second overhead is greeted by rueful laughter.

The new employment contract presents a cold and harsh view of the world. There is no loyalty between individual and organization; no commitment beyond the short term; no history beyond yesterday's results; and certainly no sentimental attachment.

Moreover, the new contract is extraordinarily one-sided. The organization gets the flexibility in staffing it requires: it can hire and fire at will, without obligation to the employee, and without guilt. The individual gets only vague promises of continuing growth and development, as long as he or she demonstrates continuing usefulness.

"They call that a contract?" one friend asked. "I mean, would *you* sign it?"

WHY WE WORK

"You can't run a business, you know, on a basis of sentiment." That's what Kenneth Thomson, chairman of Thomson Corp., said on selling *The Daily Press* of Timmins, Ontario, the newspaper where he trained as a reporter.

People and organizations are driven by very different sets of motives. Fundamentally, organizations exist to make profits for their shareholders (or, in the case of public sector and nonprofit organizations, to achieve some other set of required results). This has always been true. But traditionally this single-minded pursuit of organizational goals has been moderated somewhat by the need to attract, motivate, and retain staff, and by concerns over the organization's image in the community as a "good employer" or a "good corporate citizen."

Today, even those restraints have been loosened. In pursuit of efficiency and global competitiveness, organizations feel free to treat their people like any other "resource" — as a commodity to be purchased at a particular price and used as convenient within a particular time frame.

Understandably, many people find it difficult to think of themselves as commodities. People don't work only for material gain or for personal advancement, but for much more complex and multifaceted reasons. We work, for example:

- to do something we believe in
- to make a difference
- to have a secure and stable life
- to have dignity
- to practice a skill or craft we take pride in
- to be part of something bigger than ourselves
- to gain the respect of our coworkers
- to belong to and serve a community
- to be challenged and stimulated.

Many of these motives are so commonly observed that some behavioral scientists suggest that we are "pre-wired" by thousands of years of evolution to experience them. They are a part of what makes us human.

We are now witnessing a collision between these fundamental human needs and the new organizational imperatives. And to the extent that it fails to recognize and meet these underlying human needs, the "new employment contract" has become a source of widespread concern and unhappiness.

WHATEVER HAPPENED TO ANDROGYNY?

When I started out as a consultant more than a decade ago, one of the great new management buzzwords of the day was "androgyny." Leading-edge organizations wanted to encourage in their managers, male and female, the expression of not only traditionally "male" qualities, such as being tough, dispassionate, and competitive, but also such so-called "feminine" qualities as showing nurturance, empathy, and concern for people's well-being.

It seems so long ago. The noble ideal. It got lost along the way, somehow.

Cold. Ruthless. Bloodless. Uncaring. Over and over again these are words I hear used by people in organizations to describe their employers. Or as one manager described her senior management team, "These guys are so tough, they have hair on their teeth." Sheer toughness — including a complete and utter lack of sentimental attachments — has come to be celebrated as a virtue in its own right.

If anything, the language of management has become more masculine than ever, full of warlike metaphors: "There'll be blood on the floor"; "body counts"; "I was ambushed . . ."; and so on.

SMASH THIS CULTURE

"Everything of the past is scheduled to be traded in for newer goods."

— SUSAN SONTAG

Picture this scene: You are in a large room, the one your company reserves for all-employee meetings or major conferences. Your whole department is in the room with you. And all of you know that something big is about to happen.

There have been many consultants around lately, asking questions about your work: its purpose, your role, the value-added, the skills you need to do the work. The consultants, in private conversation, have told you of the need to "smash the culture," to break the "entitlement mentality," to get rid of the whiners and the people who can't embrace change, the people who aren't real team players, the people who aren't continuously learning, who aren't taking responsibility for their own future. This is a WAKE-UP CALL, you are told. A 25 percent reduction of staff is anticipated over the next few years.

You look around the room. Everyone looks a little tense, and the usual collegial banter is gone. Everyone is guarded in their conversation. The president comes to the podium. He is flanked by the vice president of operations, and the head consultant, the one they call The Suit.

The president makes a few strained jokes. Clearly he is uncomfortable with the "small talk," the necessary warming up of the audience. He has a message, and he's anxious to get to it: "Work as we know it will never be the same. We are going through a transformation in our business. We need to take a hard look at every aspect of how we do business if we are to survive, and survive we must. Every one of our roles will be questioned and challenged, including mine. There will be some difficult times for all of us as we take a hard look at how we compete in the new marketplace. We will survive because we will embrace change, we will . . ." He is no longer awkward, he has warmed up to his message, he is a man with a mission.

Unfortunately, you cannot say the same for the audience. The president has heard the words so many times from his consultants that he no longer quite hears them, even as he delivers them now – they have become so much management cant. But you, and the rest of the audience, have not had the benefit of this psychological distancing from the message. You hear every word. But you don't hear "exciting journey," "create a transformed workplace."

What you hear is this: "We have to smash this organization's culture – this culture to which you belong, and with which you have identified for years – because it's worthless. It's fat, antiquated, useless. And so are you. You're worthless, too. And if you identified with this organization, you're a fool."

And perhaps you hear this, too: "You may not make it . . . you may not be one of the new breed of managers who will take us into the twenty-first century."

Many people's sense of self-worth is tied to their ability to make a contribution to their organization. When the value of their work is thrown into question, they feel that their very sense of self is under attack. As John D., a marketing manager in a recently re-engineered organization, observed, "I felt like I had ceased to exist as a human being and that I had to be a good soldier and act like all this change was good for us because if I didn't, I would look like one of the old guard, someone who couldn't quite make it."

There is also, not surprisingly, anger at the organization and its "change agents." As Linda P., a forty-something corporate trainer, asks, "Don't they have any idea how offensive it is to have some twenty-seven-year-old snot-nosed M.B.A. earning $100,000 a year tell you that 'the problem with business today is not a lack of experience, but too much experience?'"

THE TYRANNY OF RHETORIC

Be a visionary leader . . . Embrace change . . . Be a lifelong learner . . . Think of yourself as an independent contractor . . . Think outside the box . . . These are the new catechisms that we are asking people to embrace.

What people hear from all this is that they are somehow wanting: they're not bright enough, adaptable enough, young enough to make it. As one middle manager observed, "I felt like I was being treated like an interchangeable piece of a process, without any human identification."

A recent example of how management jargon can trivialize the emotional experiences of employees threatened by layoffs occurred at the Canadian Broadcasting Corporation. On the heels of an announcement of huge budget cuts leading to an expectation of massive job losses, employees were bombarded with messages orchestrated by the consulting company, such as:

- "Recover, refocus, regenerate."
- "Make your sleep work for you. When you have a tough problem think about the pros and cons of it before going to sleep and direct your subconscious to work on the problem overnight. Upon awaking the problem may appear as clear as daylight."
- "Allow yourself to feel anger . . . Every exit is an entrance to somewhere else . . ."

Many employees are less than impressed with these management bromides. For example, during the recent takeover of the Chase Manhattan

Bank by the Chemical Banking Corporation, management attempted to "share the vision" with employees through a "Merger Update" newsletter. But as the *New York Times* reported, in its celebrated 1996 series on "The Downsizing of America," Chase employees found the messages in this newsletter "saccharine and platitudinous." Some distributed newsletters of their own, including one in which this advice appeared on how to ensure a job at the Chase:

"Take your boss to lunch . . . Tell him/her over and over again that your only hope, dream and aspiration is to serve for little or no pay and work inhuman hours to make this place the best banking and financial services company in the world, bar none, without par, without equal, post no bills, void where prohibited."

Re-Engineering the Human Psyche

We may be able to re-engineer organizations, but we can't as easily re-engineer the human psyche. People are not machines, able to reprogram themselves at will according to the latest management theory: they have enduring behavior patterns and motivations. When they go to bed at night, they don't say, "Oh, boy! Isn't all this change exciting? Aren't I lucky to be in on the ground floor of the transformation of our business so that we can always stay one step ahead of our competition?"

When most people think about themselves or their future they don't think in terms of "re-engineering" or "managing change" or "being a strategic partner." They think in the same constructs that people have always used in challenging situations, such as "How will I fare?" "Will I be happy?" "Will I have a future?"

Many of the current change initiatives are counterproductive, making people even more anxious about the future, more preoccupied, and less productive. It's not surprising that the 1994 CSC Index "State of Re-Engineering Report" found that 50 percent of the organizations participating in the study reported that the most difficult part of re-engineering is dealing with the fear and anxiety in their organizations.

So many people are having difficulty adjusting to the "new program" because it conflicts not only with their fundamental needs as human beings, but also with their most deeply rooted habits of mind – ways of thinking they have become accustomed to, that come most naturally to them.

Some people, as a result of temperament or experience, have the habits of mind to cope readily with today's challenges. For example, children of entrepreneurs may learn early on to cope with economic uncertainty, and therefore be less troubled by a lack of job security. Or again, children of immigrants moving from one culture to another learn to adapt to sudden and dramatic change – an experience that may prepare them to cope better as adults with change in the workplace.

CHALLENGES TO IDENTITY

Most people, however, face a much more difficult adjustment. Indeed, they may experience the changes now going on in the workplace as challenges to their very sense of self. These challenges include:

- loss of predictability
- loss of security/enforced self-reliance
- the "commodification" of self
- loss of connection.

Obviously, people vary in the degree to which they are affected by these different challenges. Some find a lack of predictability challenging and exciting rather than disturbing. They thrive on ambiguity and relish living in an uncertain world in which they are constantly reinventing themselves to adapt to shifting circumstances. They like having responsibility for their own destiny, rather than giving up control to some "paternalistic" organization. For such people, these are heady times. But they are the exception rather than the rule.

As you read through these challenges, think about *your* life — does this represent an issue that you or someone you know is dealing with?

Challenge #1: Loss of Predictability

"Will I have a job tomorrow, and if so, in what form? Will I be happy? Will my partner have work? Will I be able to pay my mortgage? Can I afford to buy . . . ?"

One of the most basic human needs is to be able to make meaningful hypotheses about the world: "If I do X, then Y will happen . . ." In this way, we strive to create order in our lives, to understand how things work and why, and to make plans for the future.

Many people were attracted to work for large organizations because of their apparent ability to offer a stable future and a predictable standard of living, along with comfortable roles and clear rules for behavior. They believed that if they worked hard and showed loyalty to the organization, they would be rewarded with promotions and job security. They were therefore willing to make sacrifices today in anticipation of rewards tomorrow. By the same token, organizations invested in training their people, confidently expecting that they would continue working for them long enough to repay that investment.

A decade of downsizing and re-engineering has shattered those comfortable predictabilities. Today, people who work for organizations must live with constant ambiguity, unable to make any meaningful hypotheses about their future.

Of course, there has always been some element of unpredictability in the world of business. But there has never been unpredictability of such depth and breadth, cutting across so many domains of people's lives. People feel that they can no longer control the consequences of their own actions. Even if they do achieve the desired goals, they can't predict the results: "You did a great job reorganizing the department. Unfortunately, you reorganized yourself out of a job." Instead of concentrating on making a contribution to the organization, the employee focuses on trying to make sense of the situation: "What's going to happen now? What does this restructuring mean to me?"

The result of this constant unpredictability, as Harvard business professor Howard H. Stevenson has observed, may well be "people too scared not only to take risks but to take any action at all."

It is possible, however, to learn to cope better with unpredictability. In later chapters, we will look at strategies to manage effectively in an uncertain work world, in other words, how to career-proof yourself for difficult times.

Challenge #2: Loss of Psychological Security/Enforced Self-Reliance

Instead of nurturing and protecting their people's careers, organizations now expect them to "hit the ground running" and then keep on proving themselves over and over again. There is no comfort zone, no tolerance for errors, no protection from the cold, harsh world outside.

Staff are urged to become more self-reliant, to think of themselves as independent contractors. For many, this is an unwelcome suggestion. "I've been with this company for twenty years," says Peter J., a forty-four-year-old engineer. "I joined because of its leading-edge technologies and the security and benefits the company provides – or should I say, used to provide. I'm now being told to think of myself as an independent contractor. If I had wanted to be an independent contractor, I wouldn't have joined a big company in the first place."

People feel the loss of protection keenly. As one long-term employee of a large organization put it: "I feel like I'm naked at the high school prom, like every layer of protection has been stripped away."

So much of our sense of self is tied to our work. When we ask people to think of themselves as free agents, we are asking them to *develop a new self-identity*. Learning to let go of your ties to the organization, distancing yourself from one of your primary sources of identity and self-esteem, can be a very painful adjustment. That's true whether you have actually lost your job or find yourself in a significantly reconfigured workplace or are worried about the possibility of losing your work in the future.

Once the new reality of the unprotected workplace sinks in, initially there is the same sense of loss and betrayal as there is when you lose your job. And glib talk about "new employment contracts" and "Me Incorporated" and "thinking of yourself as an independent contractor" doesn't really help matters. Indeed, to the extent that it tries to cover up the real pain and grief that people are feeling, it makes matters worse.

Of course, people vary in their needs for security. Some are more vulnerable than others, and have a particularly hard time adjusting to the new order of things. Take, for example, the case of thirty-year-old Shirley J., a very bright and energetic executive assistant with a large electrical utility.

Shirley had been working for this company since she was eighteen. When this company downsized and offered employees voluntary severance packages, she was eligible for twelve months' salary despite her relatively young age. She was sorely tempted to take the deal: she would surely find a new job elsewhere. But after considerable thought, she turned down the offer saying, "I know it's crazy, but I can't overcome my needs for security."

Paradoxically, when I mentioned this story to another woman of a similar age, doing similar work, her comment was, "I couldn't bear to look at myself every morning, much less accept a salary check, feeling I was so unemployable." (There is a sad epitaph to this story. The organization went through a subsequent downsizing six months later and Shirley received six months' severance.)

Challenge #3: The "Commodification" of Self

We have all had to sell ourselves at one time or another, whether in interviewing for a job, pitching a boss to get sent on a training course, or selling a piece of business to a client. What is new, though, is the need to sell ourselves hard, all the time.

People who work for large organizations now find themselves in the same position as consultants, freelancers, and other independent contractors: endlessly gathering testimonials, documenting their achievements, and making proposals for new pieces of work. Indeed, just like many consultants, they may find themselves spending as much time selling themselves for the work as actually doing the work. In today's workplace, workers have to constantly resell/market themselves — to constantly manage other people's impressions of how well they are performing.

The same applies to an even greater degree to people who find themselves in a fiercely competitive job market: it's not uncommon these days to go through more than fifteen interviews for one job.

Effectively, people need to present themselves as a desirable product — to turn themselves into marketable commodities. Some managers and professionals, however, balk at such overt and constant selling. They think, "If I'm doing a good job, I shouldn't have to let everyone know about it." And in an ideal world, perhaps, that would be true. But this is not an ideal world.

As one senior manager told us: "There were two high-level professionals on my project team. The assignment was coming to an end, and both faced an uncertain future. One of them, Terry, started to actively market his services through proposals and offers to provide support to other senior managers. The other, John, did nothing to let people know what he was capable of offering. He thought that it was 'unseemly' for a professional of his standing to have to do that, sell himself so aggressively. He told me, 'people know I'm good at what I do.' And he was very good — better than

Terry, actually. But not enough people knew it. And where Terry was able to hook up with another project team, John was let go."

One wonders at the cost to organizations of having so many talented people spend so much time on managing impressions of what they do, rather than on actually doing the work. If everyone is so busy marketing themselves, who's taking care of the needs of the business?

Challenge #4: Loss of Connection

I was going for lunch with a client in a restaurant in the mall below the office building occupied by his organization, and as we walked through the mall, we passed many people in business suits who nodded to my client. In the restaurant, again, people at several tables waved to him, and he waved back. I commented on how many people he knew in the organization. "Oh," he said, "none of these people work here anymore. They just come here to hang out."

The people in the mall had been terminated over the past three years: some with generous early retirement provisions, others with large severance packages. None had succeeded in finding new jobs. They came back there because they had nothing better to do. And because they missed the lives they had once lived and the feeling of being connected to other people.

Work, for many people, is a key source of social identity – all the more so with the increasing fragmentation of families and communities. People want to belong to an organization they value, and which values them. They want to feel connected to other people, and to contribute to something bigger than themselves. Today, many people no longer feel that sense of connection with their organizations.

Managers, in particular, may feel particularly pained by new corporate expectations – caught between the demands of the organization and their loyalty to their people. "I've been with this organization for twenty years," says one senior manager of a large transportation utility. "There are a lot of things I really liked about it . . . challenging work, working with some of the best minds in the industry. But most of all, I think, I enjoyed the sense of being part of an extended family. I have my own rich family life at home, but I also really care about the people around me at work.

"Now I have to carry out senior management's agenda — an agenda which cares only about profits and nothing for the people who make them — and I don't want to, because I don't believe in it. It goes against everything I feel is valuable about this organization, and everything I sold to my people when I hired them in the first place."

For many people, work used to be a place of friendship and collegiality. Hit television sitcoms like the *Mary Tyler Moore Show*, *Taxi*, and *WKRP in Cincinnati* celebrated the extended family of workplace friends. But today's top sitcoms, tellingly, for the most part feature just plain *Friends*. In today's fiercely competitive job market, coworkers are just as likely to be seen as rivals than as potential friends. And in any case, there's no time for socializing. As one executive assistant commented, "I used to love the banter that would take place, the easy conversation and chatting. Now everyone is so busy, anything we talk about is related to getting the job done faster."

The irony here is that just as we work so hard to foster teamwork, many people who are actually part of a team feel increasingly cut off and isolated. The nature of social interaction in the office has changed, from the casual open-ended conversations that used to take place by the coffee machine or the water cooler to intense, focused communications about the task at hand.

Restoring the Ties

In the end organizations may pay a heavy price for allowing the ties between themselves and their people to weaken. Organizations need their people, whether long-term core employees or short-term contract staff, to feel a sense of connection to their workplace. The very last thing they want to do is to deliberately discourage it.

Despite the damage that has been done to that sense of connection over the past decade, there remains hope that it can be restored, if in somewhat different form than in the past. Loyalty to others, after all, is an enduring human trait. It cannot be eradicated, even by the most drastic re-engineering. Even if people can no longer feel a sense of connection to the organization as a whole, they may still feel loyalty to their work, to their team, to their manager, or to their profession.

As we will see, the challenge facing managers will be to harness these loyalties to the benefit of the individual and the organization.

THREE

Talking About Your Generation: Pre-Boomers and Early Boomers

"I grew up thinking anything was possible. We were guaranteed a pretty good life if you were willing to work for it. Today it's different. I don't think every twenty-year-old has grown up feeling they're guaranteed anything anymore, even if they want to struggle and fight for it." — CALVIN KLEIN, BORN 1942

"A lot of my friends have more or less given up, saying there is no work. But I think there are lots of opportunities out there — as long as you're willing to take risks." — A TWENTY-SOMETHING COMPUTER CONSULTANT

*O*pportunities define a generation. The way we look at our careers and our expectations for the world of work are shaped both by the dominant economic forces at play during our early childhood and youth, and by the opportunities available to us as adults. The period in which we first entered the workplace – the early career years – is particularly crucial in forming these attitudes.

When you were growing up, how important did you think work would be in your life? How easily did you expect to find work that matched your interests and goals? Did you feel that career and financial success were basically your birthright? Were you part of a large demographic "bulge" competing for too few jobs, or of a "baby bust" generation in an expanding economy? Did you enter the workplace during a time of dwindling or expanding work opportunities?

Obviously, not all members of the same generation or subgroups within each generation share exactly the same experiences and way of looking at the world. Other factors, such as social class, personality, and geographic location, also shape our values, our expectations for success, and the way we look at our careers. Moreover, each generation shares some characteristics with immediately preceding and subsequent subgenerations.

Still, it *is* possible to make some broad generalizations about the different generations in the workplace and how they are experiencing the new work realities. There are marked generational differences today in how people view their careers, their expectations of employers, their relationships with work colleagues, and their expectations about the future.

There are no firmly agreed upon boundaries for distinguishing the different generations and subgroups within each generation in the workplace today. In particular, the exact makeup of the "baby boom" generation and the generations that followed it has been discussed and debated considerably:

- Some demographers define the baby boom generation as those born between 1946 and 1964.
- Distinguished University of Toronto economist and demographer David Foot, author of the acclaimed *Boom, Bust & Echo*, defines the

baby boom as the generation born between 1947 and 1966, peaking around 1960, followed by a "baby bust" generation born between 1967 and 1979.

- U.S. historians William Strauss and Neil Howe, invoking the concept of a more consistent peer personality, define it as those born between 1943 to 1960: amongst other shared experiences, the boomers remember the death of John F. Kennedy, the protests against war in Vietnam, and the generationally defining 1969 Woodstock Festival. These authors have labeled the subsequent generation, born in the 1960s and 1970s, as the "13th generation" (that is, the thirteenth generation since the birth of the American Republic).

I will use a hybrid definition. Rather than treating those born between 1960 and 1966 as being either boomers or "post-boomers," I will discuss them as a separate group, the "late boomers." These late boomers, in terms of their behaviors and expectations, are sometimes more like their predecessors, and sometimes more like their successors. (This definition is consistent with that of Foot, which identifies the group born between 1960 and 1966, the "back quarter of the baby boom," as a separate subgroup commonly called "Generation X.")

In this chapter, and the next, we will look at the four generations and generational subgroups currently participating in the contemporary workplace:

- Pre-boomers – people born before 1945
- Early boomers – born between 1945 and 1960
- Late boomers – born between 1961 and 1966
- Post-boomers – born between 1967 and 1975.

Each generation is reacting very differently to the new work realities. They bring to the workplace different emotions, expectations, and behaviors.

They also have different feelings and expectations about the other generations in the workplace, which can be a source of strain when they work with
members of these groups.

THE PRE-BOOMERS: THEY HAD IT SO GOOD

At fifty-three, John D. has an impressive track record. After graduating from a
good university with a Bachelor of Engineering, he joined a large petrochemical company. He moved quickly through the management ranks,
gaining exposure to different areas of the organization, before becoming vice
president of human resources. In that role he presided over a major expansion
of the human resources function, drawing upon a seemingly bottomless budget for consultants and training resources. He developed a reputation as a
strong leader – a change agent with a keen appreciation for business priorities.

In 1991 John lost his job after a merger, when the acquiring company's
vice president of human resources was chosen to head the merged function.
John found a new position, but lost it within a year because of a difference
in management philosophy with his boss, the company's president. His boss
felt that John was spending money unnecessarily on training and management development and that he wasn't delivering fast enough on his
objectives.

Since losing that position almost two years ago, John has been on the
search circuit. He has now pretty well given up, saying he's "networked-out."
The major challenge facing him, or so he has been told by countless search
consultants in the industry, is his age. "My children aren't even teenagers
yet," he says, "and I'm considered old. Not only am I just one more statistic
on the road to the new economy, but I feel like I'm living the title of a cover
story for *Fortune* magazine."

The great majority of the pre-boomer generation in today's workplace
were born, like John D., immediately before or during the war years, in a
period of low birth rates. They entered the workplace in the late 1950s and

throughout the 1960s, a time of tremendous economic buoyancy and North American predominance.

The North American economy grew exponentially during this period, and pre-boomers faced comparatively little competition for good jobs. The relatively small size of their generation, combined with a rapidly expanding industrial economy, led to a shortage of managers. People who worked for organizations found themselves in high demand, and their ascent up the corporate ladder was often rapid.

Unlike people in subsequent generations, whose career aspirations were limited as much by competition from other people as by their own talents and ambitions, for pre-boomers career progress was dictated as much by individual ambition as it was by talent. All things being equal, competition from their cohorts was not a limiting factor.

When they looked at their career options, pre-boomers saw a variety of choices. There was plenty of challenging and interesting work, and they felt that, in tandem with their organizations, they could determine their career development. They were not expected to "hit the ground running." Instead, their careers would be nurtured by the organization, and they would be provided with appropriate developmental assignments.

In many respects, pre-boomers shared the values of their immediate predecessors, who were so eloquently portrayed in William H. Whyte's *Organizational Man*. Whyte described these corporate warriors as giving up independence, individual spirit, and family in favor of security and the community of the corporation. They identified with organizational life, its values, and its norms, with being part of something bigger than themselves. Believing in the authority conferred by position in the hierarchy, and in the chain of command, they did not question the expectation of conformity.

Like their predecessors, pre-boomers' own beliefs about career and work had been shaped by their childhood memories of the scarcity and insecurity of the late 1930s and the war years – in sharp contrast to their baby boomer successors, whose values would be shaped by the stability and buoyant economy of the postwar years.

Cautious and thrifty, pre-boomers believed in the value of hard work, and expected their hard work and loyalty to be noticed and rewarded by a relatively benevolent organization, which would provide them, in exchange, with promotions, opportunities for feelings of belonging, and lifelong job security.

A Broken Promise . . . An Endangered Species

The pre-boomers now find themselves an endangered species in the workplace. None of the old rules and traditions that guided their behaviors is true any longer. Their concept of how corporations should be run — with some beneficence — has been tossed out the window. Their organizations now adhere to a management philosophy that many of them don't understand, often implemented by people younger than they are.

In the heyday of the pre-boomers, corporations engaged in exhaustive long-term planning. Today, the new corporate wisdom states that the major competitive advantage is *speed*.

Not surprisingly, many feel like dinosaurs — out of date, antiquated, trapped, with few options. As one middle manager in an electrical utility observed, "I'm made to feel that I'm corporate fat. I'm doing work that I don't like, that a couple of years ago I would have been very quick to express my concerns about. But I'm much more cautious today. I'm two years away from early retirement and I know I'm not high on the employability sweepstakes."

Some pre-boomers characterize themselves as a "lost" or "silent" generation — not big enough or sexy enough to have been profiled and feted like the boomers. Some feel self-conscious about how they are seen by younger managers. As one middle manager said, after a major re-engineering in his company, "I've been *re-injured*. I've been made to feel that not only am I worthless, but that I am actively standing in the way of progress."

Blamed alternately for corporate fatness, and then for corporate leanness and meanness, they feel tainted by the sins of management past – and not entirely without good reason. As one pre-boomer senior manager observes, "Through wave after wave of new management philosophy I have embraced and helped implement changes, including several reorganizations. Having once been one of fifteen general managers, I am now one of three. And I have finally come to realize that I have been progressively nibbling away at my own backside."

An Uncertain Future

Pre-boomers feel especially vulnerable if they haven't saved enough for retirement. They are not confident in their skills and their ability to make it in this new information economy, and recognize that they are competing against younger, often cheaper, and more technically savvy people.

According to a recent study conducted by a team of researchers at the University of Toronto, who spent three years studying the aging workforce at five Canadian and two U.S. companies, "older workers are sitting ducks," expected to bow out gracefully into early retirement when the organization needs to pare down its workforce. Older workers are typically more expensive than younger employees, and are often seen as more disposable:

- Older workers are perceived as being in worse health and taking more sick days than younger colleagues. (Actually, younger workers take more sick days than older workers.)
- Older workers are seen as having more difficulty adjusting to technological change.
- Once older workers lose their jobs, they have serious difficulties finding new work.

The reality of age discrimination in hiring was confirmed by a recent study by Exec-U-Net, an international executive networking association, which showed that the older you are, the harder it is to find a new job. Exec-U-Net surveyed over 1,500 executive search firms and 1,000 human resource executives and found that almost three-quarters said that age plays a critical role well before the age of fifty. Unemployed executives over fifty-five can expect a job search of approximately two years, where their thirty-five-year-old counterparts can expect to find an executive position within eleven months.

Indeed, some may never find new jobs, instead slipping into permanent unemployment. As one former senior manager observed: "This is *not* early retirement. I am unhappily and grudgingly unemployed."

Once fired or cast out into enforced early retirement, some pre-boomers attempt to make a shift into self-employment: consulting, running a small business, buying a franchise, marketing various business services. However, because of their work experience, and their "habits of mind," many lack the skills for success in today's economy.

The transition is particularly difficult for those who have spent many years in senior management roles where they were cosseted by armies of support staff. They were taught to think BIG – big plans, big deals, big initiatives, big programs, all of which required big resources, big staff, big capital. For many, faced with the prospect of setting up their own business, their natural instinct is to think in terms of partnerships, bank loans, and fancy brochures. Living their sheltered corporate existence, they never developed the habits of mind necessary for successful self-employment in a fluid, fast-changing environment, such as:

- taking initiative to carry out work outside a strategic plan
- working alone
- making decisions based on very little information
- being able to "hit the ground running"
- operating with minimum resources.

Often these former senior managers find themselves with rusty technical skills. In their middle- and senior-management jobs, they were rewarded for their generalist skills, not for being a specialist. They may be adept at strategic planning, managing, and team-building, but they no longer have marketable professional/technical skills to sell as independent contractors.

Many are still burdened by debt from multiple marriages, support payments, and children's tuition and weddings. And while a few do have some capital, they are nervous about starting or buying a business or franchise for fear of being completely wiped out.

Having lost the status conferred on them by their membership in the ranks of senior management, they now experience what sociologist C. Wright Mills once referred to as "status panic": the loss of prestige and social esteem conferred by professional achievement and professional belonging. Not all pre-boomers in this situation fail, of course. Those who go into a business that builds upon their own industry experience, or buy a business that uses their financial management skills, may, in fact, be very successful. But they are definitely playing in a new sandbox.

ADAPTING TO NEW REALITIES

After a reorganization, George, a vice president of human resources for a large telecommunications company, and Tom, his training manager, found themselves out of work. They struck up a business partnership as consultants, offering training seminars to large organizations. Tom greatly admired George's "boardroom presence" – his ability to schmooze with the movers and shakers, the VPs and CEOs – and saw George as his "ticket" into the offices of the decision-makers.

And George did his thing, just the way he had always done it inside the corporate environment. He was polished, slick, and smooth, very political. Always having lunch with senior people, always playing golf with them. But

45

he couldn't close a deal. Soon Tom recognized that he was the more resourceful of the two and that he had the necessary skills to sell his services himself. The partnership was dissolved; Tom scaled down his goals and continued to develop his training business. But it took George two years to sort out his confusion between presentation and content, and to understand that "big," "flashy," and "brassy" doesn't necessarily cut it anymore. Ultimately, though, he learned that it is not enough just to know the "right" people – you also have to offer a concrete, definable service of clear benefit. Building on his wide network of senior contacts in organizations, he is now a partner in a financial planning firm, selling services to senior managers.

A New Set of Loyalties

Pre-boomers still employed in organizations are experiencing considerable strain in shifting their mind-set. Intellectually, they understand they need to move *from corporate loyalty and identification to enlightened self-interest*, to become strategic in managing their careers, and look after their own best interests. But their lifelong training tells them that acting in your own self-interest is synonymous with selfishness and not being a "team player."

In one client organization, the entire middle layer of management (over five hundred people) was vaporized within three months. I spoke with one of the casualties three years after that event. Now a project director in systems for a utility company, he sees himself as one of the lucky ones: many of his ex-colleagues are still unemployed. "One minute you're there, the next – poof! – you're gone. I think the hardest part was recognizing that I'm only as good as my resume – that I have to sell myself all the time."

Again and again in workshops, I hear pre-boomers express their discomfort at the concept of self-promotion. They find it foreign, distasteful, and even unseemly to be constantly promoting themselves within an organization, looking after their own interests rather than the needs of the business.

The challenge facing pre-boomers, particularly those in vulnerable work situations, is to develop a new framework for the daily business of working. They need to find opportunities to *leverage their wisdom and experience* to the benefit of both themselves and their clients or employers — situations where they will be valued for who they are rather than being made to feel self-conscious about their age. (In Chapters 7, 8, and 9 we will look at the new career landscape and the new principles, rules, and skills for success in that landscape.) Like the early boomers who follow them, pre-boomers have to revise their expectations and definitions of success.

THE EARLY BOOMERS: THE BIG GENERATION

Peter Z. is a forty-eight-year-old executive with one of North America's largest petrochemical companies. To all outward appearances, he is extremely successful. Peter started work straight from university as an analyst and has worked his way up to his current position of vice president of marketing.

Peter's colleagues describe him as extremely capable, even brilliant — very conceptual, with a strong business sense, and an almost intuitive ability to develop a persuasive business case. His counsel is often sought out by the senior vice president and the president.

For the last few years, however, things have not been going so well for Peter. Like many men of his generation, he was slow to admit to himself that he was encountering difficulties. But matters have now reached the point where he is experiencing extreme stress on all fronts.

He is working longer and harder than ever to meet demanding deadlines, but with less and less enthusiasm. Although he is still receiving above average, and occasionally superior, performance ratings, he has also had a number of conflicts with his coworkers lately, whom he perceives as "empire building" and putting their own ego needs before the needs of the business. He is also doing work for which he is fundamentally ill-matched: work that requires political savvy as much as professional expertise, and basically plays against his major strengths.

For the first time in his career, Peter is worried about the future. He is not sure how much longer he can stand his current work situation. But given his age, gender, and length of service with a single company, he worries that it will be difficult to find a job elsewhere.

The strains Peter is feeling at work are having an impact on the home front as well. His partner says that lately he's become distant, preoccupied, moody, and irritable. He is suffering severe insomnia; having given up his fitness activities, Peter has put on thirty pounds in the past year and is basically slipping into a spiral of mild depression, losing his sense of confidence in his own competence.

If Peter were to lose his job tomorrow, and if he trusted his skills, he could be quite successful as a freelancer. But he is uncomfortable at the idea of operating without any of the traditional corporate trappings. His sense of self is tied to his corporate identity, doing work for a prestigious organization and holding a prestigious title. Without that corporate identity, he is not sure who he would be.

Someone Special

Early boomers are the true "bulge" generation, born between 1946 and 1960. They entered the workplace from the late 1960s through to the 1980s. Endlessly profiled and celebrated, the early boomers have shaped what were to become the dominant characteristics of the workplace, much as they have shaped the larger world around them.

Growing up in an era of rapid industrial expansion, the early boomers believed they could be, more or less, anything they wanted to be. They fully expected that their superior education and hard work would enable them to participate in all the goodies that society could provide.

The 1950s and 1960s were a time of North American political and economic ascendancy. Daily life was characterized by stability – stay-at-home mothers, suburban home ownership, 3.5 kids, all deftly portrayed as the middle-class model to which all could aspire in such TV shows as *Leave It to Beaver* and *Father Knows Best*.

The boomers' parents extolled the same values depicted in Whyte's *Organizational Man*, celebrating the virtues of corporate employment as the ultimate career goal. (Remarkably, only 2 percent of the Harvard graduating class of 1942, the parents of these boomers, indicated a career interest in self-employment.) It was a time when North Americans believed in their leaders and in the goodness of their social institutions, and trusted government to solve problems and provide leadership.

The early boomers believed they were special, and for good reason. They were courted when they entered the workplace. They were placed by their organizations into special development programs; moved from department to department to ensure maximum exposure to different business areas; sent on the most expensive training and personal growth programs.

Indeed, the major concern of human resource departments at this time was: were these early boomers challenged, did they feel they were growing? If they left their jobs, their employers conducted exit interviews to probe on those dimensions, to see where the organization might have failed them.

Stuck in the Middle with You

The early boomers came to expect meaningful work, rapid promotions, and handsome financial remuneration as almost their birthright. And yet by the early 1980s, the problems with this scenario were already beginning to show.

There were, quite simply, too many early boomers awaiting their turn to grab the "big brass ring," too many people chasing too few promotions. Organizations could not meet their needs for career growth as quickly as they had with the pre-boomers. They asked, "How can we keep them motivated and productive under such circumstances?" In retrospect, such concerns now appear quaint.

The problem of slow career advancement has given way to the problem of *no* advancement. Instead of moving up more slowly than they might have liked, many early boomers have hit a full stop. They have reached a career *plateau*, a point in their organizational careers from which further advancement is unlikely.

It's true that everyone eventually reaches this point in their career: the higher you go, the fewer positions there are in the organizational pyramid, and the more people competing for them. Most people hit their plateau well below the top of the pyramid. But the early boomers have, on average, plateaued earlier than the previous generation, due to both the sheer size of their generation and the relentless downsizing and delayering of organizations that have drastically reduced the number of managerial positions.

When Douglas C. joined his firm as a purchasing manager six years ago, for example, he looked above him and saw three management levels separating him from the president, and plenty of opportunity to advance in his career. Douglas is still in the same job, but as a result of re-engineering and delayering, there is now only one management level between Douglas and the president, and, he says, "A lot of people with better qualifications than I have are quadruple-parked on the few spots likely to open up." Douglas is tired of being stuck in the same job, and depressed at the thought that he has nowhere else to go.

Martha R. is a school teacher, aspiring to be a vice principal. "There are so many people chasing the same jobs, they keep pushing up the required credentials," she complains. "I have an M.Ed. and an M.B.A. What more do they want?"

And yet plateauing is no longer considered a major issue by many organizations. It's as if organizations now expect their people to be motivated merely by having work, rather than by prospects for advancement. And to some degree, this judgment is justified. Certainly, there is a critical difference between now and then in people's expectations. In the 1980s my clients worried that their people had unrealistic expectations about advancement. *Today most people have few or no expectations.*

It is not surprising, given how they were coddled and wooed in their early career years, that many early boomers are finding it difficult to deal with the new career and work realities. Where once they were special, many, particularly those in the first wave of baby boomers, born in the late 1940s and early 1950s, feel they are now *dispensable*. Where once their every feeling of well-being was fussed over, they now feel they are commodities, valued only as long as their stamina and thick skins keep them viable.

Like the pre-boomers, many early boomers have either lost their jobs through downsizing, geographical relocation, or mergers at least once in recent years, or else are worried about job loss. Virtually no one has been unaffected by the rise of the new, ruthless economy. Moreover, early boomers are at an age where they need to worry about the mobility of their skills and their overall employability – particularly if they have spent a lot of their working career in one industry or organization.

Craftsman in an Industrial Age . . . Dreams Die Hard

David K., a forty-year-old accountant, likens himself to "a pre-industrial craftsman at the dawn of the industrial age":

"I thought that if I worked hard, by this stage in my career I should be able to enjoy some of the fruits of my labor. That I would feel established in my profession, possibly be a partner in the firm. Instead, I feel that every day I'm re-earning my right to be a manager here, to work here . . .

"They keep telling me to get rid of my baggage – to look at the world without my old expectations. And I understand that intellectually. But the bottom line is that I grew up with these expectations. These were what I was socialized to believe. And these expectations are real."

Like a pre-industrial artisan, David invested his youth in developing a set of skills, aptitudes, and experience based on the world he was raised in. But technology has changed his world just as surely as the Industrial Revolution changed that of the artisan, leaving David quite bewildered.

Not only have they not met their career expectations, early boomers have also not met their financial expectations, despite having believed in and followed all the "tried and true" financial chestnuts. They bought homes, which they thought would increase in value, taking on large mortgages following the popular wisdom that "the first few years are the toughest – your income will grow, your mortgage will be increasingly easy to pay off." But not only has their income not increased as expected, in many cases it has *decreased* – along with the value of their homes.

Many are "maxed-out" on credit card debt, not to mention the costs associated with holding onto an increasingly more tenuous lifestyle: two cars to support two careers; an expensive mortgage and perhaps a second home or cottage; private schools to provide some extra protection for their children in an increasingly difficult world.

Early boomers' expectations of what they thought they would have attained at this stage of their career are colliding with what they will likely attain. They see themselves as *provisional* members of the upper middle class, a status they will hold only until there is another reorganization. They must now come to terms with a work ethic that makes employment status conditional upon their ability to remain employable, which, in turn, is provisional on *being able to "take it"* – the frenetic pace, the turn-on-a-dime flexibility, the constant requirement to "sell yourself" within the organization, and the incessant and unrelenting changes imposed by new technologies. The new employment contract brooks no coasting. Full-throttle energy is the minimum requirement.

Early boomers are feeling squeezed on all fronts. The world of corporate work is no longer recognizable to them. Younger, more technologically adept managers are nipping at their heels. Many are reassessing their values relative to career demands (see Chapter 6); their retirement security is far from guaranteed (see Chapter 7); and they fear for their children's future (see Chapter 11). When they look above them, early boomers see fewer and fewer levels in a delayered and flattened organization through which they can move. Although intellectually they realize that they must revise their perspective, old dreams and expectations die hard.

Overworked, Underappreciated

"Here I am, at what should be the best time of my life . . . a time to spend nurturing my children, developing in my profession and my career. Instead, I never see my family, and my most important relationships are suffering. And in terms of my career, although I'm told that I need to be constantly learning . . . heck, who has time for that? It's all I can do to respond to the demands, to survive. And it's not as if anyone even notices, much less appreciates it."

Early boomers grew up believing that there was a work ethic operative affirming that effort attracts commensurate rewards. As they find themselves working at a super-aerobic pace, making significant sacrifices in their personal life, they are questioning the effort–reward equation. Many are finding it difficult coming to terms with what they consider a double whammy: a declining standard of living coupled with a seventy-hour work week.

This feeling of being overworked and underappreciated – that their sacrifices aren't noticed, or particularly valued – is one of the key themes underlying the pervasive new "career diseases" that we will discuss in Chapter 6.

Because they see that their sacrifices aren't particularly valued and, more importantly, that they as people are not particularly valued, many early boomers are wondering if the sacrifices are really worth making. Some of the alternatives that they are pursuing have more in common with their younger counterparts than they might care to admit: there is a thin line between a twenty-something "slacker" and a forty-something convert to "voluntary simplicity."

Concern for Their Children

Perhaps more than any preceding generation, early boomers must struggle with an issue that reaches well beyond their own career and aspirations: the future and safety of their children. Parents, of course, have always worried about their children's future. But in the past, this concern was typically grounded in the knowledge that their children could aspire to "bigger and better" things than themselves. The focus was on providing offspring with the education and training that were the "magic bullet" to success. Today, many parents worry about a future in which their children will be much worse off than themselves.

A forty-something mother in one of my workshops recently described the horns of the dilemma as she experiences it: "Even if I encourage him to go to university or college, there is no guarantee that there will be work for him when he's finished. The whole world could be different in four years. And an undergraduate degree isn't worth anything anymore. Now you need an M.A. or a Ph.D. Kids today can't possibly run hard enough to keep up!" I think many people now believe what was unimaginable five years ago: that they, as parents, can do nothing to ensure that their children are prepared for work in the new economy.

Actually, although there are no quick solutions available, parents can use many strategies to prepare their children for an uncertain world. (Chapter 11 looks at these strategies in detail.)

Compounding their anxiety about their children's future is the fear that many have for the safety of their sons and daughters. There has never been such pure, pervasive *angst* regarding personal security to compare with that being experienced by today's parents in relation to their children. As one early boomer mother states: "I live in what is considered to be a safe, family-oriented neighborhood. Yet every time my child goes for milk, I worry. I worry about who the neighbors are. I worry about the safety of the school. In fact, there is very little I don't worry about."

I recently conducted an informal survey with thirty of my clients who have children. "What is the number one concern or worry you have about your children?" I asked them. Extraordinarily, every one of them identified an issue related to safety: from drunk drivers to child molesters, from school yard bullies to drug dealers, they saw their children under potential threat from every side.

While there is evidence to suggest that today's youth are more at risk of violence than previous generations, there is nonetheless the possibility that this notable level of anxiety is related to something else: to the pace and impact of change on the larger sense of security among early boomers. Is the fear for their children's safety somehow related to the general feeling that there is an urgent need to "get the wagons into a circle"? Given the pressure that early boomers are feeling from all quarters, it seems entirely possible.

A Good Run

But while early boomers complain about debt, overwork, and fragmented careers, and pre-boomers feel that they are being squeezed out of the workforce before they are ready, in relative terms, each of these generations has had a good run. Each, at least for awhile, commanded a more-than-fair share of the pie. As we will see in the next chapter, the next generations have not been so lucky.

FOUR

Late for the Feast: Late Boomers and Post-Boomers

"It seems that everywhere you go, there's a roadblock. There's work out there. But it's much more difficult to find. There's an awful lot more competition. And when you do find something, no matter how mind-numbing it may be, you're told you're lucky because you have a job." — *A THIRTY-YEAR-OLD MANAGEMENT TRAINER*

*T*oo late for the feast — for the abundance of good jobs and material wealth produced in the golden years of the postwar boom. That has been the experience of the late or tail-end boomers and, to an even greater degree, for the post-boomers. Reaching maturity in a much more constricted economic environment than their predecessors, their experience of the workplace has been a struggle every step of the way.

The Late Boomers – X-Plaint

Laura R. did a graduate degree in journalism in the late 1970s, with the goal of getting a job in the then booming magazine industry. But she graduated just when the recession of the early 1980s was hitting that industry hard. Advertising revenues were down, magazines were shrinking or disappearing, and no one was hiring. Laura tried her hand at freelance writing, but there was little work available, and she was competing against much more skilled and experienced writers. Eventually, after a number of stints on community newspapers and short-term government contracts in communications, she was hired as the editor of a trade magazine covering the medical supplies industry, where she is still employed. This was not what she set out to become, but she is grateful to be working in her profession when so many of her friends are still scrambling to establish a foothold. Still, she yearns to be involved in a higher-profile magazine with greater challenge, responsibility, and prestige.

If the early boomers are now feeling the strains of unfulfilled expectations, their younger brothers and sisters – the late or tail-end boomers – are feeling it all the more sharply. Born between 1961 and 1966, most university-educated late boomers entered the workplace in the recessionary early 1980s, through to the late '80s.

This younger group of boomers is the true "Generation X" that Canadian author Douglas Coupland wrote about in his novel of the same name. (Coupland was born in 1961, like the characters in his book.) But so anonymous is this generation, they have lost even their own generational title to the twenty-something post-boomers now more usually called "Gen X-ers."

The way late boomers feel about their lives and careers was shaped by the world in which they were socialized, just as it was for the previous generations. But where stability and prosperity were the hallmarks of the early boomers' childhood, the childhood of their younger brothers and sisters was marked by upheaval, and by the apparent unravelling of society in the late

1960s and early 1970s. The anti-war movement raged on college campuses, while on the home front divorce rates soared across North America.

The late boomers grew up in a time when every idea and every once sacred belief – from teacher-centered education and streamed classrooms to the right of the schools to teach religion, to the right of the United States to be in Vietnam – was suddenly open to question.

They were the children of North American economic and social decline: the first generation of latchkey children; the first generation whose parents were divorcing at a rate of approximately two to one. They grew up in the wake of Vietnam and Watergate, when government had forfeited much of the public's trust in its ability to solve problems and provide leadership.

Perhaps just as important, however, was the impact of the career opportunities available to late boomers when they entered the workplace. Looking above them, they saw the ranks swollen with early baby boomers whose career paths were already bottlenecked, and who were too young to be contenders for early retirement.

The late boomers entered the workforce at a time when organizations were just beginning to re-engineer, cutting out whole management ranks in pursuit of cost efficiencies. About 20 percent of North American job losses since 1988 has been in the ranks of middle management, precisely the level to which people in the late boomers' age bracket aspired. For many, career progress came at a snail's pace. And for some, it never occurred at all.

Many late boomers now find themselves dissatisfied with the pace of their progress within their organizations. Others are still struggling to get any sort of foothold: like so many of their twenty-something counterparts, they are still moving from one dead-end job or temporary work assignment to another. For some, the solution has been to stay in school indefinitely, continuing their education whether to better equip themselves for the job market or to postpone entry into an inhospitable marketplace.

How They Feel

Despite a good deal of discouragement, the late boomers for the most part have not given up on their careers. As compared to the post-boomer generation behind them, they entered a workplace still largely defined by traditional values. They are still operating to some extent under a more traditional career paradigm, with more traditional expectations of success.

The possibility of reaching the ranks of middle to senior management is still real to them – if they have not yet achieved it themselves, some of their friends will have done so, particularly those in more entrepreneurial and younger work environments and industries such as fashion, information technology, and entertainment. Whether or not their career expectations are realistic, they are based on what they were socialized to believe was realistic, attainable, and desirable when they were growing up.

In many ways, late boomers are caught in a sort of limbo between early boomers and post-boomers – a limbo characterized by a gnawing ambivalence. Like the early boomers, they are determined to participate in the good life. And yet they are haunted by the feeling that they will never attain it.

Dissatisfied with the rewards they are receiving at work, late boomers question the effort–reward equation just as intensely as their older counterparts, although for somewhat different reasons. To the extent that they still pursue the rewards they believe organizations can offer them – and many of them do – they feel that there is little left for them. It seems to them that the early boomers have gobbled up all the goodies: the management roles, the discretionary budgets, the opportunity to work on, or close to, the senior management team.

Not surprisingly, some have developed a "why kill myself?" attitude: they don't believe that hard work will produce the coveted rewards in any case. As Linda T., a market researcher in her early thirties, observes: "It doesn't matter how hard I work, I know I'm never going to have the same standard of living as my parents. When I look above me in the company, I see that the boomers have all the good jobs – and they're not planning on going any where anytime soon. Besides, when I see how hard they work, I'm not sure I'm ready to make those kinds of sacrifices. My personal life is important to me. But I do need challenging work. I couldn't imagine doing the same thing over and over again."

Other late boomers, particularly those who are still struggling to establish themselves, are angry and cynical – more like the next generation of post-boomers. They are resentful at the older groups whom they see as having swallowed up their future: "You've used up our resources and spent our future. Now we'll have to support you in retirement, although we'll never earn as much as you did."

When I asked a young thirty-something friend which generation had most reason to feel disappointed with their career opportunities, he responded that his generation had the lousiest deal. I thought about it for a moment and concluded that he was probably right, but not for the reasons he thought.

In fact, in terms of both his career and his overall lifestyle, he was much better positioned than those in their twenties. The difference is that the twenty-somethings had never *expected* anything better than what they have now. My friend had expected much more, and he had got at least a taste of the lifestyle he pursued. He was doing well at work, he owned a house, he and his wife had started a family. But he had grown up expecting to be bet-ter off than his parents, and now faced the possibility of having to settle for less. This discrepancy – between what was expected and what is reality – is prevalent among late boomers, and an understandable source of their anger.

Every year I deliver career planning workshops to chartered accountants who have just received their professional designation. Many of these people have more than one graduate degree to their credit and have acquired work experience in management roles elsewhere. Resentful of their early boomer bosses, they say: "I'm tired of listening to these boomers whine and complain about their $150,000 mortgages, the cost of private schools, how expensive it is to pay for a nanny. I don't think I'll ever even be in a position to complain about those things. They say we should be patient and wait our turn. The fact is, they just happened to get there first."

Many late boomers see the early boomers as a pampered mass who have blocked their prospects for career advancement. When thinking about their boomer bosses, late boomers have a belief that "there but for an accident of birth year, go I." Relative to their early boomer siblings, late boomers feel that they have been dealt a bad hand of cards, that the boomers got everything from Woodstock to great careers, while they inherited AIDS, McJobs, and a crushing national debt.

And the facts back up this perception. By the time they were thirty, the group born between 1946 and 1956 earned 30 percent more than their parents. At the same point in their career, those born between 1957 and 1964 earned 10 percent *less* than their parents, according to University of Waterloo professor of actuarial science Robert Brown.

Not only do they feel early boomers have blocked them in terms of their career progress, late boomers also feel blocked on the home front. They came into the housing market after the early boomers bid up the price of housing, so that owning a home is significantly more expensive, particularly given their relatively lower incomes. As one thirty-something actuary ruefully observed, "Here I am, part of a dual-career family and I can't afford an entry-level home in an unpronounceable town fifty miles out of another unpronounceable town, fifty miles outside of a city with public transportation."

Late Boomers' Fear
Late boomers worry about being overlooked, about their skills becoming obsolete before they've had their crack at management. They worry that they are not as technically savvy as their younger siblings, and because of their age they may be too expensive to compete against the most recent crop of graduates.

Late boomers are old enough to have invested significantly in a particular career path, so that a change of course, such as going back to school to move on to another career path, or to update technical skills, is an option only some are able to entertain. Many have young families and financial responsibilities so that a period of no earnings is frightening.

What They Want

The savvy late boomers recognize that they may well stand to benefit from the first waves of early retirement and so want to be well-positioned for longer-term career success. They may not have the readily available opportunities for advancement at the moment, but they do have significant opportunities for *learning*.

Indeed, learning may be the one word that best captures the career incentive of this group. As long as the traditional rewards of promotion and salary increases are no longer part of the equation, they look for opportunities for personal development and growth: "If I can't move ahead, then give me challenging work." "If you can't pay me well, then give me the opportunity to develop skills that will look good on my resume."

Another key word describing their hopes and expectations is *balance*. They don't want to emulate the lifestyle of their boomer bosses. "I see my bosses working sixty or seventy hours a week. They don't have a life. What's the point? I would rather spend time with my children, and do things that are important to me or the community." Or, as one marketing consultant said to her early boomer boss: "Don't hold yourself up as a model of personal sacrifice. I don't honor your sacrifices. Nor do I believe that any sacrifices I might make will be honored by you. They won't even be noticed."

Post-Boomers – Slackers? Not!

"We are hard-pressed to define any personal expectations for ourselves. They simply do not exist. Nor do we have any idea what our parents' expectations of

us are, if they ever existed. They've been very busy."

— CYNTHIA R., TWENTY-SOMETHING

"My generation assumes nothing . . . You boomers assumed too much for too long."
— JOAN C., A TWENTY-SOMETHING ASSISTANT MARKETING MANAGER

Twenty-six-year-old John D. has degrees in communications, arts, and law. But he is working as a bicycle courier while also playing keyboards in a local bar band — much to the distress of his very prominent and accomplished parents.

When you ask John what he will be doing in five years, he says that he doesn't know, and that it's not an important question for him. "What's important is that right now, I'm having fun. I'd rather deliver packages to people in suits than be one. And I really think this band could make it. But if not, that's okay, too — at least I'll know that I gave it my best shot."

If personal and political instability helped define the character of the late boomers, the same is doubly true of the post-boomers, the twenty-something generation who grew up in a world characterized by social, economic, and environmental upheaval: from fear of nuclear annihilation to the end of the cold war; from the energy crisis to the greenhouse effect and the ozone hole; from elaborate government social programs to their collapse into a black hole of public sector debt; from the sexual revolution to the fragmentation of families and the AIDS pandemic; from VCRs to video games to direct-broadcast satellites and a two-hundred-channel universe; from giant mainframe computers to laptops and personal organizers; and on and on.

Post-boomer early career experiences have been disappointing. Many are stuck in the kind of entry-level or one-step-up-from-entry-level jobs which were once the first step up the ladder for freshly minted graduates, but which now lead nowhere. Others are in temporary and contract work that doesn't challenge them or properly use their skills. Trapped in low-paying, dead-end jobs, many still live with their parents, with little hope of ever moving out.

The post-boomers entered the worst job market ever for university graduates. Employment in management and technical fields grew an average 1.8 million jobs each year during the 1980s, compared with an average of 310,000 jobs per year in 1992 and 1993.

About 20 percent of recent university graduates are *unemployed* while many others are *underemployed*. Indeed, the U.S. Bureau of Labor Statistics forecasts that nearly one-third of college graduates from the classes of 1990 through 2005 will take jobs whose content doesn't really require a degree. In Canada, economist Susan Crompton analyzed the data on male employment and concluded that a university degree is now worth about what a high school diploma was worth less than a generation ago.

No Expectations

Expectations are based, at least in part, on an appraisal of what is realistically attainable. Given the job market they have entered, it is perhaps not surprising that many twenty-somethings have *no* expectations: no expectations of rapid career growth, or corporate fairness, or a predictable future with increasing responsibility within one or more organizations.

That said, I have noticed that post-boomers as a generation fall into two somewhat different subgroups in terms of how they respond to the work and career realities confronting them:

- Apathetic, angry, and demotivated; and
- Resourceful and entrepreneurial.

Apathetic post-boomers have given up trying almost before they have begun. They see nothing left for them in an economic environment where it is impossible for them to get a secure foothold. They don't believe they will have a future. They see themselves caught in a never-ending cycle of working for low wages in a nowhere job, returning to school to upgrade, only to have access to nothing but another dead-end job – or no job.

For the second group of post-boomers, however, having few or no expectations for themselves has *freed them up psychologically*. They feel no pressure to be one thing or another, and as a result are free to choose their own direction. They are resourceful, energetic, actively engaged, and optimistic.

As Jane M., a twenty-five-year-old would-be journalist, puts it: "There are lots of opportunities, but there are also lots of risks. And the opportunities don't come wrapped up with their own little road sign which says 'OPPORTUNITY STRAIGHT AHEAD.' So you have to be much more vigilant, and develop a sixth sense for what may be possible, all the while being prepared to deal with the potholes and roadblocks."

This upbeat group of twenty-somethings holds the promise of creating a functional new work paradigm for this quicksand economy.

New Work Paradigm

I met Helen W., a journalism student, after a speech I gave about the new career realities.

What Helen found most instructive about my presentation was not the description of the new realities and implications for managing your career, which virtually everyone over thirty had responded to. ("I already knew all that stuff about the end of the job," she said.) Rather, she was intrigued by an almost throwaway comment about how we could all take a lesson from the post-boomers who are modeling new work relationships. She particularly liked the verb I used to describe the new way of working – "cobbling" together a living – which she said described her life perfectly.

A quintessentially well-educated twenty-something, Helen is multilingual, has undergraduate degrees in law and psychology, and a Master's degree in French from the Sorbonne. What does she do for a living? A bit of this, and a bit of that . . . some desktop publishing for consultants, the occasional freelance article for the neighborhood newspaper, receptionist/clerical support for some local offices, and, of course, the inevitable occasional waitressing. She says she likes the variety, although she is sometimes weary of having to constantly sell herself. But she is definitely not angry about her prospects: *she never expected anything different.*

Jared D. has an M.B.A. and an M.Sc. in psychology. He is currently study-ing everything he can get his hands on about franchising, as he is looking to establish and franchise a chain of learning clinics for learning disabled children. "At twenty-nine, I've already had four very different careers," he says. "Five if I count the film newspaper I started in high school. If I work until I'm seventy and change careers every five years or so, I'll have the opportunity for about ten different careers."

Many post-boomers, like Helen and Jared, are comfortable living with constant ambiguity and upheaval. Growing up in a world on fast-forward has taught them to expect nothing less. They think very untraditionally about jobs. They are prepared to travel to find work; to work part time or freelance; to set up their own business; to work in fields unrelated to their education. (About 25 percent of law graduates, for example, are working in unrelated fields, according to the Law Society of Upper Canada.) Some will go back to school for the sake of learning, not just to improve their job mar-ket credentials.

Indeed, examining their attitudes and behaviors can provide us with use-ful insights into strategies for managing the new work realities.

When I ask early career professionals attending our workshops about their expectations for the future, only a handful (less than 10 percent) see themselves in an identifiable job. This is a dramatic change from just a few years ago, when approximately half the participants in these workshops saw themselves as pos-sibly heading for a senior management role within their organizations.

These resourceful post-boomers still see senior management as a possibility. But so is working in another organization, or self-employment as a consultant, or being an entrepreneur, or perhaps doing a whole bunch of different things. In other words, there are many options; and nothing seems particularly more likely than anything else.

On the whole, *they see their relationships with employers as economic exchanges* in the purest sense. There is no sacrifice involved and no expectations for loyalty on either side.

LONGER-TERM PROSPECTS: WELL-ADAPTED OR ALIENATED?

What will be the *longer-term* impact of post-boomers' current underparticipation in the workforce on their work habits and beliefs? Here are some disturbing trends:

- Two-thirds of U.S. high school seniors surveyed by *Scholastic* magazine believe that the country will be worse ten years from today than it is today.
- According to one recent estimate, one-sixth of sixteen- to twenty-four-year-old Americans are "disaffected and disconnected." They see no roles for themselves in an "informated" society, and think of themselves as having an empty future.
- Thirty-five percent of college and university graduates describe themselves as underemployed five years after graduating, that is, in jobs that do not require their qualifications, according to Statistics Canada.
- There is significant rising "credentialism": a university degree is now worth what a high school education used to be worth a generation ago. Many organizations require university degrees as a minimum requirement for entry-level work.
- At a time when university education is critical to getting any kind of work, and to longer-term success in the economy, university students are dropping out to avoid crushing debt. Students face rising tuition

costs, while receiving less financial support from cash-squeezed parents. They may well ask: "Why put myself in such financial straits if it won't even lead to a job?"

Early career experiences play a significant role in longer-term career success. "Learning the ropes" – whether it be how organizations work, how to work with people of different disciplines, cultures, and ages, or the importance of honoring commitments to team members – sets the foundation for later work effectiveness.

The jury is still out on the longer-term impact of the post-boomers' delayed start on their attitudes toward work, career skills, and degree of success in the workplace. Arguably, those who are adaptable and resourceful will be better prepared in the longer term to thrive in a free-form economy. Their lack of expectations regarding career success will help them to evaluate work opportunities in terms of their intrinsic qualities: for example, challenge and learning rather than prestige and status. But not getting work they want, and being rejected for jobs, leads to an erosion of self-esteem. If you have been trained as a professional, no matter how resourceful you are, going from one dead-end service job to another takes its toll over time.

Their technical skills may also become rusty. Younger, more technically current workers may well pass them by. But those who set up their own businesses and know they can rely only on themselves, who see opportunities (with attendant risks) everywhere, will succeed, whether as entrepreneurs or independent contractors, or inside an organization where their self-management skills will serve them well.

Unfortunately, not everyone is equally resilient. For those more affected by ongoing rejection and less capable of demonstrating initiative and self-management, this lack of meaningful early participation in the workforce *will* take its toll, for all the reasons outlined.

Getting It Right

Fear of making the wrong career decisions ranks among the major stresses for post-boomers.

For example, Sharon A. is a recently qualified chartered accountant with a large public accounting firm. At twenty-eight her options seem almost unlimited. Remarkably, Sharon's firm has already indicated that they see her as being possible eventual "partner material." She is interested in specializing, but worries that changes in the business environment could render her specialization obsolete. CAs in industry can often command higher salaries earlier in their careers, and Sharon knows that she could probably make more money by leaving her firm (although longer term, she may be financially better off staying where she is). And so she hesitates, unable to make a commitment, terrified of making a mistake.

Having grown up in a very uncertain world, post-boomers like Sharon have no particular belief in traditional values and institutions. Their loyalty is to themselves, rather than any particular organization. They know better than to seek the security of lifelong employment, or a good pension plan. And yet they look for a kind of security all the same – that of making the "right" career decision.

One of the real problems that people like Sharon face is in *knowing* whether they are in the right job. She asks, "How do I know there isn't a better job out there for me, one that is better paid, more challenging, or provides more learning?" Sharon is looking for signposts, a *guarantee* that this is the *right* job for her.

The culture of scarcity in which they have been reared has raised the level of angst around the judgment calls they must make as they explore their options. Because they are starting well behind "the pack" (of both early and late boomers), post-boomers feel each career decision they make must be the right one, in case they fall even further behind. They see that the stakes are much higher now than they were for their older siblings, because the world of work is much less forgiving.

A Question of Balance

Howard P. is a forty-something manager with a staff of bright twenty-somethings whom he often finds aggravating: "They want to get ahead, they want new challenges all the time, but you can't ask them to work long hours, or to give up their weekends. When I was their age, if I was asked to work late or on the weekend, I didn't call it overtime, I didn't expect to be paid for it. I didn't ask if the work would be interesting . . . I just did it. The expectation was that if you wanted to get ahead — and we all did — then you did whatever work your boss asked you to do. End of story."

Many boomer managers like Howard P. find twenty-somethings a challenge to manage. Like the late boomers, but to an even greater extent, post-boomers want to keep their lives in balance, and question excessive overtime. I've heard many senior managers complain that post-boomers are "unrealistic," "not willing to put in their time," "too concerned about balancing their work and personal life."

This is not to suggest that early boomers don't care about balancing work and personal life. Of course they do. But the post-boomers, dissatisfied with the rewards they are getting at work now, are more skeptical about the potential rewards for working even harder.

Which brings to mind a conversation I had with a forty-something partner in a large public accounting firm. He was complaining about his young staff's seeming lack of motivation and willingness to work long hours and do weekend work.

"Where were you when you were twenty-nine?" I asked him.

"Living in Harbourfront [an expensive condominium in downtown Toronto]," he replied.

"When you thought about your future in the firm, what were your expectations for the next five to eight years?"

"I thought I would be made a partner," he answered.

In that simple statement he summed up all that was different between the two age groups. The boomer boss I talked to was motivated to do that which brought him the rewards he valued. Post-boomers are doing exactly the same thing. The big difference is that the rewards are less likely to be found inside the context of work. *It is an entirely reasonable and predictable response to invest time and effort in your personal life, if that is where you perceive the rewards to be more probable.*

An Irreverent Generation

"How can you be twenty-five years old and already so jaded?" one senior manager commented on the cynicism of his twenty-something staff about the company's motives.

Many post-boomers are cynical about organizations, and have a very pragmatic view of their relationship to their employer. Asked "What skills and attitudes will you need to be successful in your career?" the most frequent response is "You need to be loyal to yourself." They *know* no one will look after them. They see no reason to surrender themselves to an entity which, they believe, does not particularly care about their well-being, and are unwilling to put their personal lives on hold in order to accommodate corporate demands. They resist what one woman described as "the politics of overwork," where people wear their long hours and weekend work like a status symbol.

They do not want to worship at the same altar where their parents were sacrificed in waves of restructuring. This is all the more real if they see themselves, as many do, as the *abandoned children* of career-obsessed parents.

Twenty-seven-year-old Carolyn, a marketing manager with a pharmaceutical company, comments: "My father started working for a company when he was nineteen, straight out of school. He always worked really long hours.

Whenever we complained that we didn't get to spend any time with him, he'd say that the company had been good to him, and that he had to be good to the company in return. They fired him when he was fifty – threw him out like a piece of garbage.

"He hasn't been able to find work since, partly because of his age, but partly because of his long service. Employers don't think he could adapt to a new company. He's very bitter now. And he always says, 'Don't ever count on anyone else to look after you. You can only count on yourself.'"

Management schools report that students are most interested in courses in entrepreneurship and small business management. Some corporations say that it is difficult to find enough people on campus interested in being interviewed for corporate positions. A significantly higher percentage of graduating students are choosing careers in investment banking and management consulting (high impact, high-potential earnings, high risk) over more traditional corporate careers.

Post-boomers are reluctant to make a commitment to an organization or a career. Ask them how their job is going, and they will answer with a qualified and tentative, "It's going well . . . so far." It's as if they worry that no sooner will they make a commitment than it will be taken away from them. This unwillingness to commit may be a healthy defense mechanism, a means of reducing the vulnerability they experience in the workplace.

Many, in fact, have mixed feelings about working at all. A few twenty-something professionals (accountants and lawyers) I have talked to worry that their university-educated contemporaries who are flipping hamburgers envy them. They are embarrassed by their good fortune – their much higher income and the fact that they are working in their chosen profession. But they also envy the freedom enjoyed by their hamburger-flipping counterparts.

As one information scientist commented: "I keep on wondering what I'm missing – the travel, the leisure – and if one day I'll feel like I've missed out on something important in my life."

What They Want

John C., a twenty-five-year-old M.B.A., is working on contract. He has no job security and no benefits, but he describes himself as extremely fortunate to be working, particularly within an organization where there are "so many people I can learn from, so many opportunities for learning."

Motivated twenty-somethings like John are happy as long as they are being challenged. Their commitment to their work is commensurate with their opportunity to acquire skills. They ask themselves: "Am I intellectually engaged? Am I doing new and interesting things? Will it look good on my resume?"

In the face of an unpredictable future and the probability of a patchwork career, they hope that learning will lead to long-term career success. But they also see it as a way of having fun in their work lives right now. Although jobs may be scarce, they are still very selective about where they choose to work.

As June R., a management consultant, commented: "Be honest . . . either pay me well, or give me lots of opportunities for development. But don't put me in a dead-end job, pay me garbage, and then tell me that you care about me and my future in this company." In a work world where post-boomers see few traditional rewards left for them, honesty on the part of employers about what they can offer is at a premium. Post-boomers have a completely unvarnished view of corporations, and of the world.

A Failing Grade for Society

If we as a society were to get a report card for our treatment of the pre-boomers and many of the early boomers, we would not get top marks. Nor can we be praised for our performance in providing work opportunities to twenty-somethings.

There is something terribly awry with a society that sends its wisest and most mature members out to pasture on the golf courses, and its freshest, most enthusiastic, and technically savvy into the fast-food chains.

FIVE

Squished, Squashed, Sliced, and Diced

"How would I describe my feelings? I'm feeling squished, squashed, sliced, and diced." — *A THIRTY-SOMETHING MANAGER, MOTHER OF TWO YOUNG CHILDREN*

*D*O IT! DO IT! DO IT!

Louder, Faster, Quicker, Shorter.

Do More, Better, Cheaper, with Less, Less, Less.

It has become one of the most glaring paradoxes of our time: The unemployed and underemployed complaining about not having enough work, while people with full-time jobs complain about having too much.

In the post-downsized workplace, individual workloads are sharply increased and resources pared to the bone, while responsibilities have become ambiguous and expectations diffuse. We ask, "When is enough enough?" "When is done done?" Because no matter how hard or long we work, it seems there is always more to do.

Organizations demand more to achieve improved productivity and competitiveness in a never-ending quest to please demanding shareholders. And in the short term, they may get the results they seek. But they may be storing up trouble for the long term.

In this chapter, we look at the new, hyper-metabolic pace of work in the corporate world. In the chapter that follows, we will examine the *result* of this frenetic pace – an epidemic of new career maladies.

THE ENDLESS FITNESS TEST: WORKING, DOING, ACTING

Recently, I had a fitness test. Hyperventilating as the workload on the treadmill was increased to the maximum, wondering if it was ever going to end, I had what at the time felt like an epiphany: I realized that our lives have become an endless fitness test. My test was timed: I only had to go through another three minutes. But when your life is an endless fitness test, you never get to step off the treadmill.

At work in our super-lean, post-downsized organizations, we have the same amount of work to do, and fewer bodies to do it. Relentless deadlines leave us no time to pause, to reflect, or even to catch our breath. And in our personal lives, too, we juggle a flurry of daily commitments and demands. There are simply not enough hours in the day to do everything we need to do. Or as Canadian author Douglas Coupland put it, "You don't get a year's worth of a year anymore."

"Stamina – Who has it? Why do you need it? How do you get it?" asked a 1995 *Fortune* magazine article. Suddenly, "stamina" has become one of the most highly valued and celebrated of managerial attributes. Employers seek it out in new hires, while people capable of working twenty-hour days and eighty-hour weeks are the heroes of the new economy. Endurance is seen as "the quality that makes you a success in the new round-the-clock global economy."

In this view, the future belongs to a select group of "staminacs" who thrive on long working hours and constant activity. But don't worry: if you're not one of the elite now, you may still be able to reinvent yourself through proper diet and exercise.

I find it all rather ironic. I wrote my Ph.D. thesis on the subject of "Type A" behavior: the hard-driving, time-urgent behavior pattern that cardiologists Drs. Rosenman and Friedman had shown to be strongly correlated with heart disease. In those (not so long ago) days, people worried a great deal about Type A behavior, and its costs, just as they worried about "workaholism." They recognized that our society in general, and organizations in particular, rewarded the Type A, high-octane overachiever — with potentially damaging consequences. One of Canada's largest organizations provided invaluable support for my research.

Flash forward to today: No one worries much about Type A behavior or workaholism anymore. No one has *time* to worry. We have created a culture that not only seems to value hard-driving, workaholic "Type A" behaviors — impatience, time-urgency, obsessive work commitment — but almost parodies those behaviors. Step by insidious step, we have become a work-intoxicated society.

THE NEW HERO: THE CONSUMED BUSINESSPERSON

My friend Jim G., a fifty-three-year-old geologist, is semi-retired, and has been so for a couple of years — except that no one knows it. As a result of some shrewd investments, he has made enough money so that he no longer needs to work. He spends a few hours a week looking after his business interests, and takes on the occasional consulting assignment. The rest of the time he occupies himself by volunteering, taking long walks, writing poetry, and taking art classes.

Jim enjoys his new, relaxed lifestyle. But so deeply has he internalized society's belief that visible work equals visible worth that he has not told anyone about his changed work status. Indeed, even when he goes away on vacation, he tells people he is looking after overseas business interests.

Jim is a victim of the cult of busyness. We have all come to worship at its altar. Today, one's busyness is worn like a *badge of honor*, a measure of one's status in the modern workplace. Ask someone how they are and they'll usually respond with one or two predictable answers: "I'm so busy" or "Things are crazy around here."

We have entered an era where to be not *living* our work leaves us feeling we are somehow wanting. As one thirty-eight-year-old bank manager put it: "If you're not doing something, if you're not creating something, you're not adding value and you're not defining who you are."

I call this the *conceit of busyness*. People like this bank manager have allowed their very sense of self-worth to become wrapped up with Working, Doing, Acting. They have come to see busyness in itself as a mark of status: "I'm so busy, I must be worthy." Even when they seem to be complaining about the pressure they are under ("I haven't been home in time for dinner all week . . ."), they are actually making a kind of boast, a statement of identity: "I work, therefore I am . . . I'm just as busy as you, maybe even busier. And the busier I am, the more important I feel."

Success for many of us is defined by being wired, being in the know, having more phone messages, e-mails, and faxes than we can process, carrying cell phones everywhere, running into meetings fifteen minutes late.

We have become so addicted to busyness that when deprived of the never-ending assault of demands, many can't cope. One comment that is depressingly common among people who are "between jobs" is the feeling that their life is empty. As an acquaintance of mine commented, after being restructured out of her high-power job in advertising, "Sometimes I feel like

I am a phantom, that I am not real. There is nothing that gives my life shape or definition or meaning."

Work in the future will almost certainly be of a more *intermittent* nature (a development that we will look at in Chapter 7). Rather than working continuously for the same employer for a long period of time, we will move between assignments or contracts of varying lengths with different employers/clients – punctuated by shorter or longer periods of "downtime."

We will need to live with these periods of downtime, not only financially, but also psychologically. We will need to learn to use these periods as times to nourish ourselves, to reconnect with people, to explore new avenues of work and play – in sum, to regenerate ourselves and to find something other than our own busyness to validate our sense of self-worth.

TIME FAMINE – WHO KNOWS WHERE THE TIME GOES?

- The average employed person now works an extra month a year compared with twenty-five years ago, according to Harvard Economics professor Juliet Schor, author of *The Overworked American*; average yearly vacations and other paid absences decreased by 3.5 days over the last decade.
- Thirty-six percent of workers experienced a health problem because of workplace stress, according to surveys by economist Earl Berger.
- The average working couple spends twenty minutes a day together.
- The average father talks to his child for ten minutes a week.
- Despite teleconferences and e-mail, business travel continues to increase. According to a survey by the Canadian Professional Sales Association, businesspeople spent six more nights away in 1995 than the year before.
- Approximately two-thirds of working mothers and half of working fathers experience unreasonably high stress levels according to a study

of 28,000 Canadians by Carlton University professor Linda Dunberry and University of Western Ontario professor Chris Higgins.

- Americans have added nine hours of work to their work week.
- The average worker today produces about 30 percent more goods or services than he/she did a generation ago, with less take-home pay, less job security, and dimmer future prospects.

Overworked – How Do You Measure Up?

- How many hours do *you* work? (No cheating – commuting, including time spent in airports and on airplanes, counts, unless you find it relaxing.)
- Does your family and/or children and/or close friends think you work overly long hours?
- If you have children, to what do they attribute your long work hours (e.g., your personal choice; boss makes you; etc.)?

THE ENDLESS WAVE POOL

"It's like being in a giant wave pool. Every time you manage to stand up, another wave knocks you down."   *– MANAGER, TELECOMMUNICATIONS*

"When I'm working and have to think about a problem, I sit with my hands poised on the keyboard in case anyone sees me and concludes I'm just thinking and not working."   *– PLANT MANAGER*

In today's "never let up" atmosphere, we have no time to think, to reflect. As one manager puts it, "You can't plan. You can't say I don't want to do this today. It's got to be done NOW." Our culture has become obsessed with "doing," with *producing*.

When we fall into this frenzy of busyness, we start to function on "automatic." We don't think about what we are doing. We just *do* it. There is no time to *experience* the experience. We are too busy just reacting. Under such pressures, everything is flat, and there are no highlights or lows. There is no luster. We are all on autopilot.

Still less do we have time to reflect about *why* we are working so hard. We just work. And the harder we work, and the busier we make ourselves, the less time we have to examine the way we are living.

Much of this work frenzy is driven not by necessity, but rather by an ever escalating and *self-reinforcing hysteria*. Because senior managers have so little time available to think and reflect, they just react — sparking off a pointless frenzy in those who work for them, who, in turn, transmit it to everyone around them, producing a cyclone of panic.

The manager says, "This is a top priority. I want a report on ABC on my desk by Monday." And his team works right through the weekend to meet the deadline. But by the time Monday rolls around, suddenly XYZ is the new priority — and his team will probably have to work through next weekend to report on it. Meanwhile, the report on ABC goes into a desk drawer, unread.

Sound familiar? People early in their careers tend to take this sort of thing especially hard, asking, "Why can't they decide what we should be focusing on?" More experienced employees just shrug their shoulders. They no longer expect their workplace to be run rationally.

WORK ANYWHERE, ANYTIME

Money never sleeps. Business flows on ceaselessly, across markets and time zones, eroding the conventional nine-to-five workday. An amazing two-thirds of all American workers now work outside traditional work hours, while International Data Corp. estimates that more than 40 percent of large U.S. companies work under the stars at least in some aspects of their business.

The new imperative is "Beat the Clock" — a celebration of sheer *speed*. In the high-tech, twenty-four-hour-a-day organizations, the corporate culture is built on urgency and "fast enough never is." Or as Jim Sha, general manager of Netscape (where 130-hour work weeks are the norm), has put it: "The only competitive advantage is speed."

Some manufacturing companies have had round-the-clock shifts for years. What is new today is the growth in round-the-clock work amongst knowledge workers, and the blurring of the boundaries between home and work. As these boundaries continue to collapse, we will become accustomed to switching back and forth between different roles, constantly prey to interruption.

Already, the concepts of "work turf" and "personal turf" are eroding. Stress and health researchers know the importance of having a place of respite, a refuge in maintaining wellness. But we have *lost our sense of place, lost the traditional signifiers for family time, rest, leisure, hominess*. Home offices compete with bedroom furniture for space, computers fight it out with kitchen appliances. There is no sanctuary anywhere. "Teleworkers" often work in the evening, usually after putting the kids to bed, in order to complete a day's work, while elite knowledge workers complete their presentation for tomorrow's important meeting.

A new set of social conventions are emerging that blur the boundaries between work hours and "off" hours, work and leisure. Boundaries melt, priorities slip. We think: "OK, I'll just work on that report later, after I've put the kids to bed, until something else emerges that also needs responding to . . ."

When your whole house becomes your office, you can never leave the office – and you can never come home. It's not surprising that the work never seems to end. We have become *too* enabled by technology and an elastic concept of time. It becomes increasingly difficult to just say "no." We have become "wired in" all the time to meet the demands of a never-sleep, never-stop business world.

Second-Rate Work

"Welcome to the era of the half-assed job." That's how one manager describes how this frenzy of busyness is affecting the quality of people's work. It's a problem for individuals and organizations alike, because hurried work is typically sloppy work and, ultimately, less productive.

The chronic time squeeze is also eroding our *opportunities to feel good* about what we are doing. With the never-ending demands, we rarely get to finish a project to our personal satisfaction before being compelled to move on to something else. No sooner do we sort of finish something than something else is thrown at us, which we just start to get a grip on when something else is thrown at us . . . and so on.

Many people are finding it difficult to come to terms with producing what they perceive to be second-rate work. They say, "I went into this profession/work because I loved it. If I'm no longer doing work at what I consider to be up to professional standards, what's the point? How can I feel good about myself?"

But *perceptions* do not always reflect reality. Because we are so busy, we have no time to reflect on what we are really doing at work, or to take satisfaction from it. (Interestingly, when people go through a career evaluation experience in which they look at what they are doing at work and how they feel about it, they discover that they are actually accomplishing significantly more than they thought.)

THANKLESS WORK

For many, it has become a thankless work world. They say: "I am working so hard, but to what end? I am having none of my needs met — emotional, financial. I don't feel my contributions are valued. My sacrifices are not appreciated. No one says 'thank you' for a job well done. No one even *notices* a job well done."

I am constantly surprised by the number of people who will repeat the most trivial of compliments they have received. But such is the degree to which positive feedback has been eroded.

One manager, whose company was moving from Toronto to Calgary, did not want to uproot her family to move with her job, and was not enthusiastic about the new city. An outstanding performer, her experience in organizational renewal made her extremely employable elsewhere. And yet she seriously contemplated the move all the same because, as she said, "My boss really likes me, compliments me on my work, asks my advice, drops by my office to sound out ideas on me. Do you have any idea how *unusual* that is today?"

If it seems to you that you hardly get any feedback unless you have made a mistake, you're not alone. But while it may be small comfort, remember that your boss is probably just as busy, and feeling just as besieged, as you are.

Grumpy, Grumpy, Grumpy

"What does it [the pressure] do to you as a person? I think it probably doesn't make you a nicer person. You're more demanding, more uptight. You're always looking for more. You're not satisfied." – Ron Zambonini, president, Cognos Inc.

"It's the pace of life. You're late to work. You're pushing it. The guy in front and in back and to the side of you feel the same way. Somebody pushes ahead and the others give him the finger." – University of Washington sociologist Pepper Schwartz

Our pressure-cooker lives have led to a widespread loss of civility. Starved of sleep, of time for family and friends, of recognition for a job well done, people are behaving in ways that might once have appalled them: grumpy, selfish, and mean-spirited.

We are seeing increased levels of hostility and violence at work, ranging from sabotage of computer systems to "suit wars" between people "losing it." I heard from a client about one manager who was sneaking into people's offices when they were out and cutting up any clothing he could find.

One of the most common complaints I hear today is how rude everyone has become. There is no time to say "please," or to return phone calls. Ironically, many of the people who are most guilty of the new rudeness are the loudest lamenters of the loss of civility.

When people feel themselves to be under siege from every side, they may not have the resources for pleasantries. Staff say that their managers tell them to be polite to their customers, be gracious, say "please" and "thank you" to them. But these very same managers never say "please" or "thank you" to their employees.

DEMANDS, DEMANDS, DEMANDS

Be a good parent, be an effective team member, be a leader, stay physically fit, be active in the community, be supportive of your friends/partner – never before have there been so many demands on us to excel, or at least to manage, in so many different domains of our lives.

As one woman put it, "Every aspect of our life has been 'decisionalized': I have to think about which suit to wear to impress my client, which school my kids should go to next year, which car dealer to take my car to . . . Not making the right decision in any one area could lead to serious consequences for my career, my children, or my budget."

Besieged, we struggle to juggle competing business and personal priorities, an overwhelming flurry of daily demands and commitments, with fewer resources than ever to deploy in response. Nonetheless, we feel we must respond – or face serious consequences.

And no matter how hard we work or how fast we run, there are not enough hours in the day to meet all the demands. Something has to be sacrificed – and what is sacrificed is often our personal and family life.

Overcommitted, overextended, and overwhelmed, people feel like they have erected a "house of cards." If they so much as move one piece the wrong way, everything will come tumbling down. Only their sheer powers of will and organization are keeping everything together.

Neglecting Ourselves – And Our Children

"My job gets 125 percent. By the time I get home all I have left for my husband and children is the dregs." — A DIRECTOR OF MARKETING

Overwork, exhaustion, time away from things that are important to us . . . these have become hallmarks of the way we live. Our personal lives have become impoverished in the drive to keep up, "keep our show on the road":

- Fitness level is at an all-time low since 1981 (just when we most need it).
- Sleep is suffering: "We are chronically sleep-deprived . . . this is making us clumsy, stupid, unhappy, and dead," says prominent sleep researcher/ neuropsychologist Stanley Coren.
- Time with children and significant others has never been more impoverished. In a 1993 survey by the Family and Work Institute, 66 percent of parents felt that they were not spending enough time with their children (see Chapter 11 for more). There are significant increases in behavioral problems in middle- and upper-middle-class homes. Parents, overwhelmed by the pressures of their lives, don't have sufficient time and energy for their kids.

Many times people tell us they work so hard because financial and job pressures leave them no other choice. Or else people say they work this hard to provide for their children. For example, forty-year-old lawyer Carolyn, the mother of four children, routinely works twelve-hour days. At least twice a week she ends up sleeping over at the office after burning the midnight oil. She claims she is working so hard so that she can pay for her children's extracurricular activities and ensure they have all the advantages they will need to succeed. But, as we will see in Chapter 11, her children may well pay a serious price in terms of their own long-term development.

I think Carolyn really believes she is doing the right thing for her children. I don't think that this belief is motivated by greed or indifference toward her children. She has just been so busy working, and is so worried about the future, that she has never taken the time to consider what she is giving up, or to ask herself if she is really accomplishing something that is really important.

As author/journalist Anna Quindlen, who quit her high-powered job as a *New York Times* columnist to spend more time with her children, explained: "[My children] have given me perspective on the pursuit of joy and the passage of time. I miss too much when I am out of their orbit, and as they grow, like a time-lapse photograph that makes a flower out of a bud in scant minutes, I understand that I will have time to pursue a more frantic agenda when they have gone on to pursue their own."

My friend Cheryl, the daughter of European immigrants, told me that when she was growing up she would complain to her parents that they were always working at the small dress-making business they owned. She was particularly resentful in her high school years. She says, "My mother would tell me that she and my father had to work so hard to pay for my clothes and my education, and they didn't have many other choices."

Now a successful doctor, working a sixty-to-eighty-hour week to keep up with the never-ending work, she says, "I hope my children don't think I'm working this hard to buy things that we don't need, or worse, because I prefer to spend time at work than to be with them. I understand my parents, as immigrants, didn't have many choices. But I wouldn't expect my children to be as forgiving of me."

ARE WE WORKING OURSELVES TO DEATH?

I attended a conference a few years ago when corporate America was just beginning its extended romance with re-engineering. Presenters from two leading, highly profitable, high-technology companies talked about their experiences.

The presenter from the first company explained that, as re-engineering was a high priority activity demanding considerable time and effort, executives selected for the re-engineering team were no longer required to carry out their normal day-to-day activities. This would allow them to focus completely on the process.

The presenter from the second company explained that in order to keep costs to a minimum, re-engineering duties were added to the existing workload. When asked by the previous presenter whether this situation didn't cause an increase in stress, the speaker casually remarked that this was indeed the case. In fact, two employees had recently suffered heart attacks, one fatal. "It's unfortunate," she said, "but it's a cost of doing business."

What I found most amazing was that no one showed any sign of surprise at the price the company was prepared to pay in the cause of greater efficiency.

In Japan, they have a word for sudden death caused by overwork. They call it *Karoshi*. It is typically associated with the "salary-men" who work for large organizations, who have traded their personal lives for eighty-hour work weeks and what is literally a drop-dead existence.

The relationship among work, stress, and mental and physical health is complex. Many books have been written addressing this issue and it is impossible to do proper justice to it here. A few highlights from the research literature:

• Epidemiologists conclude from empirical research conducted around the world that increased work loads are causing increased illness (cold, flu, bronchitis, poor immune functions, high blood pressure) and death rates. In the United States, health activists say that overwork kills 30,000 workers annually.

- It is not only the *amount* of work, it's also how we work and live. Susan Michie and Anne Cockroft of London's Royal Free School Hospital and School of Medicine, writing in the *British Medical Journal,* conclude that "increased pace of work over the preceding five years and a lack of social contact with colleagues during spare time were . . . associated with an increased risk of myocardial infarction [heart attack]."

- More fatal heart attacks occur at 9:00 a.m. Monday than at any other time.

- Cary Cooper, professor of organizational psychology at England's University of Manchester, refers to a new workplace phenomenon: "presenteeism," the opposite of absenteeism, the malady you get from going to work. Employees no longer perform effectively because they are working long hours, or showing up for work despite illness. They feel a need to be seen to be working long hours in order to obtain a promotion or out of fear of being fired.

CAREER MALAISE

Can people sustain this kind of grueling pace indefinitely, no matter what the cost to themselves or their families? I don't think so. Mental health experts now recognize that work has as much of an impact on emotional well-being as family experiences and personal relationships.

Everywhere I go, I see an epidemic of career distress. Teachers in Saskatoon, accountants in Auckland, clerks in Chicago, managers in New York . . . everywhere, people are asking, "WHY AM I WORKING SO HARD FOR SO LITTLE . . . SO LITTLE EMOTIONALLY, FINANCIALLY, AND PERSONALLY?"

People are re-evaluating their work and personal lives. They are looking within themselves, questioning even their most closely held values. They are experiencing a kind of existential angst — a crisis of meaning. And, as we will see in the next chapter, they are asking:

"Why do I work?"

"How can I better meet my needs for an emotional and spiritual connection?"

"Is this really how I want to live the rest of my life?"

SIX

Singing the New Career Blues

*D*o *you look forward to going to work in the morning?*

Have you completed a project to your personal satisfaction in the past year?

Are you proud of the quality of work you are producing?

Are you confident about the future?

Over the past few years, I have posed these questions to thousands of managers and professionals at speaking engagements and in workshops across North America. Typically only a handful of people will answer "yes" to any of these questions. Many, in fact, publicly volunteer such statements as "I feel like I'm losing it" or "I'm just holding on by my fingernails."

My research indicates that approximately 75 percent of managers and professionals today are:

- overwhelmed by the new demands being made on them at work
- overstretched
- feeling that the organization "doesn't care about them"
- worried about the future
- having difficulty responding to new workplace demands.

So if you're feeling overwhelmed, you are not alone. Career and work distress have become pervasive as once-privileged, highly educated, middle-class managers and professionals everywhere are singing what I call the "new career blues." In this chapter, we look at these modern maladies.

BLAMING THE VICTIM

Last year, I was pleased to be invited to work with a group of senior human resource practitioners from different organizations on a task force on stress in the workplace. But when we got together, although there was widespread agreement that there were tremendous levels of stress in organizations, everyone wanted to focus on the individual. They asked, "How can we help individuals manage stress better?" rather than, "What can we do to help reduce the overall level of stress?"

The approach disappointed me. Having done my Ph.D. thesis in an area related to workplace stress, I have some ideas about how individuals can better manage stress. But it seems to me that an approach, no matter how well-intentioned, concentrating exclusively on the individual is one that blames the victim. It leaves people thinking, "If only I were stronger, I could cope better" – that they are somehow personally inadequate or suffering from a psychological deficiency.

The current level of workplace distress is not due to the weakness of individuals. Rather, it stems from a variety of economic, social, and demographic changes that have affected our work, and our expectations about what work and career should be like. Helping people to cope with their personal stress through increased physical fitness or relaxation techniques may be helpful. But it is hardly enough.

SHEDDING LIGHT ON CAREER MALAISE

Most of us are reluctant to discuss our own career blues. It's "personal," after all – not the sort of thing we want to discuss, particularly not in work environments that celebrate toughness and resilience. We suffer in silence, believing that everyone else at work is coping just fine, blaming ourselves for our difficulties.

That's why it's so important to discuss career distress and how widespread it has become. The most common response on discussing the new career "diseases" in our workshops is relief: "I thought I was the only one, that there was something wrong with me . . ."

These new career blues can be grouped into two broad categories:

1. Feeling besieged and out of control, including:
   • Burnout (or "Running on Empty");
   • Boredom (or "It's the Same Old Song");
   • Conflict between work and personal life (or "Piece of My Heart").
2. "Career angst" – that is, doubts about one's work and purpose – including:
   • Career vertigo (or "A Simple Twist of Fate");
   • Career regret (or "I Threw It All Away");
   • Crisis of meaning (or "Is This All There Is?").

These different forms of career blues overlap to some degree, but each has its own distinct constellation of characteristics, problems, and concerns. As you read the descriptions, see if you recognize anything of yourself. Pinpointing sources of career distress in your own life is a vital first step on the road to career renewal.

At the same time, think about the ways in which the different syndromes might apply to friends and coworkers. If you are a manager, think about the people who report to you. This will give you a better understanding of "where they are coming from" and, where appropriate, an opportunity to provide them with more effective support.

BESIEGED

"I feel like a tightly rolled-up tube of toothpaste. You know that if you jump on it you can always get one last squirt." — PROJECT MANAGER

As we saw in the previous chapter, many people feel "squished, squashed, sliced, and diced." At work, this experience of operating under impossible pressures can ultimately lead to burnout. In our personal lives, too, we may be struggling to meet impossible demands.

Burnout: "Running on Empty"

- Do you look forward to going to work in the morning?
- Are you energized by what you are doing?
- Are you finding it difficult to respond to workplace demands?
- Do you have energy left at the end of the day to do things important to you?

Besieged by multiple demands, producing what they perceive to be second-rate work, people feel their lives are out of control. They are too busy managing day to day, *reacting* to events, to derive any pleasure from their lives.

Paradoxically, although they are so overstretched, they may at the same time feel understimulated: underchallenged, not learning anything new, with nothing to look forward to.

For some people, the problem is the sheer *volume* of the work. For others, it is the too-rapid pace – they can handle a heavy work load, but prefer to work on one or two tasks at the same time, rather than juggling multiple tasks. (As we will see in Chapter 8, it's important to match up your work with your own style, including your own natural pace.)

At the extremes, some people publicly volunteer such statements as "I feel like one of the living dead." This comment, made by a thirty-year-old at a recent conference for women M.B.A.s, was greeted with vigorous nods of recognition from her fellow workshop participants.

Boredom: "It's the Same Old Song"

- Are you so engaged and absorbed in what you're doing that your work-day seems to fly by?
- Has your work lost its luster?
- When you think about your work, does it feel like you're in perpetual reruns?
- Does your work lack challenge?

Been there, done that, got the coffee mug. With limited career mobility and scarce resources, people are doing the same work longer, and have had a lot of "administrivia" added to work loads – leading to feelings of being bored, stale, and underchallenged.

It is a paradox of our time that we can be both bored and overworked. We think: "How can I be bored with so much going on around me?" But actually, it's quite possible to be both overworked and understimulated, thinking about the same thing day in day out, talking to the same people, using the same skills, not learning anything new.

At the extremes, boredom becomes *burnout*.

Conflict Between Work and Personal Life: "Piece of My Heart"

Ann S., a vice president of marketing for a large utility, had always managed to maintain a strong family life. But lately she is close to the breaking point: "I come into work early, stay late, but never catch up. When I have to travel, the work just piles up higher. My boss is mad at me because I'm not delivering on time, my partner is mad at me because I'm never home, and my kids are upset because they hardly see me."

Recently, participants in workshops conducted by my firm have been asking us whether we also offer training for partners who don't understand the new demands being placed upon them. That's something we have never been asked before.

- Are your personal relationships suffering as a result of your workload?
- Do you wish you had more time for family and friends?
- Do you feel your work is causing you to make significant personal sacrifices?

Chronic time famine, combined with relentless demands on all fronts, makes it almost impossible for us to balance our work and personal life – or to have any sort of life at all. (For some tips on balancing work and personal life, see "Be a Ruthless Time Manager" in Chapter 9.)

CAREER ANGST

My firm has been delivering career planning/self-management workshops for more than a decade. As well as some core activities, workshop participants have the opportunity to choose additional options that best fit their own needs.

Typically, in the past, participants would use this time for "hard-core" self-assessment, such as exploring their skills in more depth, rather than "softer" areas, such as looking at their values. Now, the reverse is true, and people are keen to look at and talk about these issues.

The change is particularly striking among groups of senior male managers, who, in the past, preferred to play it close to the vest, not talking publicly about "you know, personal stuff," such as the need for affection, friendship, spiritual growth, community involvement, and so on. Now they are anxious to share their concerns. They no longer see their values as peripheral to their career decisions, but as central.

Why has concern about values become so widespread? I believe it is, in part, because we are being forced to think hard about what we do at work and why. This is the first time people have been told that no one else can make career decisions for them. If we look to our organizations for guidance, we are told, in effect: "Don't ask us. It's your responsibility. You are 100 percent responsible for your own careers and career choices." And so we ask, "If I am free to be one thing or another, why did I *choose* to do this?" And we may find it hard to answer that question.

When we do start to look at our careers, we may be shocked to see the extent to which our lives revolve around our work. We realize that we are making all sorts of sacrifices – giving up weekends, postponing vacations indefinitely, not spending the time we would want with partners and children, always rushing – for very little reward.

As a result, we may start to question *everything*: from the nature of our original choices to the extent to which we are living up to our personal values. Suddenly, everything is up for grabs.

Career Vertigo: "A Simple Twist of Fate"

At age thirty-eight, Ed H. is vice president of finance and administration for a major petrochemical company. But at night, often, he lies awake wondering: "I'm from a family of doctors. How did I end up working for an organization? What am I doing working for this company? For that matter, why am I living in Calgary? And why I am married to this woman sleeping beside me? *How did I get from there to here?*"

Suddenly, Ed can no longer understand his career; he no longer believes that his life makes any sense.

- Do you feel that you just "fell into" your work?
- Do you feel that you made an active choice to pursue particular career options, or was it more of an accident?
- Can you explain the underlying logic that has led you to do the work you are doing now?

If you find it hard to explain to yourself how you came to be in your current line of work, you are not alone. Like about 80 percent of managers and professionals, you are suffering from a form of career blues I have labeled "career vertigo," probably the single most common form of career distress today.

When you suffer from career vertigo, you look back on your career and see no conscious choices, only an apparent sequence of accidents. You cannot find any underlying logic to what you have become. Asked how you ended up in your line of work, you say, "I just *fell* into it."

For example, here's a partner in a large public accounting firm explaining his choice of career: "Why did I become a CA? Because one accounting firm had the best display at the careers fair in university – the best posters, the nicest recruiters, and so on. At that stage in my life, I didn't know what to do, and accounting seemed like a reasonable choice. After all, you could always get a decent job, couldn't you?"

If your career choice was an accident rather than a matter of choice – if you really did just "fall into" doing what you are doing – you might well ask yourself: "How do I know I wouldn't be happier doing something else?" Suddenly, *everything seems arbitrary*. You see how the world might have ended up very differently, given only a relatively small change in circumstances. The very underpinnings of your life feel fragile, as if you have no moorings.

Accident *can* play a powerful role in our lives, and not only in our career choices. People end up married because they happened to be in a particular place at a particular time, or to have a mutual friend. But we are not powerless victims of fate. Whether in romance or in our careers, we are always making choices whether we are aware of it or not.

When we look at our career history, what we discover is that for the most part we have gradually moved toward what we are doing now through "successive approximations." When we are good at something, we tend to enjoy the work, to receive reward or praise for our skills, and to seek out similar work in the future. By the same token, if we are unsuited for something, we tend not to perform very well and don't get the rewards or "reinforcement" to make us persist in this line of work in the future.

As one woman put it at the end of a career-planning workshop, "I've been in the training field for fifteen years now and yet when I came in here I thought there was no particularly good reason why I had become a trainer. But when I look back over my career history, I realize that I have always enjoyed and been good at standing in front of a group and giving presentations, teaching, helping people articulate problems, and helping them make changes. In each job I've had, I would unconsciously seek out those opportunities. And as I moved through my career that was the work I kept getting good feedback for."

As a general rule, most people do not make fifteen-year career "mistakes." Sometimes, of course, after spending ten or fifteen years in the same line of work, people may find themselves in situations which are no longer a good match for their skills, interests, or values. Or else they may reach a point where, for one reason or another, it becomes "time to move on," and make a shift to another field. But that doesn't mean that they would have been happier doing something else all along. It just means that it's time to explore new horizons.

Career Regret: "I Threw It All Away"

Thirty-year-old Norma C. was an executive assistant to the president of an electrical utility. Three years ago she turned down a generous severance package offered by her company as a voluntary buyout as part of a major downsizing. Many of her friends chose to take the package, but Norma didn't want to venture out to an uncertain job market.

Since then Norma has been endlessly revisiting her decision. She looks at her former coworkers, some of whom have gone on to apparently more "glamorous" jobs, and thinks they are much happier than she is. Lately she has begun to blame her employer for not having explained to her fully the terms of the buyout and has become increasingly bitter and preoccupied. At the same time she has not done anything to change her own work situation, which she describes as "unfulfilling."

- Do you feel that, but for one event, your life would have turned out differently and you would have been happier or more successful?
- Do you feel that if you revisited your life and did one thing differently your life would be better today?
- Do you feel that circumstances have prevented you from achieving your full potential?

Career remorse is a form of second-guessing, in which we endlessly revisit decisions that we have made or things that have happened to us: "If only I had completed my M.B.A."; "If only I'd been willing to take a risk in that start-up situation with . . ."; "If only my company hadn't been acquired by . . ." Or, as they used to say in the movies, "I coulda been a contender."

We make the best career decisions we can, based on our own inclinations, circumstances, and the information available to us at the time. Sometimes we make mistakes. We back the wrong horse. We get derailed by forces beyond our control. And sometimes things don't work out the way we hoped.

As human beings, we are constantly explaining ourselves to ourselves: "I voted for Party X because they promised to cut my taxes"; "I came to work for this company because it offered good job security"; "I studied at night school because I thought I would get a better job." But when it seems like our judgment has gone awry, we may be unable to do this. It is then that we may become trapped in a spiral of regret – blaming ourselves, or other people, for what has gone wrong, rather than taking steps to put it right.

Crisis of Meaning: "Is This All There Is?"

For years, Jack M. assumed that by working hard he would achieve the good life for himself and his family, and that the exchange would be worth it. As long as his work gave him a sense of accomplishment, Jack was happy enough with the bargain. But lately he is questioning to what end he is working.

The sudden death of a close friend has led Jack to think long and hard about the real purpose and meaning of his life: "My work no longer provides me with any sense of accomplishment. I can't see that anyone benefits from it other than the company's shareholders. I don't identify with the values of the organization. I don't like the people I work with. I make a good living, sure. But if I died tomorrow, what would I leave behind me? I can't help thinking, there must be something more . . ."

- Do you sometimes feel your life is empty?
- Do you wonder if you could be doing something more meaningful with your life?
- Would you like to do work that contributes to growth (yours or others') and/or community and/or the betterment of society?
- Do you feel that you should be serving something greater than profit?
- Do you feel out of sync with organizations – do you increasingly see them as cold, soulless, . . . driven by profits at the expense of human beings?

Weary, unhappy with what they see going on around them at work, people question how they are living: Was this really what I wanted? What could give me a greater sense of meaning and purpose?

They experience their work environments as *soulless*, their employers as morally bankrupt. The fragmentation of families, the breakdown of communities, and the erosion of religious faith have led to a great spiritual hunger. People are looking for more, looking for a connection. There has been an upsurge in the popularity of charismatic speakers and self-help gurus; books on spirituality and the soul crowd the bestseller lists; and lunchtime attendance at church and Bible classes is reportedly on the upswing, as people try to find a sense of being in touch with something beyond themselves. "Rah rah" motivational after-dinner keynote speakers on "How to be successful" are giving way to speakers dealing with a sense of meaning and purpose.

Witness the success of poet David Whyte, author of the business book bestseller *The Heart Aroused*, who admonishes corporate audiences to get in touch with their inner life: "Don't die on the shore. The stakes are very high; the stakes are your life . . ."

WORK – ANOTHER GOD THAT FAILED

"It's hard to get excited by another 1,000 tons of newsprint going out the gate."

– *GENERAL MANAGER OF A PULP AND PAPER COMPANY LOOKING AT A CAREER CHANGE*
INTO THE VOLUNTEER SECTOR

For many, work has replaced religion, community, even family, as the main source of meaning in their lives. But now work, too, has failed us. Instead of feeling that their needs for belonging and social interaction are being met, people find themselves tied to their computer terminals in an increasingly impersonal workplace. Meanwhile, long work weeks deprive them of quality time with friends and family. In essence, work is no longer satisfying deeply held emotional and psychological needs.

Under such circumstances, people are asking hard questions about work, their values, and the values of their organizations – the very values they once extolled. Marsha L., for example, has spent her working life employed in progressively more senior positions in different corporations. Politically conservative, Marsha is very articulate about government interference, and celebrates free enterprise and the right to make a profit without being encumbered by government regulations. She has always been particularly impatient with the "entitlement mentality" of staff who "feel the world owes them a living."

Marsha now finds herself working for a boss who is long on visionary ability but short on human sensitivity. If you want to be excellent, he believes, you can't qualify it by being available only certain hours. "You're either there or not," he says, "and if you want to be a player, you're there." Unfortunately this means impromptu evening meetings, routinely scheduled breakfast meetings, frequent weekend meetings, and a constant stream of e-mails to her home.

"Five years ago I would never have said something like this," Marsha says, "but I now remember the days when I used to complain about paternalism, entitlement, and bureaucracy with fondness. I want a work world where ruthlessness and coldness aren't the only attributes that get you ahead, where short-term profit and a desire for an immediate return to the shareholders don't drive all business decisions."

RETHINKING WHY WE WORK

"The material progress that was supposed to free us has left us more enslaved. For all the hype about going for the gold, we are so weary at the end of the day that going for the sofa is as good as it gets." – JOE DOMINGUEZ AND VICKI ROBIN, YOUR MONEY OR YOUR LIFE: TRANSFORMING YOUR RELATIONSHIP WITH MONEY

"[I want to] make decisions based on the voice that speaks from our heart and not that great, inchoate 'they' out there that dictates career paths and life goals based on a cookie-cutter view of success, and a disdain for personal happiness as an end in itself."
— ANNA QUINDLEN, *"WHY I QUIT"*

Many people are searching for alternatives to the traditional values of work and consumption. They have lost faith in the central tenets of postwar North American beliefs: that work will set us free from want, and that working longer, harder, and faster will give us even more of what we want. They are seeking work they find personally meaningful, which will make a difference in people's lives and affirm the value of being human — not work so all-consuming that it crushes all other opportunities for human interaction and self-expression.

Whose life is it, anyway? That's what many of us are asking ourselves these days. Recently, a friend of mine commented after leaving a very demanding job that she was going to take the next few months to figure out who she was and what she wanted. "This is the first time," she commented, "that I put myself into the equation . . . I have spent the last twenty years looking after children, meeting financial obligations, looking after parents. Somehow I lost myself in the process."

A 1993 Gallup poll found that one-third of Americans said that they would take a pay cut if they or their spouses could work fewer hours. A 1995 poll by Merck Family Fund showed that many people have actually made such a change: 28 percent said that over the last five years, they had voluntarily made changes in their lifestyle that resulted in their making less money.

(If you're evaluating how and why you work, see "Rethinking Your Relationship to Money" in Chapter 9.)

WORKPLACE DEPRESSION . . . A MODERN EPIDEMIC

In this chapter, and the one that preceded it, we have looked at what people are feeling about the new workplace realities, and how they are adapting to them, and at the pervasive career distress amongst middle-class professionals and managers. As we've seen:

- People feel out of control, unable to make predictions about their future. They see little relationship between what they do and what happens to them.
- Many have no sense of personal satisfaction. They are not finishing work at the level they would like. They feel they are not making a meaningful contribution.
- Their self-confidence has been eroded. They are beginning to question their competence and feel they are losing their "edge." They worry about the future.
- People are cynical about their employers, and pessimistic about their futures.

Broadly speaking, I have just described some of the clinical symptoms of depression. Or to put it another way, if the opposite of depression is excitement, anticipation, and joy, then these emotions are clearly lacking in many of today's organizations.

This poses serious challenges for the future productivity of organizations, and perhaps more importantly, for our society's ability to meet people's legitimate needs for some level of joy, challenge, and fulfillment in their work.

In the chapters that follow, we will look at what you can do as an individual and as a manager, and what organizations can do, to combat this malaise and promote career renewal.

PART TWO

Renewal

SEVEN

Welcome to TempWorld

"*D*evelop a metaphor or mantra which describes the new career."

This is the challenge I posed recently as a keynote speaker at a human resources conference. Several hundred attendees, representing a broad range of industries, organizational levels, ages, and career stages, generated approximately fifty metaphors.

When you think of future careers, what is your overriding image? If your images have elements of danger, risk, and fierce competition, then you are thinking along the same lines as the attendees at that conference. Their metaphors had a number of underlying themes:

– **Shifting relationships:** For example: "The new career is like dancing:

sometimes you lead, sometimes you follow, sometimes you just sit on the sidelines waiting to be invited to the party."

— **Danger:** For example: "The new career is like a house in a horror movie, with scary monsters behind every door, and trapdoors opening up under your feet."

— **Intense competition:** For example: "The new career is like life in the jungle. It's eat or be eaten."

But if there was one theme that best captured the emotional tenor of these images it was the *loss of protection*. The metaphor that the group as a whole voted the best and most apt because it represented both the positive and negative went like this:

"The old career was like an animal in the zoo, protected, fed, and nurtured. The new career is like an animal in the wild. You have to look after yourself, and your survival is always at stake. You're competing with other animals all the time for scarce resources."

A harsh picture. But one with at least some redeeming features: "An animal in the wild is in a more natural, organic state. You're not living in cages. You're free to run your own lives, free to roam. Sure, you have more uncertainty to deal with, but you also have more possibilities."

The social Darwinism of these images is consistent with most people's beliefs about the new world of work — and with the title of the latest book by Intel CEO Andy Grove: *Only the Paranoid Survive*.

LIKE A DATE . . .

I like to liken the new career to a date, the old career to a marriage. And each has some good and bad aspects.

Many of us crave the relative security, comfort, commitment, and intimacy provided by marriage. But marriage can also be, well, predictable.

The good news about a date is that it's exciting: you don't know how it will end until you get there. The bad news . . . you always have to hold your stomach in.

There are some other good things about dates, even the ones that don't work out so well. You may learn new things about yourself and other people. You may go to new places. And if things don't work out, it's a lot easier to end than a marriage – and you won't suffer the same emotional hangover afterwards.

Like it or not, you have to prepare yourself to live in an uncertain work world. Because above all else, the watchword for the new career is *temporary*. Everything shifts rapidly, everything is in flux, nothing is forever. What you do at work, the skills you use there, where you work, who you work with – everything is temporary.

Or, to paraphrase Andy Warhol, in the future everyone will have a good job – for fifteen minutes.

Welcome to TempWorld.

NEW WORK ARRANGEMENTS

To manage your career in the future, it's crucial to understand the shape of careers to come. As the metaphors above make clear, there are some tough realities associated with the new career. But there are also some tremendous opportunities – if you understand the new work realities, and you can position yourself to take advantage of the options available to you.

One almost needs a glossary to understand the numerous new configurations of work: regular part-timers, occasional part-timers, permanent temporary, temporary permanent, just-in-time workers, contract workers, leased workers, outsourced workers, and, less charitably, "disposable workers."

One of the most often-quoted statistics is that by the year 2000, less than 50 percent of the workforce will be employed in conventional full-time jobs.

The majority will be part-time, temporary, or contract workers. Already, such "nonstandard employment" makes up a third of all Canadian jobs. Let's look at the different types of new work arrangement.

The Temp in the Armani Suit

The headlines say it all: "Outsourcing is here to stay." "The temp biz boom."

Our society is entering an era of permanent temporary employment. Organizations have embarked on a deliberate strategy of reducing the size of their "core" workforce (see "The Core Employee" below) and making up the difference as required by drawing on a pool of "contingent" or temporary workers. For organizations, there are advantages to this strategy:

– **Flexibility:** Having just-in-time workers means you have the right people when you need them. Organizations can allow for the peaks and valleys of demand.

– **Reduced overhead:** Temporary workers are cheaper to hire, are paid no benefits, and can be disposed of without severance.

– **A buffer zone:** The contingent workforce cushions the organization from global economic fluctuations and competitive changes. There is no risk to the organization in staffing up. Contingent staff, who can be cast aside at the first sign of difficulty, will absorb any shocks.

– **A trial run:** Organizations can "audition" people for permanent positions. For example, Advocate Placement Limited, which has more than 850 lawyers available on demand, says that nearly 50 percent of their placement hours have led to permanent work.

– **Quicker adaptation to changing skill sets:** Recently, for example, the distribution center of a large Canadian retailer introduced new technology to reduce costs and be able to get business delivering goods for other stores. Two hundred employees were let go. Those with the technical skills to work with the new system were then rehired as temporary workers; the rest were not retained.

Get rid of permanent employees, hire temps to replace them – that's become the new cost-cutting formula. When AT&T CEO Robert Allen announced the impending loss of 40,000 jobs, insiders ruefully observed that AT&T would shortly stand for "Allen and Two Temps."

As a result, the temporary or "contingent" workforce has become one of the fastest-growing segments of the economy. The largest single employer in the United States is the temporary employment agency Manpower, with half a million workers; the U.S. Department of Labor forecasts that the temporary labor market will increase by 57 percent by the year 2005, from 1.6 million to 2.6 million jobs.

The nature and scope of temporary work are changing, too, as temping climbs from the secretarial pool to the executive ranks. Traditionally, most people temping have filled low-wage clerical and light industrial blue-collar positions. But temporary employment in professional and technical fields now makes up approximately 20 percent of the temp payroll and is the fastest-growing segment of the temp market.

Upmarket temps, specialists in anything from law, medicine, accounting, computers, graphic design, or engineering, migrate from one project to the next. In Santa Clara County, the heart of California's high-tech Silicon Valley, contingent employment has accounted for *all* new job growth since 1984.

Having entered the contingent ranks, even highly skilled technical and professional workers may now face economic insecurity and downward pressure on wages. Real wages in technical occupations in temporary agencies have declined by nearly 28 percent over the past five years, according to the U.S. Bureau of Labor Statistics.

Former permanent staff who become contingent workers may go through a difficult psychological adjustment. Some feel left out in the cold: merely disposable workers, cheap labor, "treated like used Kleenex, or Post-It notes." But there can be positive aspects, too, as we'll see below.

NO WONDER PEOPLE MAY THINK TWICE BEFORE HIRING

According to Shamel Rushwin, vice president of manufacturing for Chrysler Corporation, hiring a unionized employee who will remain with the company for life is a $7 million decision. The cost rises to $9 million for a salaried employee.

Part-Time Work

Part-time work is on the increase. In fact, in 1995, 19 percent of all Canadian jobs were part-time, up from 12.5 percent in 1976. (It has been suggested by some economists that the figure may actually be as high as 25 percent due to the vagaries of classification.) The young account for the largest segment of this part-time workforce. And 45 percent of all Canadian workers under twenty-four had only part-time jobs, more than double the number from 1976.

People work part time for many reasons. Some are in school, some prefer the flexibility. But a growing proportion of those working part time do so because they cannot find the full-time work they want, with about one-third saying they would prefer a full-time job.

With this shift from full-time to part-time work comes a decrease in wages, as well as a reduction or disappearance of benefits such as health and dental insurance.

"Cobbling Together" a Living – Multiple Job Holders

Statistics actually underestimate the number of part-time jobs, because of the growing number of "hidden part-timers," people counted as full-timers because they hold two or more part-time jobs.

Joe L., for example, works twenty hours a week as a bookkeeper at a distribution center for a clothing manufacturer. At the end of his six-hour shift he rushes across town to a five-hour shift for a transportation company. He says he does it for his kids. But since he hardly ever gets to see them, he's beginning to ask himself, "What's the point?"

Similarly, twenty-eight-year-old Mary J. has three jobs. On Monday, Wednesday, Friday, and Saturday she works for a tony leather goods store. On Tuesday and Thursday she is a bicycle courier. In her spare time, she is trying to make it as a writer, and freelances for a Web magazine.

"Cobbling together a living": This will increasingly define the new worker. Multiple job holders include:

- Creative, entrepreneurial twenty-somethings scrambling to get a foothold in the job market to acquire some skills, learn, and gain resume-building experience.
- Newly disenfranchised full-time employees, some of whom held well-paid, though not necessarily highly skilled, jobs, others of whom held middle-management jobs that have disappeared. Lack of skills, or age, has forced them into low-paid and insecure work.
- Fifty-something "early retirees" who can't afford to retire. They still have debts to pay off, or ongoing expenses, and need another ten years of income to retire comfortably.
- Highly skilled victims of re-engineering or retrenchment who find themselves in their peak earning years becoming "consultants" working from home, doing a bit of this and a bit of that while "between jobs" – where they may remain indefinitely.

IMPLICATIONS OF THE NEW WORK ARRANGEMENTS FOR ORGANIZATIONS

"I spend three-quarters of my working day telling new contract employees where the washrooms and cafeteria are."   – PROJECT DIRECTOR, BANK

Although the new work relationships described above may provide organizations with greater workforce flexibility, they strain the real assets of the organization.

When disposable workers replace long-term employees, something is lost, something that might best be described as *wisdom*. This wisdom is a kind of collective institutional memory made up of "rules of thumb," ways of doing things, knowledge of common problems and how to fix them, and an intuitive understanding of relationships with customers and suppliers.

Typically, this wisdom is concentrated in the ranks of middle-management staff – the first to be displaced in favor of lower-paid temps in the event of a reorganization. Once their wisdom is lost, things may not get done the way they used to be done, and relationships with customers can deteriorate.

Something else is lost, too: commitment to the organization and its goals. Contract workers, concerned about where their next paycheck will come from and who their next employer or client will be, typically don't have the same loyalty as full-time employees.

Teamwork also suffers from this lack of commitment. Contract workers think of themselves as being "at the bottom of the food chain," unable to share in the close-knit working relationships and *esprit de corps* of full-time team members.

Reliance on temporary staff can also involve threats to security. A friend of mine told me how he knew of a major corporate takeover about a month before it was announced in the newspaper. He heard about it from a temp in his office, who had just been working at one of the legal firms involved in the deal. With the rapid turnover and broad mobility of temporary staff, leaks of inside information like this could well become common – with potentially serious consequences.

Positive Aspects for the Individual

Undoubtedly, contract work has its drawbacks for the individual, including the anxiety of worrying about earning your living each and every day. But there are some positive aspects to life as an independent contractor, including the opportunity to spend more time with family and friends, or to pursue personal passions.

Paradoxically, too, you may feel a *greater* sense of security in your life than when you worked for an organization. Rather than waiting like a passive victim for something terrible to happen – to be re-engineered, downsized, or restructured out of a job – you become an active player in managing your own life.

As one marketing consultant put it: "As an employee, my life depended on the whims of my boss or the attitudes of each new group of consultants hired to reinvent the corporation. I was functioning in a permanent state of anxiety that drained my energy, reduced my performance, and threatened to ruin my life. Now that I work for myself, I'm much less anxious, even though I frequently face times when I have no work."

You may also escape some of the vicissitudes of life as a full-time employee, in fact, be *more* secure. As one contract worker commented: "The organization where I work has gone through three downsizings since I started work there. The instructions come from above to reduce the department from fifteen to twelve employees. Each time I'm spared, because I'm not officially counted as an employee. My future doesn't even come up for discussion."

Increasingly, the ability to change your mind-set and look at yourself as a free agent will be a key to feeling you are in control of your life. (In Chapter 9, we will discuss the new rules for career success in a free-agent society.)

The Core Employee

When less than half of the available workforce is in full-time employment, it will no longer make sense to think of a full-time job (what has been referred to as "standard employment") as the norm. But this does not mean that no one will have a job anymore.

The future will probably look something like a scenario outlined by British management expert Charles Handy, under which there will be both "core" employees and "contingent" employees. The core employee is an essential executive or worker who is supported by outside contractors and part-time workers. Core employees will do the work that most intimately describes the main purpose or mission of the organization – the *core* work.

Examples of such core employees include actuaries in a life insurance company, CAs in a public accounting firm, and chemical engineers in an oil refining company – in contrast to the support people in these organizations, such as trainers, finance people, and lawyers. These core staff will have high levels of pressure, but their work will be relatively secure, and they will be paid relatively well because their skills will be highly valued by the organization. In contrast, non-core employees are more vulnerable to the ups and downs of the business.

This is not to suggest that a core employee will be guaranteed a job for life. If you do decide to pursue this option, you will still be vulnerable to business changes, mergers, and fluctuations in your industry. But you will have more protection than non-core staff.

To be an effective core employee, you will need the ability to withstand pressure; to work very intensely; and to maintain your skills at the cutting edge. If you don't keep up with developments in your field, you will be vulnerable to younger, more technically savvy people as new technology is introduced to your industry.

New Career Patterns

Zigzag Careers – Moving Between Different Life Spheres

People used to think of their careers in terms of ascending a career "ladder," straight upwards, rung by rung.

There are no career ladders anymore. But neither are there any obvious images to describe the shape of the new career. Think of a lattice, perhaps, or a child's game of hopscotch, zigging and zagging along, or a game of Snakes and Ladders, or a jungle gym. In the new career, you will probably move from side to side at least as much as you move up and down – not only in your work, but between other life domains as well, such as education, leisure, and volunteer work.

Perhaps you are a core employee for a while. Then something happens: a downturn in the business or new technology renders your work obsolete, or the company decides to replace you with someone younger, cheaper, or with a different skill set. What now?

Perhaps you get a series of short-term assignments as an independent contractor, selling your services to a previous customer or competitor. Perhaps you get hired by another company. Perhaps you set up your own home office and have multiple clients.

But what if the technology that rendered your job obsolete has also rendered your skills obsolete? What do you do? Perhaps you will go back to school, or take some courses, or volunteer to get the missing management skills that will offset your technical weakness.

Then again, perhaps you will decide to take "time off" between work assignments to travel, or learn to paint, or write a novel, or volunteer at a hospice, or work in your garden . . .

Actually, I've never been comfortable with the phrase "taking time off." Time off from what? *We talk as though human activity is valuable only to the extent that it either contributes directly to the economy, or else prepares us to do so.*

Obviously, you will still need to do paid work to support your other interests. But increasingly, in the future, you are likely to look at work as just one of several equally important domains of your life. Rather than seeing periods between work as mere "downtime," you may well welcome the opportunity to pursue other interests.

Serial Careers

"The pace of technical change is so fast now that we must be prepared for [people] to change not only [their] job but [their] entire skills three or four times in a lifetime."

This sounds like a mantra for the year 2000, but, in fact, it was prophesied in the late 1960s by British cyberneticist Sir Leon Bagrit.

As new industries and technologies emerge, as government policies change and demographics shift, new work will be created and other work will become obsolete. The result is that the average person starting work today will have five or six different careers. Everyone from Newt Gingrich to Bill Clinton to business writers is trumpeting this "trend."

When I make this statement in workshops most people's response, regardless of their age, is one of discomfort. They ask: "Does this mean that my career has a shelf life, that I am hot-wired to destruct after four or five years and that everything I know will no longer be valid? Will I have to go back to school to reprogram myself to become something completely different? If I'm a lawyer, will I have to become an accountant? If I'm a marketer, will I have to go back to school to become a gerontologist? Will I constantly have to reinvent myself in a never-ending series of guises to meet endlessly changing and new market demands?" It's as if they fear that they will have no core, that they will *lose the essence* defining who they are and what they do.

It's true that future careers will be shape-shifting, reconfiguring, and elastic (in ways discussed in more detail in the next chapter). But you will not be completely reinventing yourself every four or five years. You will not have to develop a completely new set of skills. Instead, you will be *reconfiguring* the skills you already have. As your work changes, certain skills and competencies will be called to the fore according to changing business needs and work demands, while the importance of others will recede.

Think of your different skills and interests as *modular building blocks* that can be fitted together in different combinations. As you move through your career, the way in which you configure these skills and interests will no doubt change, allowing you to play more to certain strengths in one position, other strengths in another. But your essence – your core strengths – will stay more or less the same. (See "Reconfigure Yourself" in Chapter 8.)

Goodbye Traditional Retirement

Although we have been sold the dream of retirement at age sixty-five, of a life of bucolic leisure – the well-deserved reward for a lifetime of work – for many, that dream is increasingly untenable, both for psychological and financial reasons.

Organizations will continue to use earlier and earlier involuntary retirement to pare down their workforce and reduce overheads. (Some organizations, astonishingly enough, are encouraging early retirement for employees as young as forty-five.) But many people who are asked to take early retirement can't afford it and don't want it, having large debts, ongoing expenses, or inadequate savings. They will return to the workforce in some capacity, although they may have to settle for lower-paid and often part-time work to "bridge" their way to retirement.

If, that is, they retire at all. With people living longer and staying active longer, there is growing recognition that work life doesn't necessarily have to end, even at age sixty-five.

When retirement benefits were first introduced in the nineteenth century in Europe (later in Canada and the United States), it was never expected that many people would live long enough to collect them. The Canadian Old

Age Pension Act was introduced in 1926 for people seventy years and older at a time when average life expectancy was sixty-one. Today pensionable age is sixty-five, with average life expectancy at seventy-five for men and eighty-one for women. Similarly, when Franklin Roosevelt introduced the Social Security Act in 1937 (to get more older men to retire in order to create work for the unemployed), the pensionable age was sixty-five — but the average American died at sixty-three.

Retirement at sixty-five was always an arbitrary concept, based on an artificial concept of a "finishing line" to one's life's work. But there is no finishing line — life's activities do not come in neat, finite bundles of work followed by play. The future will see a much less sharply defined transition, one that better reflects people's interests and needs.

Moreover, the financial reasons for continuing to work may be compelling. Indeed, many Americans believe that they are more likely to see a UFO than to collect social security. And certainly government pension plans in both the United States and Canada are undergoing radical restructuring to avoid massive deficits.

That makes it all the more important that individuals save for their retirement. Financial planners recommend people save 10 percent of their gross income for every year that they work in order to enjoy a secure retirement. The average private sector Canadian employee today saves considerably less — about 5 percent. And with growing debt and employment difficulties, people are increasingly dipping into their meager retirement funds.

At the same time, there has been a significant decrease in the number of people covered by private company–sponsored pension plans. In 1982, 84 percent of American workers were covered by fixed payment pension plans. Now only about half are. This trend is set to continue, as long-term employment becomes the exception rather than the rule.

Retirement at age sixty-five, then, is becoming an increasingly impractical concept. For many people, it is simply unaffordable. So whether through choice or circumstance, many people over the official age of retirement will continue to participate in the workforce in one way or another. This can only benefit society as a whole — stemming a profound loss of knowledge, experience, maturity, and wisdom.

LIVING AND WORKING IN TEMPWORLD

The New Nomads

"As a nomadic member of the meritocratic class, I maintain a mobile lifestyle, flowing as easily as capital or information between the moneyed pockets of the nation's various urban centres. A loyal knowledge worker, I'm ready to pack up my roller blades and mountain bike at a mere beeper message from my boss, to be hermetically transported to yet another hip, urban playground filled with like-minded members of my psychographic."

— KEITH WHITE

Gwen P., a thirty-seven-year-old information consultant, works for a large, international consulting firm specializing in re-engineering. She changes assignment every six or seven months or so. While on an assignment, she lives from Sunday night through to Friday afternoon in whatever city the client is located. On Friday night she goes home.

Where is "home"? That depends. Gwen is married to a career soldier who is restationed every few years. When I met her, she was about to fly out to a new home that she had only seen once before, for a couple of hours.

Didn't she find it difficult, I asked, living this kind of lifestyle? Not really, she said. As long as she was doing interesting work, she was completely indifferent to her location: "From Sunday night to Friday I rent myself out completely to my client. I work all the time. So whether I am working in a city with an opera company or a marina, or a town surrounded by miles of wheat, really makes no difference to me. I guess if I cared about anything it would be how long the plane flight home was. But even then, if it's one hour more or less, I don't really care."

Gwen's whole personal identity is tied to challenge, learning, and achievement. Like a sports star, she is a "free agent": a hyper-mobile migrant worker of the new global economy, always ready to go where the work is most challenging and rewarding. For Gwen, concerns about family, community, or place are mere sentiment. She belongs to no neighborhood, no community, no country. Nothing holds her back.

Of course, also like a sports star, Gwen is ultimately disposable: if her services are no longer necessary, or become too expensive, she will be cast aside. But Gwen is confident that no matter what happens, she will always land on her feet. There will be a place for her, somewhere – even if she has to travel halfway around the globe to find it.

In a wired economy, knowledge workers like Gwen need to be ready to go at a moment's notice, mercenaries chasing opportunity wherever it may emerge. French futurist Jacques Atalli has described these "liberated nomads" as the new winners in our society: members of the knowledge elite who require only their imagination and their electronic products to function anywhere.

It's hip to be a new nomad. Business magazines celebrate their glamorous itinerant lifestyle, limited only by their ambition and talent. Cosmopolitan, jet-setting independent contractors, empowered by their laptops, cell phones, electronic organizers, aerobic heart monitors, and Internet home pages, are chasing opportunities and capital on the frontiers of the global economy; they are the true children of the new electronic capitalism.

As Edward Castleton has written: "The world has transformed itself into a place without space, where time zones are more important than trade zones, and where an address on-line is a thousand times more significant than any petty street coordinate. Busying themselves with faxes, voice mail, e-mail, and the Internet, this new class (cyber-elite) couldn't care less where they physically happen to be . . . there is, for example, no difference between Sunday and Monday in [high-tech guru Nicholas] Negroponte's workweek. Work follows him everywhere, and he follows it, jacking in with his laptop wherever he happens to be."

But not everyone finds the free-agent lifestyle so congenial. Sandra L. was fifty years old when her Toronto-based company re-engineered her out of a job. She spent a year looking for another job in her own city, where she had lived her whole life. After she had exhausted all opportunities for work in Toronto, she reluctantly cast her net farther afield.

She has now found an exceptional job. Unfortunately it is in Chicago. So at an age when she feels she should be starting to make the transition into her later career years, she now has to start all over again to re-establish herself in a new community with new friends. Her husband remains in Toronto looking after an ailing business. Her aging parents still live there, too. Sandra has had to walk away from what she feels are the most important responsibilities in her life.

In Sandra's story, we see acted out all that is emblematic of the free-agent society: the dissolution of community, the loss of family, the nagging sense of dislocation. Of course, some would say that Sandra is one of the lucky ones: at least she found work. Actually, "luck" hardly entered into it. Sandra found work because she took an *activist* stance. In her openness to change and ability to cope with disruption, she exemplifies some of the qualities required of the new worker discussed in the next chapters.

Professional Gypsies

David K. is a senior vice president at the corporate head office of a large bank. For the past four years he has had no fixed official function or job description.

"What floor are you on these days?" I asked him recently.

"The twelfth, the fourteenth, and the seventeenth," he responded.

Moving from office to office and assignment to assignment, David has a number of different internal clients who pay part of his salary. Because his assignments have varying durations, ending at different times, he is always having to resell himself to find a new client to pick up the slack so that he can maintain a full work load.

Despite his senior level, with more than twenty years of experience with the bank, David knows that he is only as good as his last project, and that he will remain employed only if he keeps his skills up to date.

Twenty-seven-year-old Dan R. is thrilled that he is working for what he describes as the "employer of choice," and he is determined to continue working there. Although, strictly speaking, he is a contract employee, he has spent two years within the company and everyone thinks of him as a regular employee. His strategy for keeping his work: "I find pregnant women who are doing interesting work and I understudy them, so when they leave I'm the natural choice to take over while they're gone."

David and Dan are on the front lines of the new career, displaying the independent, activist behavior required to manage your career successfully in TempWorld. On a day-to-day basis they are responding *adaptively* to some of the more frightening aspects of the new career, a subject explored in more depth in the next chapter.

The Endless Audition

"You are only as good as your last hit." What was once true in Hollywood will become the new mantra defining most of our lives. In a world of intense and ruthless competition from every side, you are competing not only with colleagues, but also with independent contractors, the unemployed, and virtually everyone else in the world who, either alone or as part of an organization, can provide the same services as you cheaper, faster, or with a higher level of quality.

"Will someone younger, more energetic, slicker, more technically adept replace me?" This is a legitimate question that will increasingly concern us.

The era of the "safe" career, where you could eventually hope to reach a point where you could relax and rest on your laurels, basking in past accomplishments, is gone forever. In a work world whose defining characteristic is "toughness," there is no more margin for error, no tolerance for mistakes. You will constantly need to prove yourself, to sell yourself as the most worthy and capable of doing the work. Work becomes an endless audition, in which you are only as good as what you did yesterday at five o'clock.

The only way to continually re-earn credibility is to turn yourself into a commodity: making yourself the most attractive, up-to-date, "value-adder" possible; constantly selling yourself so that others will buy you, your services, and your approach to doing business.

"Did you like my driving? Was I courteous? Did I arrive on time? Was my uniform clean? Did your goods arrive in perfect order?" When I think of what will be required in the future, I think of this print advertisement for a moving company that appeared a few years ago — with a few modifications: "Did I add value? Did I show that I understood your needs? Was I flexible, timely? Was I responsive? Did I demonstrate superior levels of customer satisfaction?" This will be the new hymn.

The End of the Job

Organizations used to compile elaborate "job catalogs" that described all of their jobs in some detail, including the responsibilities and the skills required. A decade ago I wrote an article for a human resources magazine arguing that these catalogs were a waste of time and money: no sooner would a job be described than it was out of date, so that organizations would end up preparing people for the jobs of yesterday.

When I wrote this, it was heretical. Job catalogs were deemed to be a central piece of career-planning processes. How, organizations asked, could people plan their careers if they didn't know what was available for them? Today one would be hard-pressed to find many people who expect such stability that their organization's jobs could be reliably and meaningfully described with any useful shelf life.

Indeed, in the very near future, very few of us will have something called a "job" at all. Jobs, after all, are rigid and highly structured. As such, they are no longer sufficiently flexible for a fast-moving business environment where companies and industries can disappear or emerge almost overnight.

Project work, outsourcing, contract work, and short-term assignments are rapidly becoming the primary way of doing business. It will no longer make sense to think in terms of jobs with fixed "job descriptions." Instead, you will have a constantly fluctuating mix of responsibilities – "packages" of "deliverables" for which you will need to continually upgrade your skills.

This trend toward "de-jobbing" was first widely publicized by consultant William Bridges in his groundbreaking book *Job Shift*. Bridges describes how today's organization is being transformed, from a structure built out of jobs into a field of work needing to be done.

In Chapter 9, you will learn how to redefine what you do from a job into a series of *roles*.

Project Work

In most organizations today, project work is becoming the rule rather than the exception. A project team configures a group of people around a defined piece of work for a defined span of time. Some will work exclusively on a single project throughout its life span. Others are "time-shared" – working on a number of projects at once, and dropping in and out of active involvement on an as-needed basis at different phases in the project's development.

When I think of a project team, I think of an amoeba with its permeable boundaries: fluid, changeable, expanding, and contracting. Project teams come together quickly and disband just as rapidly when the work is done, much like a Hollywood movie production. Just as screenwriters are succeeded by casting directors, set designers, cinematographers, actors, and film editors, the size of the project team waxes and wanes: new specialists come on board, while others move on.

Working in a project environment requires some special skills, including:

- **Quickly establishing relationships:** By its very nature, the working environment of a project team is typically characterized by short-term alliances rather than long-term relationships. You need to be able to establish relationships quickly, and to get along with people from diverse specialities and cultural backgrounds.

- **Juggling multiple tasks:** You may find yourself working on several projects simultaneously, using different but overlapping skills and having different schedules. Keeping on top of everything by prioritizing competing demands on your time will be critical to your success.

- **Dealing with geographically dispersed team members:** Depending on the size of your organization, on some projects, you may see your fellow team members rarely, if ever. You will need to be able to maintain effective communication through phone, fax, e-mail, and video conferencing without the benefit of face-to-face interactions and the relationship-building opportunities they provide.

- **Stamina:** Project work is typically fast paced and intense, with demanding deadlines and up-to-eighteen-hour working days. Priorities may shift rapidly, leaving team members scrambling. You need to be very fluid and elastic, and to have a lot of stamina, to thrive.

- **Self-knowledge:** You need a ruthless concept of your own skills and strengths and where they fit in, so that you can focus your efforts where you will be adding most value.

— **Knowing when to say "no":** Because project work is so fluid, it can become a never-ending roller-coaster ride. The work never really ends. Sometimes you will need to just say "no" to excessive work demands.

— **Focusing on the work, but marketing for the future:** When your current project ends, you want to make a smooth transition to your next project. And not just to any project, but to the *right* project — the one that will provide you with the greatest challenges, exposure, and skill-building opportunities. That means walking a delicate tightrope between focusing on your current work, and positioning yourself for the next step. If you lean too far toward marketing yourself, you may spark resentment among your coworkers and risk spoiling your network for the future.

FINDING THE RIGHT PROJECT

Many of our project-based clients have established what they call a "resource pool." After completing a project, staff go into this pool, where they have a certain period of time in which to find a new assignment. If they fail to do so, they will be outplaced.

If you find yourself working in this kind of organizational structure, you may want to avoid the resource pool, which means looking for your next project before the current one wraps up. Moreover, you will want to find the right project — the one that will do the most to help you enhance your skills and maximize your career options.

Projects vary considerably in their length, prestige, and importance, and in the opportunities they offer to develop new skills. Two people, for example, might start out with very similar skills and reputations. One gets onto a high-profile project team, say, working on the president's pet project; the other is assigned to something more mundane like improving an accounting process. A few years later, the two have completely different visibility in the organization, skill sets, and career prospects.

Always try to attach yourself to the project that is the most leading edge, uses the newest technology, and adds the most to your abilities, in particular, skills and knowledge that are most transferable to other work settings. Determine which project will be best for you, and market yourself for a role on that team. That means identifying your key skills and strengths, your achievements, and the ways in which you can make a contribution — and make sure that the appropriate people hear about them.

You may resent the need to constantly market yourself, and prefer to focus on the work at hand, asking, "How can I get anything done, when I'm spending half the time trying to sell myself for my next project?" But the reality is that if you fail to market yourself, you are much more likely to end up back in what some describe as "the dreaded pool."

Skills Obsolescence: A Shelf Life for Technical Skills

A graphic artist acquaintance of mine spent his life learning about typefaces and design. He is virtually unemployed now. Any twenty-two-year-old art college graduate with a personal computer, he says, can do the work better, faster, and cheaper.

Similar skills obsolescence has overtaken architects who spent years learning how to draft and now use a computer-assisted design (CAD) program; doctors who used to do EKG analysis by hand; and so on.

With the explosion of scientific knowledge and information-processing power, the pace of skills obsolescence is constantly accelerating. Half the technical skills of today's graduates will be obsolete within three to seven years of graduation, according to Canadian futurist John Kettle. In rapidly changing fields such as biogenetics, most of what you know will be outdated in four years.

Obviously the more technical your field, the more vulnerable you are to skills obsolescence. Staying abreast of the latest developments is clearly an imperative.

THE TEMPWORLD MANIFESTO

In TempWorld:

- You will always have to re-prove yourself.
- Success is contingent on your last hit.
- You are affected by external factors and may move up and down economically subject to those factors.
- Your skill portfolio, interpersonal skills, and resilience will help safeguard you against external factors.
- Relationships will be fluid; you will have changing alliances as you move in and out of different projects, assignments, and work situations.
- There will be more commuter families as individuals go "where the work is," leaving others behind.
- Communities will weaken as people leave family and friends to chase work opportunities globally.

If you want to thrive in TempWorld, you will need to take personal responsibility for your career and your life. Understand future work trends so that you can be best positioned to seek out and maximize opportunity.

THE VIRTUAL OFFICE

Work anywhere, anytime – these are the new dictums.

That may mean working out of a customer's office, whether to stay close to the customer or because the customer's office is closer to your own home. It may mean telecommuting, working 10,000 feet in the air, or working from a car or hotel room or airport lounge or your bedroom.

The virtual world is one without traditional borders, whether physical walls, structured organizational units, national boundaries, or time zones. To meet the needs of the most demanding and fastest-moving customers, quickly formed virtual enterprises are established and work is reconfigured in whatever way required to get the job done yesterday.

Virtual teams will do most of the work: constantly reconfiguring teams will come together in cyberspace from across the city or across the world to work on a project or a task for anything from a few hours to a year. Telepresence, e-mail, and groupware will replace traditional face-to-face contact, providing seamless communication of information regardless of physical location.

That's the theory, at least. It remains to be seen, however, whether these virtual teams will function as advertised. Just how important is face-to-face contact to the successful conduct of business? The deep-rooted human need for that contact may place effective limits on how far we can move into this virtual future, at least for certain types of work.

That said, many of our clients have redefined the office in order to reduce overhead costs, provide more natural support for spontaneously forming work groups, and better meet customer needs: "Why pay to provide offices, heat them, clean them, and decorate them if no one is ever there?"

Sometimes the new office is highly practical, and can even involve fun and creative solutions. For example, the sales representatives of one pharmaceutical company are constantly traveling, and don't need permanent office space. When they need to get together as a team, they meet at their "own" table at a local Chinese restaurant.

But no matter how practical, the drive toward the officeless office may accentuate the sense of a cold and impersonal workplace. At the extremes, some organizations have eliminated the entire concept of personal belongings at the office. Staff store personal papers in a locker, check out electronic equipment as required, and "hot desk" it at the first available workstation. It's almost as if these organizations are saying: "From now on, any evidence that you exist as a human being outside of this business, with your own personal tastes, interests, and connections in the world, will be forbidden. Kill that tacky coffee cup, forget the pictures of your dog, dump the wilted houseplant, throw away your Rolodex . . . *Welcome to the new officeless office.*"

In theory, this sort of arrangement is liberating: maximizing the use of technology and the sharing of information. It is spontaneous, informal, and unstructured, allowing staff to build on spontaneous face-to-face meetings and reconfigure the workspace as required to meet the needs of the task. But not everyone thrives under such informal arrangements. Many people like to nest, to feel they belong to a larger community. They are uncomfortable in a work environment that feels too cold and impersonal. The new approach to office organization eschews sentiment, family relationships, and emotions. It is not surprising that many people find it distasteful and at odds with life.

Offices ought to be both work friendly and life friendly. Whether at home or work, office space needs to be in sync with individual human needs – and if that human need is for a coffee mug with a tacky cartoon, so be it.

WHAT DOES THE NEW CAREER MEAN TO YOU?

Below, you will find a description of characteristics of the New Career. Read through the list, and select any three pairs that appeal to you personally. Think about three implications of each for yourself, for example:

"AEROBIC"
"I need to increase my personal stamina."
"I need to be prepared to work long hours."
"I need to be able to demonstrate a higher level of energy in my interpersonal relationships."

"HOPSCOTCH"
"I expect to spend more time moving sideways rather than upwards."
"I'm going to be jumping around a lot."
"I won't always be able to see where I'm heading."

THE NEW CAREER

IS	IS NOT
Date	Marriage
Transient	Permanent
Mutating	Stable
Borderless	Framed
Surfing	Cruising
Aerobic	Anaerobic
Unpredictable	Predictable
Hopscotch	Career Ladder
Resourceful	Compliant
Freewheeling	Structured
Selling	Sold
Impression-Managing	Relaxed/Secure
Risk-Taking	Safe
Team-Focused	Department-Focused
Resume-Building	Company-Building
Lego	Fisher-Price
Networking	Company Picnic
Hyper-Flexible	Stuck in Role
Entrepreneurial	Corporate
Self-Managing	Company-Guided
Independent	Dependent
Hyperactive	Active

YOUR NEW CAREER

The "TempWorld" depicted in this chapter is anything but temporary. It is about to become the dominant form of work. Instead of a lifelong career, you will have a *self-managed career* in multiple settings. Your career will probably be longer than it would have been in the past, punctuated by intermittent periods of education, leisure, and volunteer work.

But for all the changes, you can still have a challenging and personally rewarding career. You may still have something called a "job"; or you may be a member of a self-managing work team with shared responsibility for a range of tasks; or you may work on one or more different "projects." You may be a freelancer on a temporary contract, or a "core" employee with semi-permanent status. But, as long as you have the necessary attitudes and skills, you will still have opportunities for satisfying and meaningful work.

EIGHT

Become a Career Activist

*E*veryone in the workshop introduced themselves along with their job title except for Louise C., who said, "I don't have a title or a business card – I'm never on any assignment long enough to get one." Louise is thirty-one years old and has an M.B.A. Currently working for a life insurance company, she goes from project to project, often working on multiple projects simultaneously. "If it's Tuesday at 11:00 a.m., I'm working on the new pension product."

Louise describes herself as a "scout" and a "scavenger." She says: "In a very tight job market I think I'm lucky to have work. I'm always on the lookout for new ways to leverage my skills, to let people know what I can do, and how I can add value for them."

At the age of twenty-six, Maria C. already has three degrees to her credit, including a graduate diploma in human resources management. She approached my client, the director of human resources for a public accounting firm, with a proposition: "Hire me to handle your day-to-day headaches. In return, I'd like to be included in your management meetings. When you think I've proven myself, I'd like you to consider me for a professional position."

Tom B., previously a vice president of marketing for an insurance company, is forty-five years old, and has been on the job-search circuit for about nine months. He was offered a job that, at first blush, appeared to be a great opportunity. But after some serious introspection he made what he describes as a "gut-wrenching decision" to turn the job down. "I'm someone with strong needs to run my own show," he says. "The job reported to the parent company – I wouldn't have the autonomy I require to feel good about my work."

To the astonishment of his coworkers, Wayne C., a thirty-nine-year-old systems engineer, just took a demotion, in order to move from operations into system design. Wayne was very comfortable in operations, but worried that he was becoming *too* comfortable. The new area would stretch him, as well as offering greater prospects for future mobility.

All of these people are on the frontier lines of the new career, taking an *activist* stance in managing their work lives.

One of the key principles of career intelligence is to become a *career activist* – defining yourself independently from your organization, and taking charge of your own career choices. But to make informed choices, it's crucial to *know yourself*: your key strengths, interests, and values.

In this chapter we will look at four key principles in managing your career:

- Be a career activist: craft your own future.
- Know yourself: know who you are, what you are good at, the contents of your personal portfolio, what you have to sell. Redefine your experiences to identify underlying themes and skills.
- Know what you love: know what is most important to you.

- Be who you are: see yourself as capable; develop a personal success paradigm.

DISPELLING THE MYTHS

Before we look at the key principles of managing your career, let us first examine some enduring and ever-popular myths that many people have about careers in general, and their own career in particular. I am constantly amazed to hear these myths expressed by people of all ages and from all educational backgrounds and organizational levels. Seeing through these myths to look at the world of careers objectively and realistically is a crucial first step toward becoming a career activist.

"The Grass Is Greener"

Perhaps the most widespread career myth of all is the idea that other people in other jobs don't work as hard as you do; make more money; are able to make a more satisfying contribution at work; get more appreciation for their efforts; and just generally have more fun.

If you feel this way, you are probably overestimating how much fun other people are having at work, while underestimating how much fun you are having personally. As we've seen, people everywhere complain that they are overworked and underrewarded. The pressures you are experiencing are not unique to you, but are part of the new business realities.

Moreover, when you stop to assess your own situation objectively, you may well discover it is a lot better than you thought. One of the most frequent comments I hear from participants in our career planning workshops is: "I never realized how much I liked my work." Once you go through a process of self-assessment, you may be pleasantly surprised to discover that there are many aspects of your work you do enjoy; you are actually having more fun than you thought; and you are making a more significant contribution than you thought.

"There Is a Perfect Skill Set for the Future"

I am frequently asked questions such as: "What skills/educational experiences do I need to get ahead/to keep my job/to become a manager?" and
"Should I do graduate courses or get more experience to become . . .?" It's
as if people assume that there is a "magic bullet" or all-purpose tool kit that
can be applied across the board, a talisman capable of protecting them from
the vagaries of the economy and ensuring that they will thrive. It is interesting that when I respond to this question by asking "What are you good
at? What is it you want to do?" I typically receive a blank stare.

There *is* no magic bullet, no right skill set that can be applied willy-nilly
to all situations, or that all individuals can equally develop. Everyone has
unique aptitudes. As a general rule, you will do best by excelling at what you
are already good at rather than trying to develop yourself in an area where
you have little aptitude (see "Play to Your Strengths" below).

Indeed, it's not even true that the same work demands the same skill set.
Different people may do the same job in quite different ways and still
be effective. This may seem to fly in the face of current corporate wisdom,
especially if your organization, like many others, has developed competency
profiles for different levels and types of work – seven to nine skills or attributes needed to work at a high level of proficiency, such as "productive team
player," "visionary leader," or "influential communicator." But if you
are very gifted in one area, this often compensates for relative weaknesses
in another.

For example, if you are particularly talented at quickly establishing
credibility and trust, this can go a long way in compensating for poorer organizational skills. There is no such thing as the perfect, "must-have" skill set.

"There Is a Perfect Job Out There for Me – How Do I Uncover It?"

Just as some people seek the perfect skill set, others believe that somewhere
out there is a "perfect job" for them, uniquely suited to their strengths and

aptitudes. If you tell yourself this, you will be paralyzed when it comes to making any kind of career decision.

"Should I specialize? Should I do an M.B.A.? Learn another language? Move to another city? What courses should I take to increase my chances of finding the right job? If I take this job, enroll in that program, how do I know that there isn't another job or program that would represent an even better match with my skills?"

Early career professionals, in particular, fear that by making the wrong decision, they will take themselves out of the running for their perfect job. Believing there are few career opportunities left for them, they worry they will be even farther behind the eight ball if they make the wrong choice. And as the career stakes get higher and opportunities more limited, increasingly I am seeing this syndrome amongst older people too.

The reality is that there is no such thing as one "perfect" job or work situation. *There are good matches and bad matches, better matches and worse matches, sometimes even great matches.* But no matter how great the match, there will always be a number of career options that could be equally engaging to you, although quite possibly for different reasons.

One work situation, for example, might be interesting – even exciting – because it presents tremendous learning opportunities; another, because it gets you exposure to an important piece of new technology, even though the work itself may be less intellectually challenging.

"There's an Easy Answer"

People think that selecting a career path or making career decisions should be easy. Wouldn't it be nice if you could just feed your personal data into a computer, which would then spit out the answer – "You will be a French teacher in the suburbs of a city with 20,000 people . . ."; "You will be a CA in a midsize firm, specializing in the hospitality industry . . ." Or, if you could go to a career counselor, who, when you ask, "What should I be when

I grow up?" would look deep into your eyes and give the verdict: "Assistant vice president, marketing, in a pharmaceutical company manufacturing generic drugs." But there are no easy answers.

Selecting a career path is hard work. So is making career decisions. You need to conduct a rigorous self-assessment and take a hard look at your options. And as we see later in the chapter, you may also need to make some difficult trade-offs.

"There Are Clear Career Paths"

Some people still believe that the purpose of career planning is to tell them how to get from Job A to Job B to Job C, or what their next step up the ladder should be. This is a hangover from an era in which organizations offered clear career paths for people to follow. But today, for most organizations, the organizational chart of the future looks something like this:

?

As we've seen, we are now living in TempWorld — a world where there are no clearly defined, structured jobs. In TempWorld, work changes constantly in line with business needs, and those individuals with the best skill sets to meet those needs are "plugged in."

Organizations do still engage in succession planning, ensuring long-term continuity by identifying and grooming qualified candidates to fill senior management positions. But they no longer treat their succession plans as though they were carved in stone. They recognize, for example, that three years down the road the company might not need a "VP Finance" but instead a "VP of Intellectual Assets" and that the person currently slated for the former slot may not be the best candidate to fill the new one.

Using Career Intelligence to Manage Your Career: Four Key Principles

1. Be a Career Activist

"I wouldn't allow myself to be abused in a relationship — why would I put up with being abused in a job? When you're doing work for which you're not well-suited, or work which doesn't make you feel good about yourself, over time it feels like abuse." — DIRECTOR OF HUMAN RESOURCES

The path to career renewal begins with becoming a career activist.

It is ironic that work, which plays such a critical role in our life, has become the last arena for personal activism. We don't hesitate to take an activist stance in relation to our health, our personal finances, or our children's education. If our children were to have a problem with school, for example, most of us would act immediately and forcefully to protect their interests. In areas that affect us personally, we stand up and protect our rights, and strive to control our own destiny.

But, strangely, we don't adopt the same posture when it comes to looking out for our own career interests. *It's as if we don't see ourselves as being worthy of protection.* We allow our path to be shaped by other people, by circumstance, or by our own inertia. We tolerate long periods of anxiety, anger, and abuse at work, until the discomfort level is no longer sustainable or until it's almost too late. Then we start saying such things as, "If only I had been more careful/done this earlier, etc."

We are not passive in terms of initiating projects, or looking for cost savings for the company, or in letting ourselves get away with sloppy work — only in managing our own careers. In part, perhaps, we are just too tired, busy, distracted, and pressured to look after ourselves. But we are also, typically, ill-prepared to think like a career activist.

In fact, we *do* have control over many aspects of our careers, if we only choose to exercise it. We will still be affected, of course, by external factors, such as fluctuations in the economy. But becoming a career activist can help you weather and even thrive through these ups and downs.

Becoming a career activist means:

- Writing your own script rather than waiting for someone to write it for you.
- Being vigilant on your own behalf, identifying and preparing for opportunities, rather than expecting anyone else to guide you along or do reconnaissance.
- Becoming an *independent* agent, defining yourself in terms and concepts that are independent of your job title, your organization, or what other people think you should be. Rather than thinking of yourself as a level 10 computer programmer for Acme Software, for example, you need to see yourself as a software builder who has chosen to lease your skills to Acme Software in order to develop project management experience and increase your marketability.
- Being entrepreneurial – looking for opportunity, undertaking enterprises that provide opportunities (as well as risks).

Becoming an activist is not a luxury. It's the key to your future career success. "You are responsible for your own career"; "Think of yourself as working for yourself"; "You need to be self-managing." There are different ways of saying it, but they all come down to the same thing. *You* are the person in control of your own future. *You* have to plan and manage your own career. No one else can do it for you. And the only security you can depend upon is knowing that your own skills are strong, current, and marketable, and that you have the *inner resources* to manage through the ups and downs of life.

"What is the difference between independent consulting and working for an organization?" is a question I'm frequently asked by people just starting out, looking for a job, or contemplating a change. The answer now is *increasingly little*.

It's no longer possible to be a passive player in your own career management. You have to take responsibility for ensuring that you remain marketable; that you have the funds to support yourself when not employed; that your skills remain up to date; and that you will be able to afford to retire when you want to.

That means being strategic in looking at the range of opportunities you can pursue and in maximizing their potential value for your own growth, learning, and development. It means knowing what you have to sell and cultivating those assets. It means looking after yourself.

Being a career activist also means thinking about the landscape of work and opportunities in a radically different way. It means being prepared to live in an uncertain work world where the only certainty is *you*: your skills, your flexibility, your capacity to adapt to change. That requires optimism and belief in yourself.

Successful career activists behave more like a guerrilla than a soldier in a regular army. You need to be:

- informed, vigilant, and flexible
- passionate and engaged
- an unconventional thinker, with no preconceived concepts
- opportunistic – always on the lookout for windows of opportunity
- mobile, fast, and fluid
- well-informed about both your own strengths and the environment in which you operate
- able to turn advantages into opportunities.

2. Know Yourself

I was surprised when my friend, a self-employed public relations consultant for the past eighteen years, told me that she was looking for a job. "I miss the people interaction. I want to work in an environment where I'm not spending as much time by myself. And I want more structure in my life, a place to go every morning."

It is most unusual for someone who has been self-employed for eighteen years to discover that she should have been employed by someone else all along. And my friend is someone who has always been entrepreneurial, who doesn't take direction very well, and is uncomfortable with any kind of authority. It didn't make much sense to me to think that she would be better off in an organization.

In fact, a job would not be the solution to her problems. She was not suffering from not being part of a team environment nor from the need for more structure. Simply put, her problem was that she wasn't busy enough. She needed to get more work and find other ways of being involved with things outside of herself.

To manage your career effectively, you need to identify the unique talents and personal values that define who you are, what you do, and what you care about. You will then be able to match up your strengths and preferences with the right environment to achieve maximum work satisfaction.

Develop a personal work ID – liberate opportunities

Arthur W., an engineer by training, was director of manufacturing for a pharmaceutical company. After a thorough self-assessment, he was able to successfully sell himself as a director of management information systems. His new role fit well with his technical skills: his familiarity with technology, his ability to liaise between technical and nontechnical colleagues, his knowledge of the manufacturing process, and his personal love of high-tech "toys." But he might not have even contemplated such a move if he had continued to see himself strictly as an engineer in a manufacturing environment.

As jobs and roles change, one of the crucial challenges facing us is to look beyond our job titles and identify our key underlying skills. We need to separate our work identity from our jobs and job titles and exchange it for a *personal* "work ID" based on our skills, attributes, interests, values, and personal preferences. The job is only the vehicle through which we express those skills and attributes, and the job title only an outline of what we do at work.

Knowing yourself thoroughly – your interests, skills, values, and work preferences – will help you identify opportunities that play to your strengths and interests, as well as new skills and knowledge that you may need to acquire in order to ensure your productivity and employability. You will also realize what is most important for you in a work situation: what makes your work meaningful and makes you feel good about yourself.

Self-knowledge liberates opportunities. The more you know about yourself, the more options open up to you. If you think of yourself purely in terms of your job title or current position, whether as director of marketing or manager of human resources or whatever else, you confine yourself to opportunities that are essentially the same (and that may not even exist in the future). But if you see yourself as the *owner of a unique set of talents, skills, competencies, and experiences* that you can use in a wide range of settings, you expand your range of options exponentially.

Kelly P., for example, a marketing manager for a company selling high-tech medical instrumentation, was able to look at herself as having a portfolio of skills – technical, interpersonal, financial, managerial – that she could apply in a variety of work settings. As opportunities expand and contract in her industry, she may find herself at times selling more of her marketing skills rather than her technical know-how. At other times it may be her technical expertise that is most in demand.

Know your personal portfolio

I like to think of everyone as having their own personal self-managed career portfolio containing the unique combination of assets that defines them alone. This combination will ultimately determine what you have to sell.

Given that no one is perfect, your portfolio also contains personal liabilities – personality quirks that interfere with your effectiveness, and skills and abilities that are not as honed as they might be. To find continuing satisfaction and success at work, to protect yourself from career trauma, and to ensure your future marketability, take stock of your career assets and liabilities. It's important to be able to clearly describe your own strengths, work preferences, and values to find work that best plays to your strengths and assets.

This is not necessarily easy. Having witnessed countless individuals complete the self-assessment section of my *Career Planning Workbook*, I know it takes a lot of time and discipline. Fortunately, many tools and services are available. Career counseling can be arranged through a variety of public and private agencies and independent contractors. Shelves in the business section of bookstores and libraries are positively bursting with self-help career books. Spend time and invest effort to take stock of your skills, interests, and preferences. It's the essential foundation to managing your career successfully.

The "5 Ws"

One useful way of thinking about the self-knowledge you need is a model I borrowed from journalism to use in my *Career Planning Workbook* – the "5 Ws":

Who?
What?
Why?
Where?
When?

These "5 Ws" uniquely define who you are, what you do, what you're good at, and what you care about. As you read them, brainstorm or write down words that capture your own interests and skills in terms of these dimensions. By examining each dimension, you will build a picture of your personal work ID. You can then learn how to enhance your career and life satisfaction; discover your most important skills, values, and preferences; and gain a clearer sense of where you are now, where you want to be, and what you have to do to get there.

Who?

John P., a marketing manager for a life insurance company, used to enjoy his work, moving from project to project within a freewheeling team environment. But since he was moved to a special project examining the feasibility of introducing a new product line, he has been spending his days crunching numbers, interfacing only with a computer terminal. John is becoming more and more depressed, and says he wants to make a career move. Although *technically* well-suited to his new assignment, he is unable to function effectively in a work environment that provides him so little people interaction.

Linda J. has just received her accountancy designation, along with her own office cubicle – and none too soon. As a student she had been driven to distraction working in the "bullpen," an open office environment with no walls and no privacy. Linda needs to be able to go into a room, shut the door, and be by herself in order to get her work done. Prolonged people interaction is draining and ultimately devitalizing for her.

Are you more like John or Linda? Do you get your energy from being around other people? Or do you see yourself as more of an introvert, preferring to spend time working by yourself?

What kinds of people do you want to work with and for? How much interaction, and what kind of interaction, do you want to have with your boss, colleagues, clients, and others? Do you work better in a team or on your own? Do you prefer more structured or freewheeling social interactions? These are questions you need to answer.

What?

Promoted from a project management role to general management, Marilyn P. found herself feeling dissatisfied and disconnected. In assessing her preferences throughout her career, Marilyn realized that whether it was creating the high school yearbook or developing a new software program, what she was best at and what gave her energy was project management.

What are *you* good at? What do you have to offer in terms of skills and competencies – both technical and general skills?

Technical skills are specialized skills, knowledge, or abilities acquired through education or on-the-job training such as computer programming, designing a training program, doing a feasibility analysis, and conducting a focus group.

General skills are portable, independent of industry or job, the product of a number of factors, including on-the-job experiences and personal aptitudes. General skills include the ability to build a team, deliver a presentation, counsel a friend/team member/staff, or to quickly establish rapport with people.

About once a week I receive a call from a lawyer thinking about becoming an executive recruiter, or a teacher who wants to be a corporate trainer. Many people think of the technical component of their job as being synonymous with their entire job: if they become unhappy, they think they need to change careers. However, when they examine the source of their unhappiness they typically discover that it's not what they actually do that is bothering them, but that one or more of the other "Ws" is out of sync. That's why it is so important to accurately identify the underlying themes and characteristics which best capture your own unique profile of likes, dislikes, and strengths.

Ted P., for example, was a software developer in a large technology company. After his department was reorganized to work on a project team basis, Ted increasingly became unhappy. At first he thought that he was simply tired of his job, and he considered moving into sales or distribution.

But, on reflection, he realized that he still liked software development — it was the freewheeling, spontaneous, project team environment that he disliked. He was able to transfer to another part of the organization where he could do the same work within a more structured environment.

Why?

Sarah L., a well-respected magazine editor, was offered a promotion to publisher of the magazine. Flattered by the recognition, and drawn by the promise of a higher salary, she accepted. But she quickly realized that she had made a mistake. She was spending all her time courting advertisers and balancing budgets, while her staff were doing the work she most enjoyed, determining the shape and direction of the magazine. Sarah valued money and prestige, but she also valued the opportunity to use her creativity and professional skills even more.

Why do *you* work? Our values play a crucial role in determining how we feel about ourselves and our work. Increasingly, people are questioning their values in light of the frantic pace of their lives.

How well does your work meet your personal values? What is it that you really care about? It's important to reflect carefully on what is truly important to us. Otherwise, like Sarah L., we may discover that what we *think* is important and what really *is* important to us are two very different things. Staying in touch with our values can help us avoid making mistakes in managing our careers.

When you ask early career professionals about their number one value at this stage of their work lives, many of them will say "money." But after they go through a meaningful self-assessment, they typically discover that while money may, indeed, be important, other things are equally or more important: for example, having the opportunity to work in an environment where they can learn, having time for friends and family, or contributing to something they believe in.

Our priorities change and evolve over time, reflecting new life stages and experiences, like establishing a relationship, rearing a child, or dealing with the death of a loved one. Unless we stop to re-examine our values from time to time, we may be unaware of the ways in which we and our world have changed.

Often people carry around old scripts, continuing to make decisions based on what was *once* important to them. In career planning workshops I hear people bemoaning missed opportunities: "I had a great opportunity to participate in an exciting but slightly risky venture. I turned it down, because I was still clinging to the idea that I needed security above all else. That was true when I had no savings, a big mortgage, and a young family to support. But it isn't true anymore."

When was the last time that you reflected on how your values might have changed? What is important to you at this point in your life?

Where?
Dave W. was a hugely successful regional sales manager. He was rewarded with a promotion to corporate head office, but he quickly realized that he had made the wrong move. He became listless and depressed, yearning for the shirt-sleeved informality of his previous job, and the excitement of "being where the action is."

What kind of work setting suits your work style and allows you to perform most effectively? For example, do you prefer a head office environment or a field environment? Where do you prefer to live? Would you be happier in a large urban center or a smaller community? It is becoming common, in career planning workshops, for people to rate location as one of their top priorities.

Some people are looking for a lifestyle and a geography that will support their preferred lifestyle, whether it's a personal passion for skiing or a love of gardening. Work becomes secondary to living in the desired location. Others discover that they would prefer a smaller town to a larger urban center. They complain about the time it takes to get anywhere, the long commute. Or they react against what they see as the increasing alienation of big city living, and seek a better sense of community.

When?

Jane M., formerly a training coordinator, was promoted to executive assistant to the vice president of human resources. In that role, people approached her throughout the day with a barrage of questions on everything from their pension plans to expense-reimbursement claims. At the same time, she had demanding deadlines on other assignments.

As she tried to cope with the many competing claims on her time, Jane became increasingly frantic and her performance deteriorated. Her boss told her she had a time management problem. Jane's problem, however, was not one of poor time management skills. Rather, she needed more control over the *pace* of her work.

Do you prefer a fast-paced work environment where you constantly juggle priorities, or do you prefer to have more discretionary control over your work? Would you rather work on one or two things or on many things simultaneously?

We each have our own *individual rhythm of work*. Some of us get our energy from having a hundred things on the go at once: the more frantic the pace the more alive we feel. Others need to focus on just one or two tasks at a time. If that's true of you, that doesn't mean you get less work accomplished in the long run, just that you accomplish it differently.

Still, given the ever accelerating pace of business – with more work to be done by fewer people, and ever more demanding deadlines – there's no doubt that those who enjoy a higher pace of work are more likely to flourish.

Reconfigure yourself

In the future you will likely have a number of quite different "careers" (see Chapter 7). As your work shifts to meet changing business needs, certain skills will be called to the fore, others will recede in importance.

Tom C., for example, a meteorological research scientist working for an environmental protection agency, found his speciality rendered obsolete by new technology. After conducting a rigorous self-assessment and learning that he had strong investigative, analytical, and data-gathering skills, he found work with the military, collecting data on threats to the environment from chemical weapons. This enabled him to apply his existing research skills to solving a different set of problems.

You may know people who appear to have made a radical career shift. But on closer examination, you will probably find that the shift is less dramatic than it looks, and that they have simply reconfigured their skills in response to a new situation.

Thinking of your different skills and interests as *modular building blocks* means that the way in which you configure these blocks may change, but their essence will stay more or less the same.

When you look back on your career history, you will typically see underlying themes or core strengths, whether "start-up," "change agent," "expert," "project manager," "troubleshooter," "implementer," "marketer," or whatever else. You will find that you have demonstrated many of the same core aptitudes, competencies, and psychological preferences in every job and role, although in different combinations.

Rather than attempting to become something you are not in response to changing market demands, the challenge is to redeploy the key underlying characteristics that uniquely determine who you are.

Look at Yourself as a Business

In assessing opportunities and defining what you have to offer, think of yourself as a business enterprise. Most of us are very hard on ourselves, seeing ourselves in a light typically much harsher than others see us. Looking at yourself objectively as a business helps you recognize your unique assets.

Evaluate your career portfolio to identify assets and potential liabilities. What are your distinctive skills and strengths? What value do you add? Are you constantly vigilant in seeking opportunities and market niches for your services? What specific steps can you take to overcome or limit personal liabilities?

Think of yourself as a corporation of one, with a number of different departments, and you as the product:

- Marketing: What key assets do you have to sell? What market niche can you exploit? What opportunities can you take advantage of? Do you have a marketing plan? What is your product worth? Have you developed creative and effective ways of selling your services?
- Research and development: What are the areas in which you're going to learn and develop? How are you going to keep your skills on the leading edge?
- Production: What services are you going to offer?
- Promotion and public relations: How are you going to promote your product?

3. Know What You Love

From his early childhood, Alvin B. was a keen model-maker: model cars, model railroad layouts, model street scenes. When people asked him what he wanted to be when he grew up, he would say, "I want to be a model-maker. Or run a store that sells model kits."

Eventually though, under pressure from his parents and teachers, Alvin chose a "real" career: architecture. At least he would still be drawing up plans and building things. And so, after struggling through architecture school and graduating with mediocre marks, Alvin found work with a firm of architects.

Alvin worked for the firm for several years. He was not very good at his work, nor did he seem to improve. And he was miserable most of the time. Just about the only part of his work he enjoyed was making models of buildings to illustrate proposals. He was extraordinarily good at building these models. But that was not, in the end, enough. When a recession hit, the firm was downsized, and Alvin was first out on the street. His former employers did, however, offer Alvin a contract to take on all their model-making on a freelance basis.

Ten years later, Alvin makes models for many of the leading architectural firms in town. He earns a good living. And he loves his work.

Do what you love. Follow your bliss. We've all heard this type of apparently impractical advice for job seekers. But what sounds impractical is actually, when you think about it, very practical. All things being equal, the chances are that – like Alvin – you will do better and be happier doing work that you love than work to which you are indifferent, or that you actively dislike.

"I want to be a bestselling novelist."
"I want to be a famous movie actor."
"I want to be a TV talk show host."
"I want to be a major league baseball player."
"I want to be a brain surgeon."

There are limits, of course, set both by your abilities and aptitudes and by market conditions. If you really want to write a novel, for example, do so by all means. But don't expect it to be a bestseller, or even, necessarily, to be published at all. And don't give up your day job.

Finding work that you love is not as blissfully easy as the peppy self-help books might suggest. You may have to make considerable sacrifices and difficult trade-offs. But becoming an activist in your career means you will be in a position to make choices. And if you never even look for the work you love, your life will be poorer for it.

First, though, you have to *know* what you love. Knowing what you love doesn't mean you are guaranteed to find work that matches your passion. But it is a good first step. Let's look at some key criteria.

Know what is important to you

We have already seen how crucial it is to understand the "why" of your work. Knowing your personal priorities and values is crucial in ensuring your career satisfaction.

Ken P., for example, was an ambitious young software engineer with a number of important – and apparently conflicting – priorities. He wanted to "look out for number one": he wanted prestigious work that would pay well, meet his needs for challenge, and offer significant opportunities for recognition. At the same time, he wanted to contribute something of social value to the broader community.

Ken was able to reconcile his needs and values by finding work in the health care sector, working on leading-edge patient management software and becoming an expert in the field. He earned a little less than he might have in industry, but received significant recognition for his work, and a far greater sense of satisfaction.

Go for flow

When was the last time that you were so completely engaged and absorbed by your work that all of a sudden you looked up and said, "My God, five hours couldn't have passed!"? This is what University of Chicago psychologist Mihaly Csikszentmihalyi calls "flow" – a state of mind so engaged and focused that time passes unnoticed.

Ideally, work should be a primary source of engagement, pleasure, and self-esteem. Indeed, for many people, work is the most important source of positive life experiences. Csikszentmihalyi's research shows that people are three times as likely to report positive experiences at work than at leisure.

When you achieve a state of flow, the result is a sensation of confidence, of being in control, of being totally absorbed or focused. In order to reach this state, you need to balance your individual skills and abilities against the challenges of a particular task or activity.

This sense of vitality derived from work is by no means a privilege reserved for the knowledge elite. Csikszentmihalyi interviewed thousands of people around the world, from lawyers to cooks to dancers. Many of his subjects were actually doing relatively routine work: a mechanic, for example, had "transformed a mindless routine job into a complex flow-producing activity."

"Work is one of the best ways people can express themselves," writes Csikszentmihalyi in his book *Flow: The Psychology of Optimal Experience*. "But it won't happen without your participation. You have to ask yourself what you want out of life and find a job that is at least in part expressive of your own best abilities."

In other words:

- Any work can lead to total engagement depending on how you appraise it.
- In order to achieve flow you need to know what really engages you.
- Your aptitudes and what you care about should be well matched to the work at hand.
- Look for opportunities to challenge yourself in your present work: Can you remold your work so it stretches you?

4. Be Who You Are

"As far as I'm concerned," one client commented, "if I have to change my life when I arrive at work each morning, that's slavery." By that definition, many of us are in slavery, changing who we are every time we come to work, always careful, always defensive, always "in role."

A friend of mine, a successful senior manager, recently quit her job. Warm and expressive with her friends and family, she found herself becoming increasingly "cold and hard" to survive in an unrelentingly tough corporate environment. "It was getting to the point where I no longer recognized myself. I had to get out of there or go crazy."

Don't try to be something you're not. Be who you are — your *authentic* self. Find an organizational culture that reflects your personal needs and values, an environment that allows you to be you. You'll be happier. And in the long run, you'll probably be more successful.

One study, for example, looked at the characteristics of fifty-five successful women executives who held powerful positions in major American corporations. One of the most striking things they shared in common was their honesty and directness. They didn't pretend to be something they weren't. They expressed their own individuality. They weren't defensive or "political." And their careers flourished as a result.

Refuse to worship the new market god

Five years ago, you would routinely hear parents, in discussing their children's future, make comments such as "I don't really care what they decide to do as long as they're happy." I never actually believed people when they said this, but I valued the sentiment. I don't hear anyone make this comment today. It's almost as if the stakes have become so high that people feel that happiness as an end in itself is an indulgence one can ill afford.

We used to think of the economy in terms of goods and services produced in the service of individuals. Now we think of feeding the individual to the economy. As Russell Baker, writing in the *New York Times*, observed, "The market is now our supreme power. It is a God that requires human sacrifices to keep it satisfied."

The market, of course, has always determined what is desired, fashionable, valued, and profitable. But people didn't slavishly worship it as a god – they argued with it, struggled with it, debated its merits. Never before has a person's measure of worth and "fitness" been so intimately tied to their economic viability.

People turn themselves inside out to fit into positions that are a fundamentally awful match with their skills, interests, and values because they are so terrified of being without a job. They make career choices on the basis of "It will look good on my resume." They work excessive hours at the expense of their health, their children, and their personal relationships.

We evaluate activities as being worthwhile to the extent that they "add value" for customers or produce a profit. Time not devoted to these activities is seen as "dead time." There is no time for casual conversation, the pursuit of a goal out of pure intellectual curiosity, or debate purely for the pleasure of debate.

We apply this production obsession even to our children's education so that everything is measured by its potential economic utility. For example, it's no longer "Jill is learning all kinds of interesting things about the tundra" but "Jill is in a group doing a project (which happens to be on the tundra) where she is learning interpersonal, time management, cooperational, and team-building skills."

At some point, we have to step back, and refuse to worship blindly at the altar of the market god – to do what we want to do rather than contorting ourselves, pretzel-like, into whatever shape the market currently happens to demand.

Play to your strengths

We each bring to the table a unique set of skills and attributes, which meaningfully describe who we are and how we can add value. When we stray too far from these core strengths, we invite trouble.

Increasingly, I see people worrying because their organization has decided that in order for them to be successful they have to possess certain attributes and competencies. For example, they need to "be creative," to "have good leadership skills," or to "be able to withstand enormous pressure." In evaluating themselves against these competencies, people often identify one or two areas where they are not as strong, relatively speaking. They ask: "How can I become more creative? How can I be a better leader? How can I become more effective under pressure? What does it mean if I have a liability or weakness in a particular area?"

Self-help books and motivational courses would have us believe that we can be whatever we want to be, if we only try hard enough. I think this is *psychologically naive*. We are all different, and each of us has our own unique portfolio of strengths and aptitudes.

It has been said that the process of becoming older is one of becoming more of what we are, and less of what we are not. Or as Sigmund Freud observed, "The child is the father of the man." Psychologists who have conducted longitudinal studies have found that for the most part as we get older we do not change significantly in underlying core personality and behaviors. For example, as a general rule, the shy child becomes the introverted adult. The extroverted child becomes the gregarious adult. Children who are playground leaders often end up in leadership roles, theatrical children who are attracted to the performing arts may become trainers or public speakers, and so on.

Knowledge work typically requires a composite of skills and attributes. Sometimes a particular career path will involve doing some activity or using some skill that does not play to your strengths or interests. But work is *elastic*. As we noted earlier in this chapter, being gifted in certain areas, such as leadership and creativity, can often compensate for relative weaknesses in others. If you do have a liability in a particular area, try to find ways of minimizing the demand for that area in your work.

Why not try to correct the weakness? With concerted effort, you may be able to develop skills in areas in which you have difficulty. But you may be better advised to focus on what you are already good at, and spend your time developing further skills in those areas, rather than focusing on areas where you have no underlying aptitude. As a general rule, *you will get more return for your investment of time and effort by becoming better at what you are already good at.*

In sum:

- Find environments that play to your strengths.
- Become even better in areas you're already good at.
- Be patient when you're learning in an area that doesn't play to your strengths but is a must for your work. Don't expect the same learning gains for equal effort compared with areas where you already have a demonstrated aptitude.

Believe in yourself
Understand and believe that you have a future that is yours to create. Believe in yourself, that you have the emotional, cognitive, and interpersonal will and way to set meaningful goals and accomplish them. Develop a sense of yourself as:

- someone who is capable and skilled
- someone with something to sell
- someone with special talents and gifts
- someone who can make a contribution
- someone who can surf the waves of change
- someone who can play in the new career sandbox

- someone who has the inner resources to call upon in times of difficulty, knowing he/she will come out at the other end okay.

In short, develop a personal identity as a competent, effective human being. How we define and appraise a situation will play an important role in determining how we feel about it and manage it, and ultimately our success. For example, when Mary's company decided to sell off her work unit the managers were offered the opportunity to buy it. Mary and a number of her colleagues saw this as a tremendous opportunity, a chance to be their own boss, in charge of their own destiny. Although nervous, they were also euphoric. But others could not get beyond the insecurity, and decided to look for another job. Mary and her colleagues went ahead with the buyout, and today are the owner/managers of a thriving enterprise.

Often when people are confronted with a change in their work situation, they overestimate the scope of the change, the negative consequences associated with it and overreact: "I'll never be able to cope"; "Things will be completely different around here." Be realistic in your appraisal of change and your ability to manage it.

DEVELOP YOUR OWN CONCEPT OF SUCCESS

"I don't have to worry any more about moving up. I don't have to worry that people will think less of me for not being on the fast track. I don't want to be a senior manager. I've never been terribly ambitious, but I've always felt pressured to play the game. Now I no longer have to feign an interest in getting to the top."

— *A FORTY-SOMETHING ENGINEER*

One of the silver linings of the new work paradigm is that it liberates you to develop your own personal success paradigm. As a career activist, you decide what you need to do to earn an income, how you define meaningful work, how much money you need, and how you define "success."

Common Career Dilemmas

As the song goes, "You can't always get what you want." Sometimes we have to make tough career decisions that involve difficult trade-offs. Whatever your situation, *self-knowledge and understanding of the new work landscape give you the basis for making informed career decisions.* You may not come up with a "perfect" solution. But you will come up with a solution you can live with, that on balance makes the most sense. The following are five common career dilemmas.

Career Mismatch: "Should I Stay in the Wrong Job?"

Elvin T. was previously a highly rated sales manager, reporting in to the vice president of marketing, a position to which he was temperamentally and intellectually well-suited. As a result of a downsizing, however, he now reports directly to the CEO. In that capacity, he has to play a much more *strategic* role in marketing, and instead of being an implementer he has to develop the plan.

Lynda G. used to love her work as a compensation specialist until a restructuring led to a reorganization of the human resources department. Her job changed into a generalist position in which she is now expected to consult on a wide range of issues about which she knows little and cares less.

Bad fit. Poor match. Like a square peg in a round hole. Being out of sync . . . These are different ways of describing one of the oldest career problems in the book, but one that has become more common than ever. Reorganizations and downsizings, combined with a tight job market, put people like Lynda and Elvin into positions for which they are fundamentally ill-suited.

All too often after downsizing, faced with the need to get work out, organizations take an empty job and an available person and put them together. Rather than having people examine what they are really good at, what they care about and what their strengths are, they simply do a cursory matching based on superficial information. ("Jim knows pulp and paper, he's a technician, let's move him into maintenance.")

It used to be that when you were offered a new job one of the first items on the agenda was to ask yourself, "Is this a good match? Does it play to my strengths? Will I be happy/challenged doing this?" Today, beset by insecurity, people tell me they feel they can't afford the "luxury" of refusing work that is a bad fit — to do so would be somehow indulgent.

You will pay a serious price for a mismatch. Given the importance of work in our lives, *few things are more emotionally damaging than doing work that does not play to what we are.* We've all been there. And the effects of a bad match can persist for years after it has been remedied — loss of self-esteem, doubt in one's abilities, heightened emotional sensitivity.

If you feel mismatched to your work, self-assessment is absolutely crucial. Take a hard look at the key dimensions that underlie your work — the "5 Ws." You may well discover one or two minor things that are out of sync. Then examine options for improving the match.

Ask yourself: "Can I shift this work so that it is a better match? Can my boss (or someone else) help me reorganize the work?" And most important: "What is the cost to me personally of continuing in this job? What is the cost to those dear to me?" If the cost is significant, do something about it now. It may not be easy — nothing really important is — but it will be worth it. It's not a luxury; it's a necessity.

Balancing Financial Needs Against Core Values: "I Know What I Love But Who Will Pay the Kids' Tuition?"

People are torn between meeting their personal needs for growth, spending time with their families, doing something personally important to them, and putting food on the table. High mortgages, debt, and work insecurity all make people nervous about pursuing what they love.

There are no easy answers here. It's all very well to say, "Do what you love and the money will follow." But if you are a sole-support parent, or have significant financial commitments, you may not be prepared to take that leap of faith.

Remember that any decision you make is not necessarily for keeps – you are not its prisoner for life. For example, you may decide to pursue a path that puts financial needs over personal needs until your kids have gone to university, or until you have completed a particular educational diploma.

Weighing Up a Geographical Transfer: "A Three-Year Sacrifice, Great for My Daughter and My Long-Term Security, But I Hate This City"

A friend of mine who worked for a company that moved its head office from Boston to a small city was offered a bonus as an incentive to move for a minimum of three years. My friend was very involved in the social and cultural life of Boston. She lived downtown and participated in many urban activities. Small town living definitely didn't appeal. But she was fifty-one years old, and the sole-support parent of a fourteen-year-old daughter.

After assessing the job market and her own personal assets, she concluded it would be difficult to find work that produced an income similar to the excellent salary she was currently receiving. After some equivocation, she decided to make the move, reasoning that her "daughter will have the opportunity to be part of a small community and to be a real star [she is a gifted tennis player]. It will be a great learning experience, and we'll be that much further ahead financially. After three years, I can take early retirement and live where I want."

Settling for Lower Professional Standards: "I Love My Craft – I Don't Want to Do It in a Second-Rate Way"

Beset by extraordinary time pressures and demanding deadlines, forced to produce work with scarce resources, people find themselves doing work that is not up to their standard (see Chapter 5 for more on the impact on people of having to turn out what they regard as "second-rate work").

Sherry P., for example, a management development trainer, says, "What's important to me is being on the leading edge of my field. But without the time or budget I needed, I was not delivering the quality I wanted." Unable to live any longer with the compromised work, she decided to leave her job and go out on her own. At the same time she was realistic. Knowing it would take her a while to equal her former salary, she sold her house. That way, she explained, "I won't be forced into doing something I don't want to do just to pay the mortgage."

Making the Decision to Put Your Own Needs First for Once: "I'm Tired of Being on Hold . . . It's My Turn Now"

David's company planned to sell off his business unit and offered managers the opportunity to buy it. David had always had a strong desire to run his own business, to be in charge, to be his own boss. But he came from a family that valued, above all, the security of a regular paycheck, and his wife still firmly believed that only a large organization could offer such security.

Despite his family's concerns, David became part of the buyout and remortgaged his house to raise his share of the financing. "I've spent all my life putting other people's needs first, and I don't regret it. But I feel I've met all my financial responsibilities. My kids have finished university, and I've saved enough for retirement. If this doesn't work out we won't be destitute – I'm not betting the entire farm on it. But I don't want to be a bitter old man when I'm sixty or seventy, wondering what would have happened if I'd taken the opportunity. There is no security anymore, other than what you create yourself."

All these dilemmas involve some kind of values conflict – meeting one value means another is not met. Resolving a career dilemma comes down to knowing what is most important to you. Clarify for yourself:

- what you cannot give up ever;
- what you could give up now in the short term; and

167

- what you can give up entirely, knowing that in the longer term it will open up more opportunities and enable you to meet more of your values.

There are no easy answers, no quick bromides. Making the right decision requires time, effort, and careful self-examination. But the payoff is worth it.

NINE

Twelve New Rules
for Career Success

"*I* enrolled in a Health and Safety program three years ago because they told me that there were lots of good jobs in this area. I spent two years commuting an hour each way to community college. I've been unemployed now for over a year. I've applied for over a hundred jobs and I've only got to the interview stage a few times. Why did they tell me that there were jobs? Don't you think they were being irresponsible? I did everything they told me to do — how come I'm not getting work?"

I received this call when I was a guest on a call-in TV show about the new work realities. The caller talked in a very angry voice. To be honest, I was not surprised that he was having difficulty finding work. He appeared oblivious to some of the most important new rules for career success in today's extremely competitive job market:

- He talked about an authoritative "they," who were somehow responsible for his career destiny.
- He made no attempt to identify his real strengths, to research opportunities, and to determine his own best course of action; instead, he relied on what "they" told him.
- He saw the job market as being stable: "they" could make accurate predictions about job openings in a particular field.
- He had no passion for pursuing this particular line of work. Presumably if "they" had told him that flower arranging was a hot area, he might equally well have become a florist.

The workplace has changed, and the rules of career success have changed along with it. In the last chapter we looked at four principles for using career intelligence to manage your career. In this chapter we look at the new rules and strategies for putting those principles to work.

1. Ensure Your Marketability

- If your current work assignment ended tomorrow, how quickly could you find a new one?
- Are your skills up to the standard set by the external community, or are you evaluating yourself against internal corporate standards?
- Are you confident that your skills and knowledge are sufficiently current that you could sell your services to another employer/client?
- Do you search for opportunities to enhance your marketability?
- Do you have a full tool kit, or portfolio, of skills? Are you always

looking for opportunities to fill up your tool kit to ensure your longer term marketability?

Forty-five-year-old Jim L. was formerly a middle manager in a company that eradicated its entire middle management ranks. It took him eighteen months to find another job – and two years to recover emotionally: "Never again will I be caught with my pants down. Every six months I take out my resume, and if I can't think of one thing I've accomplished that I can add, I know that I've been slacking off."

It may no longer be realistic to believe that job security exists anywhere anymore. But you can have security in the *marketability* of your skills. To make yourself marketable:

- Think of everyone you work for as a *client* rather than a boss.
- Know your product: you and the skills you have to offer – your assets, strengths, and potential liabilities, and how you can add value to an employer or client.
- Know your market: both current and prospective clients.
- Be able to communicate your strongest selling points to your market.

Examine the work you are currently doing and ask yourself if it is providing experiences or new skills that enhance your marketability. If not, seek out assignments and projects that offer you opportunities that will make you more marketable in the future. *Always make the most of your current work situation.* If you don't, it may be your last.

Look for opportunities to leverage your skills and experience, identifying business niches and unexploited areas where you can add value. But avoid overspecializing (see "Are You More of a Specialist or a Generalist?" below). Instead, be flexible and adaptable – ready to try new ways of working, even if those ways of working are initially uncomfortable for you, or different from what you are used to.

Have a Fallback Position

I remember friends of my parents who ensured that their three daughters grew up with more than just a profession such as social work or teaching. Each one also had another skill area to fall back on if necessary, such as teaching music or dance. Twenty years later, each uses those skills either to supplement their incomes, or as a significant leisure activity.

- Could you readily change career directions if required?
- If you lost your main source of income tomorrow, could you success-fully move on to another course?
- If there was a downturn in your industry or profession, could you transfer your skills to pursue an alternative career direction?

The old adage is true: don't put all your eggs in one basket. Have a *broad repertoire of skills* within your portfolio, so that if your primary career doesn't work out, or you get temporarily derailed, you can switch to your fallback position.

Your fallback may be a set of skills you use only occasionally now, but which could translate into a new career. Perhaps you work in marketing, for example, but you're also a whiz with database programs. Or it could be a sideline business with a potential for growth: selling vitamins out of your garage, or moonlighting as a consultant. The point is to have something to fall back on if Plan A doesn't work out.

Build Broad Networks

For many, the shape of work to come will be short-term assignments and multidisciplinary project teams. This will require both geographical mobility and the ability to constantly resell ourselves. It will be more important than ever to nurture a wide range of relationships.

- Do you cultivate relationships with people outside of your profession, employer, or industry?
- Do you cultivate and nurture relationships with a broad range of people?
- Do you stay in touch with people just for the sake of staying in touch, or because of their economic utility (e.g., you only call them when you are looking for a job)?
- Do you feel comfortable "networking," or do you see it as phony and insincere?

I'm amazed at how parochial many people are in their networking. Psychologists hang out with psychologists, bankers with bankers, lawyers with lawyers. As a result, they develop a very narrow view of the world. In a work world where *breadth* will be one of the key requirements for career success, expanding your network horizons will increase your understanding of critical business and social trends.

Develop a broad network of contacts both inside your workplace and outside it by participating in professional associations, social-interest groups, and community organizations. Broad networks give you a broader perspective on your work, as well as enrich your life.

Getting involved in *multiple* networks will help you develop a reputation for breadth and flexibility. And from a purely practical point of view, it makes little sense to network only with people in your profession or industry. If there is a downturn in your area, you could find yourself in a network of people all looking for the same kind of work as you. The broader your networks, the more opportunities are potentially available if you need to make a career transition.

Perhaps, like many people, you're uncomfortable about networking. Perhaps you think of it as being manipulative and exploitative – *using* other people to help you get ahead. Or perhaps you feel it is somehow unseemly for you as a professional to have to "schmooze" or "glad-hand." You think of networking as fundamentally insincere – feigning interest in someone when all you really want is to use them for your own ends.

Networking is about more than glad-handing, "using people," or handing someone your business card as soon as you are introduced. Indeed many of the most effective networkers don't even bother with their business cards. Simply put, networking is about developing *mutually supportive relationships*. It is as much about being there for someone else as about "using" someone else to get ahead.

When you are networking, the other person is as likely to be the beneficiary as you are. You might learn about a possible merger at a customer's company, for example, while your network buddy finds the name of a great contact for raising money for a community association you belong to.

The exchange of information may or may not lead to an immediate payoff. Relationships take time to nurture, and one doesn't enter every relationship looking for something of immediate economic value. Don't measure your networking by its economic utility or the immediacy of the payback.

Every relationship can be worth cultivating, whether with family, friends, coworkers, or customers, if you think of it in terms of a mutually rewarding information exchange with the potential for long-term support and value. Look at "value" not purely in commercial terms, but in the much broader sense of community, emotional support and a personal connection.

Exec-U-Net, for example, a North American–wide association of senior managers and professionals from diverse disciplines, has shown the broad value of networks in helping people do everything from finding job leads to reaching a decision about where to retire and facilitating entry into a new community.

NETWORK ETIQUETTE

There are five or six people who call me every year or so . . . depending on their circumstances. I call them my "fair-weather friends" because they only call when they are having a problem at work, or are worried about their job and want advice or leads to new positions.

We all know people like my "fair-weather friends," who measure everyone's value in terms of their potential economic utility and payback.

Where does networking end and "using people" begin? This is a difficult issue. To some degree, your personal taste and style will determine what you are comfortable with.

We all know people who, as soon as they have been introduced, will "download" all their personal specifications: job title, phone and fax numbers, and e-mail address. But it is possible to be introduced to someone and shake hands without immediately exchanging business cards. Use your judgment when meeting people in a social situation. And remember, *your business card is not an extension of your hand.*

Some other tips:

- Send a thank-you note if someone has been helpful to you or generous with their time, showing your appreciation for how they helped you. Over and over again I hear about people who reaped very significant benefits because they took the time to send a brief note.
- Send a newspaper or magazine article as an "information brief." Networking is about information exchange. In a time-starved society where managers and professionals have little time to stay on top of everything they need to, these briefs are appreciated.

Market, Market, Market

In ensuring your marketability, perhaps most important of all is being able to market yourself and sell your services to a broad range of people. You're only marketable to the extent that people *know* what you can do and how you can add value.

- Are people you work with aware of your important accomplishments, skills, and work experiences?
- Do you keep people informed of your significant work accomplishments and experiences?
- Are you staying in touch with the people you should – are you keeping your network alive?
- Do you stay in touch with people to remind them of your skills and how you can add value (or do you just assume that they should know or remember)?
- Do you feel comfortable marketing yourself or do you feel that is "below you," or that it shouldn't be necessary?

Some people say that every interaction is a sales call, every person you meet is a prospect. Like it or not, this is a harsh reality of the new economy. But just as you may feel uncomfortable about networking, you may experience the same discomfort about marketing yourself. You may think: "I shouldn't have to let people know that I'm good at what I do. If I'm good, talented, and produce results, that should be enough." Or: "If I am working on a project, I'm being paid to accomplish a particular set of objectives – not to focus on getting my next assignment." Unfortunately, if you fail to market your abilities and achievements, you are likely to see your career progress stall.

A friend of mine was upset because a regular client had hired a competitor to do some work she thought she could have done better and cheaper. Her client hadn't realized that she offered that particular service. "If they had read my brochure," my friend said, "or if they had just asked me, they would have known I offer that service."

My friend was right – in principle. But in practice, contracting out that piece of work was only one of fifty different things on her client's mind. The client can hardly be blamed for not being fully apprised of every service of every potential supplier. My friend should not have left it for her client to read the brochure, but should have taken the time to anticipate her client's needs.

To market yourself effectively, *don't assume what is obvious to you is obvious to others*. Point it out. Don't wait passively to be asked what you do – take the initiative in selling your services. Don't assume that if you have told someone something once, for example, that you have a particular skill, they will remember it. Remind them, at appropriate intervals.

Keep people informed about what you are doing. Look for opportunities to exchange information with them about your work. Don't assume that everyone already knows what you are doing, and what you have achieved. Get to know your clients – whether customers, managers, or team leaders – well enough to anticipate their needs.

Most people tend to err on the side of modesty when it comes to marketing themselves, even though they understand its importance. Where do you draw the line between being obnoxiously self-promoting and keeping others informed about special skills and how you could add value to their enterprise? As with networking, there are no hard and fast rules. This is a question of taste and the acceptable rules of behavior in your occupation.

2. Think Globally – Cultural and Linguistic Versatility Count

Today's technology allows you to work anywhere, anytime. And in a global economy, you may have to. In the borderless work world, where the entire world is a potential market, the ability to speak other languages and be comfortable with other cultures will be crucial.

- When you think of work and your future, do you think of it locally, nationally, or internationally?

- Where are the geographical boundaries of your work?
- How many languages do you speak?
- Do you read international journals or belong to international associations that keep you abreast of international trends?
- Are you on-line, exchanging information worldwide (e.g., are you on a bulletin board or part of a discussion group)?

A friend of mine, an architect, after struggling for a few years in what he described as "a dying profession" ("they're no longer building office towers – they were all done in the '80s") has secured a new livelihood by going on-line and networking to find new clients as far away as Saudi Arabia. He still lives in Toronto but travels back and forth to the Middle East.

Globalization means an expansion of work opportunities, making you less reliant on the local economy. People who move to find work have always gained special skills in self-management as they are forced into greater self-reliance. A twenty-three-year study at York University, for example, found that the biggest single influence on a young person's future success is moving away from home – whether to or from a big city. "Movers" were far more likely than "stayers" to be in the middle or upper class, as defined by income, occupation, and educational level. Leaving their original community had far more impact on their success than their family's social status, what their father did for a living, or where they were born.

Living and working internationally helps you gain richer concepts not only in the mechanics of business, but also in the principles of life and work. As organizations increasingly move into new international markets, they will be looking for individuals who can adapt readily to other cultures while interfacing effectively with North American management. Cultural and linguistic versatility will therefore be a tremendous asset in your portfolio. Any multicultural exposure that enables you to move between headquarters and emerging global markets will improve your marketability. And people who have learned a second language at their grandparents' knees will be valued commodities (see also "Learn a Language" in Chapter 11). Increasingly, an international tour of duty will be a stepping-stone to career success.

3. BE ABLE TO COMMUNICATE IN POWERFUL, PERSUASIVE, AND UNCONVENTIONAL WAYS

"Get to the point — I don't have all day. I'm tired, my boss is breathing down my back. You're one of twenty-five things I have to attend to today . . ." People with finely honed communication skills have always been valued. But advances in telecommunications, geographically dispersed project work, and everyone's information overload mean that the *nature* of communication and how we need to communicate is changing.

- Can you quickly capture your listener's attention and get your message across?
- Can you use words to paint a picture, tell a story, make information vivid?
- Can you write clearly, persuasively, and with impact?
- Can you zero in on key concepts and translate them appropriately for your listener's requirements? (Or do you tend to embellish needlessly and bury vital points in a pile of superfluous information?)
- Can you quickly establish relationships and credibility with people you've never met without face-to-face contact?

An international art dealer friend of mine told me that she is now selling much of her art on the Internet rather than through face-to-face communication, and she has had to learn a completely new set of communication skills. In the past, she would build relationships and establish credibility with people over time through a combination of "schmoozing," charm, and professional expertise. To do the same thing on-line, she says, "I had to learn to use the written word the way I speak. I had to learn how to become an evocative writer – to charm, to talk about the feeling of a picture in a few powerful and suggestive words."

A consultant who has turned his charming British accent to positive advantage in running a business from his home complained about new technologies. "E-mail has no accent," he says. And video phones, when they arrive, threaten to expose the ramshackle state of his office. He needs to develop new ways to build rapport with future clients.

One of the critical skills for career success will be being able to communicate graphically, compellingly, and quickly in both oral and in written form. These skills will serve you well in working on multidisciplinary project teams with people you have never met, capturing people's attention, and quickly building rapport (see Chapter 7 for more on project teams).

4. Keep On Learning

With constantly changing work and shifting skill requirements, "lifelong learning" will be more than just a catchphrase. It will be a necessity.

- Are you feeling stretched in a positive way?
- Are you experiencing "flow" (see Chapter 8)?
- Can you describe what you have learned in the last six months?
- Can you describe what you hope to learn in the next six months?
- Are you aware of the most recent trends in your field and their implications for your longer-term success?
- Do you know what skills and knowledge you need to develop in order to ensure your future success and employability?

We have always been responsible for ensuring we had the requisite skills to get ahead, and for keeping our skills up to date. However, this used to be a *shared responsibility* between the individual and the organization: you would identify your needs, and the organization would provide the necessary tools, training, and developmental experiences as appropriate.

In our hit-the-ground-running culture, current expectations are that you will do whatever is necessary on your own time to ensure the currency of your skills. The organization offers no guarantees that your learning will ensure your employment security. It promises only to try to provide an environment where you can work with people you can learn from, and opportunities to gain skills that will be valued inside your organization or in other work settings.

Some rules of lifelong learning:

- Take responsibility for what you decide to learn.
- Stay current in your own field, and continue to develop skills and knowledge outside it.
- Be an agile learner.
- Benefit from your on-the-job experience.
- Seek opportunities for learning both inside and outside your workplace.
- Take courses, read books and journals, develop and practice new skills.
- Look at periods of full-time education between periods of work not as "time off," but as smart career moves preparing you for the future.

When considering learning, don't confine yourself to "traditional" institutions or modes of learning. Perhaps the most important learning "event" of recent years has been the number of people who have become computer literate — something achieved almost exclusively outside the traditional classroom.

As more and more educational institutes are going on-line, offering diverse learning experiences over the Internet, including graduate degrees, it will be much easier to meet the need for lifelong learning.

KEEP ON LEARNING – ON YOUR OWN TIME

A division of a Fortune 500 company sent a memo to employees that encouraged them to increase their global competitiveness by taking foreign language training during the workday. Six months later, everyone who had taken the offer was fired. Apparently, management concluded that if someone had the time to take a course during the day, they were obviously underemployed.

5. UNDERSTAND BUSINESS TRENDS

I am always amazed at how many people have only the narrowest knowledge of specific trends in their profession, and even less knowledge of broader business trends – whether economic, demographic, or cultural. I routinely ask people, "What business magazines do you read?"; "What international trends will affect your business?"; and "Globally, what is your major source of competition?" Even among senior managers only a handful of people say they are as well informed as they should be.

- Do you regularly read business magazines or the business section of your newspaper?
- Can you identify three trends that will have significant impact on your industry in the next five years?
- Do you know what new technologies might shape your industry in the next five years?
- Do you know what the potential threats are to your industry/profession?

In a very complex and rapidly changing work world, it is crucial to be aware of key trends in business, society, and politics. Not having the time to keep up simply doesn't cut it as an excuse. Read the business press or keep current through electronic media, and keep track of the fast-changing economic and social landscape. Understand the competitive environment. Get information from a variety of sources and maintain an independent and critical perspective.

TAKE EDUCATED RISKS

If you're a keen follower of business trends, you may be able to position yourself for a financial windfall. Start-up companies in "hot," high-growth areas, such as high technology, often offer stock options in lieu of a higher salary, thereby attracting talented people they would otherwise be unable to afford with the promise of future wealth when the stock is publicly traded, or the company is acquired. Sometimes these stock options prove to be very valuable (witness the number of millionaire secretaries at Microsoft). Obviously, this strategy is not for the fainthearted, nor for those who need a higher base salary. But if you're both a risk-taker and a shrewd student of business trends, you *could* do very well for yourself.

6. PREPARE FOR AREAS OF COMPETENCE, NOT JOBS

Recently someone suggested computer animation as a possible future career to my teenage son – a hot field with a current skill shortage, which would be a good match for his storytelling, graphic, and media abilities. He said, "The work I choose now might not even exist by the time I'm old enough to do it. Or if it does exist, the technology may have changed to require completely different skills." Intuitively he understood a key maxim of the new economy: Don't prepare for jobs, prepare for areas of competence. Just as many of the jobs of yesterday may now have vanished, so the "hot" jobs of today may not exist in the future.

Labor market projections are notoriously unreliable. Jobs evolve and vanish, sometimes almost overnight. A recent story in a business magazine profiled the rising stars of the new global economy. Half of them were in occupations most people probably couldn't pronounce, much less understand exactly what they did.

Even the traditional "safe" occupations have been dramatically affected by the new economy. Such professions as lawyers, teachers, chartered accountants, and doctors all face new and unpredictable challenges to their security.

For example, within accounting firms, traditional tax and audit services – now largely automated – today account for only a small percentage of the work. Firms now offer services in broad multidisciplinary fields. Organizations no longer make financial information the sole indicator of corporate value, but consider other elements such as intellectual capital. And as the kind of information organizations are looking for broadens beyond the purely financial, employers may equally consider professionals with a technology background, and M.B.A.s in finance or organizational behavior, as well as chartered accountants.

To see how difficult it is to make accurate job predictions, look at the teaching profession. Because of the large number of baby boomer families having children in the 1980s – the so-called baby boom "echo" – there were rosy predictions about the demand for teachers in the 1990s. But government deficit-cutting has forced school boards to eliminate special needs and gifted programs, and many young teachers are having a tough time finding work.

At the same time, teaching provides an interesting example of how the drying up of opportunities in one area does not mean the disappearance of all opportunities. Savvy teachers are earning income through private tutoring, profiting from anxious parents who want to help children secure a foothold in the new economy.

As for lawyers, the class of '95 in Ontario reported a 64 percent employment rate by January 1996, compared with only 57 percent in 1990 and 61.5 percent in 1985. At first glance, it might appear that studying law was becoming a better occupational choice in 1995 than in 1990. However, in 1995, 26 percent were, in fact, employed in *unrelated fields*: their education in law has ended up being about competencies, not about their final job.

It takes at least five years to become a lawyer, four to eight years to get the specialized education required for most professional designations. Given the speed of change, it is not surprising that you cannot rely on forecasts of where the "hot new jobs" are going to be.

It no longer makes sense to prepare yourself for future jobs and job titles that could vanish in a blink. Instead, focus on developing core competencies that are likely to be in demand in the future. *Define yourself by what you do and how you get it done, not by your job title.*

Think Roles Not Jobs

I have a friend who always complains about how she doesn't have a "real" occupation to "hang her hat" on. Her job title is "internal consultant." When she is at a party and people ask her what she does, she doesn't know what to say. That's because she plays a variety of roles that are *independent of technical content.* She's an advisor, problem-solver, and facilitator. Her practical intelligence combined with broad business understanding enables her to establish credibility with any work group. She is excellent at helping people work through complex problems, getting rid of all extraneous information, and identifying key issues. She quickly establishes rapport with senior managers and gains their respect for the quality of her advice. She is in high demand, and constantly receives calls from recruiters.

- Can you describe three to five roles that you perform in your day-to-day work?
- Can you identify three roles that you play that are independent of your particular job that you could transfer to another work setting?

Leader . . . Change Agent . . . Coach . . . Problem-Solver . . . Individual Contributor . . . Troubleshooter . . . Start-up . . . Team-Builder . . . Innovator . . . Consensus Builder . . . Mentor . . . Implementer . . . Facilitator . . . These are all examples of roles we might play. And the first thing you might notice about them is that they are all independent of technical content. If you have the qualifications and talents to fill these roles you will do well in the new economy.

Obviously, these roles are not mutually exclusive. Almost certainly you will find yourself playing several roles at the same time.

It's important that you can identify the different roles you play and how they can be applied in other work environments. And when you are thinking about roles, think about all the domains of your life. A minor role as a fund raiser for a community theater, for example, might be later parlayed into a major work responsibility.

NEW SKILLS FOR THE NEW WORKPLACE

New rules and new work realities call for new skills and personal attributes – primarily self-management skills. These are the skills that employers are looking for, that will determine your future success in the new economy.

Consider the following list of skills.[1] Which items describe you? Use this information to identify what you have to sell, as well as areas for improvement.

Resourceful/Enterprising	Innovative/Creative
Opportunity-Seeker	Gymnastically Flexible
Time-Urgent	Resilient
Market-Driven	Independent/Self-Reliant
Globally-Oriented	Challenge-Seeker
ROI Thinker	Ruthless Time Manager
Self-Confident	Balancer of Work/Personal Life
Committed/Enthusiastic	High-Impact Risk-Taker

[1]From *Career Planning Workbook,* BBM Resources Consultants Inc., Toronto, Ont. © Barbara Moses & Associates 1995.

Obsessively Customer-Orientated	Compelling Communicator
Problem-Solver	Insatiable Learner
Self-Promoter	Leading-Edge Professional
Team Worker/Leader	

7. LOOK TO THE FUTURE

As we've seen, you can't rely on the accuracy of long-term occupational projections, nor should you try to make career choices based on what kind of work you think will be "hot," rather than what you are best suited to do. But it is still helpful to monitor demographic, economic, and cultural trends.

If you can use the same set of skills in one industry or another, for example, it makes sense to chart a course for the industry that is apparently expanding, rather than one that is about to shrink. Similarly, in choosing between similar occupations – college teacher vs. industrial trainer, for example – gauge the likely demand in each area. You may still decide to enter the occupation or industry with apparently poorer prospects, because it represents a better fit for you in some other way, but at least you will be making an *informed* decision.

Based on current trends, here are some of the fields that should be fairly buoyant.

- **Medicine:** The health care system will continue to undergo radical restructuring to reduce soaring costs while meeting demands imposed on it by an aging population. Many of the new openings will be at the lower end of the scale, for example, home care workers and nursing assistants and aides. But there will also be openings for occupational and physical therapists, pharmacists, and radiologists.

  Demand for specialities that will help keep an aging population active and youthful-looking, such as plastic surgery and physiotherapy, will also increase. Entrepreneurs will also be able to benefit from shifts in delivery of health care by exploiting markets for ever more sophisticated high-tech equipment – particularly equipment and tools that keep people in their homes longer and out of expensive hospital beds.

– **Education:** As we noted, school boards are cutting back on the employment of teachers, but educators and entrepreneurs alike will be able to profit from the growth of private tutoring services and centers.

Increasingly, people recognize that there is no "finishing line" for education: lifelong learning has become a necessity for effective career management. A 1996 survey sponsored by the Royal Bank of Canada found that 62 percent of employed Canadians surveyed said that they had taken at least one adult education course in the past year, with people who already have some postsecondary education up to four times more likely to sign up for courses than those with only a high school education. Adult education also increases with age. Forty-three percent of working Canadians over age forty are enrolled in courses, compared with 29 percent of those eighteen to twenty-nine. Clearly, adult education is a growth area; teachers, trainers, course developers, information technologists, subject-matter experts, adult education and learning specialists, career consultants, graphic artists, and people who design, manage, and staff resource centers are among those who should benefit from this trend.

– **"Edutainment":** The growth of electronic media, particularly the Internet and CD-ROMs, and the emphasis on lifelong learning, add up to tremendous opportunities for people who can combine the excitement of computer graphics and animation with educational content – everyone from the entrepreneurs who package and market the products to computer programmers, graphic artists, animators, and educators.

- **Recreation:** We have become a society that consumes its leisure much as we consume everything else. As leisure becomes an increasingly scarce commodity, and as we become increasingly tired and jaded by overcommitted lives and high-octane careers, we will look for correspondingly high-impact recreational experiences. This, coupled with interest in fitness and the environment, should provide opportunities ranging from packaging exotic walking tours in ecologically rich locations to serving as personal trainers, coaches, and instructors.

- **The environment:** Five years ago, few had heard of environmental law. Now it is one of the hottest practice areas. The profound and growing interest and concern in preserving the environment should lead to opportunities for industries and companies that can combine innovative products with environmentally friendly practices or who offer "green" alternatives to existing ones. Government regulations play an important role in this area; these are influenced by industry pressure groups, the state of the economy, and the leanings of political parties. But given the concerns of today's children about the environment, one can reasonably expect this trend to continue.

- **Personal anything:** Excessive work demands, growing depersonalization, and time pressures will put a premium on any service or product that helps a person look or feel better – whether it's personal fitness training, nutrition consulting, or a shiatsu massage. Similarly, anything that helps people *do* things better – perform better at work or manage their lives better – will be increasingly at a premium. With many managers too busy and preoccupied to fulfil their traditional role of coaching and mentoring their staff, people will look to outside sources of help, such as personal coaches, to give them an edge in a harsh and unforgiving marketplace.

Other "hot" areas include biotechnology, pharmaceuticals, communications, and computers. There are many excellent sources of information about trends from varying perspectives such as economics, demographics, and marketing. Use your general knowledge of business trends to identify potential growth areas in the economy.

8. Build Financial Independence

To manage your career effectively, you must also manage your personal finances. When your finances are in good shape, you can make career decisions based on what is really important to you. But when you're struggling, money can change everything: "I really don't want to take this job, but I've got to make some more money . . ."

- Are your most important career and life decisions driven by money?
- Are you "owned" by your debt?
- If you lost your income tomorrow, do you have sufficient savings to tide you over until you find a replacement source of income?

A financial planner can help you take steps toward financial independence. Most financial planners recommend that people save about 10 percent of their pre-tax income to be fiscally fit, and keep six months' salary in the bank.

Think Income Streams, Not Salary

Recently, I conducted a workshop in Ottawa with about a hundred scientists in a telecommunications organization. I was surprised to learn that about half the people had started home-based businesses such as catering or selling cosmetics and nutritional supplements. Ottawa is not a city that one traditionally thinks of as a hotbed of entrepreneurial activity. Clearly, people had been moved to action by the massive downsizing of the federal government.

It's important to start thinking of having multiple income streams. This is how many immigrants traditionally thought about "making a living," whether it was secondary or additional income from renting part of their house, buying vending machines, or doing bookkeeping in the evenings. It has only been quite recently, in historical terms, that North American workers have expected to support themselves on one predictable income source. With the reconfiguring of the economy, this is starting to look like a historical blip.

Indeed, a recent survey conducted by Royal Bank found that about half of the people who indicated that they plan to start a small business in the next year intend to use their new business to supplement their regular paychecks.

Rethink Your Relationship to Money

- Do you find yourself surrounded by lots of stuff, yet unable to afford to do things that are important to you?
- Would you be willing to give up income in order to work less? Would you be able to?
- Are you making significant personal sacrifices to maintain a particular standard of living?
- Does all the stuff you buy contribute to your family's happiness, and if not, could you give up buying it?

You might want to take a lesson from the "Voluntary Simplicity" movement, in which people have actively decided to pursue a life outside the continual invectives of "Buy, Spend, Consume." Evaluate your purchases and "skinny down." Ask yourself: What do I really need? Will redoing the kitchen really make my life better? Do I really need a new car?

Susan A., for example, describes herself as a "sporadically successful marketing consultant – 'sporadically' being increasingly the operative word." In a growing competitive market for consultants, Susan is still getting the lion's share of the available work. But she feels that her position is precarious. Clients are more demanding, and expect more for less, and recently she has been passed over on some contracts she had been counting on. Chronically tired, Susan would like to be in a position where she could work less. But financially, she is in no position to do so.

Among other things, Susan has a large mortgage on her house. "I'm starting to think that it owns me," she says, "rather than the other way around." By moving to downscale her expenses now, she hopes to preserve as much as she can of what she describes as a relatively affluent middle-class lifestyle, while also making more personal time for herself.

Some people are making even more radical changes in their lives, rejecting consumerist values in search of a better way to live. "I was working longer and harder," says Joseph L., a fifty-something dropout from the corporate world, "and I was still falling back economically. I didn't like my job anymore. I didn't know if I was going to have a job tomorrow. And one day I said, 'I don't want to do this anymore.'" Joseph and his wife sold their house and most of their possessions and went to live in a small town in the B.C. interior, where they run a crafts store.

If you're re-evaluating how you are living, recognize that there are no quick and easy answers here. If there were, then philosophers, writers, and psychotherapists would not have been wrestling with these issues for so long. That said, there are some steps you can take to bring your life back into greater harmony with your most important values.

- Carefully review your personal values. Know what is really important to you. Ask yourself: What do I really care about? Are my values being met?
- For everything you do, ask yourself: Why am I doing this? Is this

meeting my need for *personhood*? Will it help me in my chosen role?

- Be ruthless in evaluating how your current lifestyle is contributing to satisfying your deeply held values. For example, in making a purchase, ask yourself: "How much of my life energy is this really worth?" As Vicki Robin, co-author with Joe Dominguez of *Your Money or Your Life*, has so eloquently observed, "We have been trained since infancy to solve our problems with products . . . We identify money with emotional needs that money can never fulfil."

Useful resources on simplifying or downscaling your life include *Your Money or Your Life* by Joe Dominguez and Vicki Robin; *Voluntary Simplicity* by Duane Elgin; *Time Out: How to Take a Year (or More or Less) Off* by Bonnie Miller Rubin; *How to Survive Without a Salary* by Charles Long; *Simplify Your Life* by Elaine St. James; and *How to Get Off the Fast Track* by M. M. Kirsch.

9. Think Lattice, Not Ladders

As we saw in Chapter 7, careers used to be thought of as "ladders," with people climbing up one rung at a time through the ranks of an organization. But downsizing and delayering have carved out half the rungs in the traditional career ladder.

The career ladder is now more like a lattice: you may have to move *sideways* before you can move up. In a lattice *everything is connected*. Each step will take you somewhere, though sometimes in unpredictable directions. You must measure progress in unusual and novel ways. Each new work assignment should contribute to your portfolio of skills, increasing both your breadth and depth, while you stay motivated and challenged.

Be creative in seeking out new opportunities. For example, when forty-two-year-old Tom L. was told that he would never "make partner" at his accounting firm, he looked for opportunities not only to keep himself challenged, but also to maintain his visibility and value to the firm. Every two years or so, Tom "leverages" his position and takes on a high-profile assignment, thus making himself an indispensable contributor to the firm.

If you're feeling stuck in your current role, consider the possibilities for job *enrichment*: a lateral move into a new work assignment that offers opportunities for learning and development; opportunities to mentor younger staff; participation in task forces; and interesting educational programs.

In some cases, you may have to move downwards in order to move into a new career direction. As we saw in Chapter 7, you may be zigzagging not only between different jobs, but also different life spheres – work, education, community activity.

Track your career progress by your work, not your level. Judge your progress not by your job title or level, but by the depth of content of your work, its importance to the organization and to customers, and whether you are still *learning* and having *fun*.

10. Decide: Are You More of a Specialist or Generalist?

One question I am asked frequently is "In the future will I be better off as a specialist or a generalist?" The answer is "Both." You need to have strong enough specialist skills to get you in the door – something that makes you unique and puts you in a position to add value to a client. But that is no longer enough.

You also need to be able to use those specialist skills in high-pressure environments; to carry out your specialist skills in teams working with people from different disciplines; and to organize your work, manage your time, keep a budget, and sell a project. So the question is not so much "specialist or generalist?" but "Should I be more of a specialist or more of a generalist?"

- Do you want to grow and develop within your speciality?
- Do you prefer to *broaden* rather than deepen your skills and knowledge?

For some people, there's very little to decide. Some people are clearly more interested in the technical content of their work, whether it be psychology, marketing, or computer programming (see Chapter 8). Good salespeople, for example, often don't want to become sales managers. They prefer to keep on doing what they do best rather than develop broader skills. Other people, though, have both strong technical skills *and* broader career interests. Which way should they go? It's not a clear-cut choice.

Because of their broader skills, generalists have more flexibility than specialists, meaning more career options. Technical expertise narrows the potential market for your services. In a sense, choosing a career as a specialist is like putting your entire investment portfolio in one stock. What if the bottom falls out on your chosen profession?

And yet: this is an era in which *expertise counts*. To meet customer needs, organizations need people with in-depth skills and knowledge. It's not enough just to be smart. As a result, good specialists in "hot" professions are a scarce resource. Organizations compete to attract them, and usually treat them better than people who are more easily interchangeable.

There are advantages and disadvantages on both sides. If you do think you want to specialize, do so cautiously:

- Conduct a searching self-assessment to make sure you have what it takes to rise to the top of your profession.
- Take an equally careful look at market conditions to make sure that you are investing your career assets in an in-demand speciality.
- Stay on top of the newest trends and information in your profession.
- Don't give up on your general skills.

Choose a path that plays both to your strengths and the business environment. But don't carve your path in stone. Career trends are fickle, and the desirability of specialists or generalists is subject to fashion.

Two years ago one partner in a public accounting firm told me that all of his technical skills came from a floppy disk, and that he needed to possess high-level generalist skills. Now, because of the competition chartered accountants are experiencing from management information specialists and the ready availability of financial management systems, he says the challenge is to have a market niche in which you are sufficiently specialized so that you become famous as an authority in it.

FIND A MENTOR

Successful people usually have a mentor: someone who takes an interest in their development and helps support their career progress.

A mentor is typically older than you (possibly only by a few years) and has a more developed career intelligence. A mentor acts as a sounding board, coaching you in effective behaviors, providing insight into corporate politics, sometimes opening doors for you and acting as an advocate on your behalf. Perhaps most crucially, a mentor will give you honest feedback. Your mentor may be your current manager, but will more commonly be a previous manager; a manager in another area of the organization (giving you access to other areas); an external consultant; or someone you worked with on a project team with whom you developed a rapport.

11. BE A RUTHLESS TIME MANAGER

"There isn't enough of me to go round."   *– A FORTY-SOMETHING BANK MANAGER*

- Do you have a clear concept of what is important to you and consciously make decisions about how you spend your time in relation to this?
- Can you, and are you prepared to, say "NO" to excessive work demands?
- Are you satisfied with the amount of time you are spending with people and activities that are important to your life?

- Are you allowing important relationships to suffer because of excessive work commitments?
- Can you allow some things to go "undone" without experiencing undue stress?

We are working in a work world where fast enough never is, and where speed is prized above all else. With so many demands on us, it's crucial to be ruthless in managing time.

Evaluate every time commitment: Ask yourself: Am I doing this because I *really* need to, or just because it's there? How important is this work? By spending time here, what time am I sacrificing on something else equally or perhaps more important?

Become vigilant in saying "no": Learn to determine which requests for work overload are really important. People often tell us that they are working so hard because they have no choice – it is expected of them. What would happen if you said you couldn't attend that Saturday morning meeting? Or that today you have to be out of the office by five o'clock? I often ask people what would happen if they did say "no" to what they believe to be unreasonable work demands. Typically they respond with a blank stare. They really haven't thought about consequences – they just *assume* they have no choice. Often when we encourage people to explore the consequences of refusing what they perceive to be unreasonable or excessive work demands, they discover that there are no actual significant consequences. Remarkably, the company stays in business, the team meets its objectives, the work gets done.

Know your limitations: Being busy is not an end in itself. Work strategically. If you are working excessively long hours over an extended period of time, are you still productive? Are you making good decisions? Are you creative? What is the effect of giving up sleep on your long-term well-being and effectiveness in all the important roles of your life? At some point everyone stops being productive. The body might be there but the mind is not — it left a long time ago from sheer fatigue.

- **Refresh yourselves on weekends:** Turn off the cell phone. Go some place you can't be reached. Make at least one day of the weekend — and preferably two — sacred. If the new work realities mean that you must sometimes work odd hours seven days a week, learn to pace yourself. Take Wednesday off, or two half days, if that's when the work load lets up.

- **Become more dispassionate in your relationship to work, and define yourself independently of it:** If work defines who you are, then in a work world where demands never end, you will constantly have to respond. If you can see yourself independent of work, you will be able to look at work demands in a more objective way and maintain balance.

- **Set priorities:** Recognize that it is absolutely impossible to do *everything* very well. Learn to set priorities, focus on what is most important, and allocate your time commitments accordingly.

- **Seek flexible work arrangements to maximize personal/family time:** For example, if you can work at home or at a customer's office one day a week, you can reduce your commute time, and have more time for yourself and your family.

- **Make time for personal priorities:** See if you can free up more time for personal pursuits by delegating less important tasks to others, or not doing them at all. For example, at home, could your partner or children cook more, or could you buy more prepared foods? Try to combine desirable activities. If you want to spend more time with your children *and* make a greater contribution to your community, perhaps consider volunteering to coach one of their sports teams.

– **Evaluate alternatives to your current grueling pace:** Try downscaling your lifestyle so that you don't need to earn so much money. See "Rethink Your Relationship to Money," above, for some references to books on downscaling and "voluntary simplicity."

Just Say "No"

A client of mine wants to start the "Just Say No" campaign:

Just say "no" to excessive overtime, missed vacation days, bosses who berate you because you're not prepared to have Saturday breakfast meetings.

Just say "no" to seventy-hour work weeks, working on the weekend, behaving as if your work is more important than the well-being of your family or other people important in your life.

Just say "no" to assuming quality time is more important than quantity time.

Just say "no" to feeling like you're uncommitted or lazy because you're only prepared to give your job forty-five high-octane hours.

Talk About Being Gymnastically Flexible: Some Paradoxes

Following these new rules can lead to some interesting conflicting demands. For example, you may find yourself having to "be a team player," (cooperative, interpersonally skillful), while at the same time having to "be a maverick" (independent, nonconforming, able to rise above group-think).

Similarly, you have to "act like an insider" (demonstrate loyalty and commitment to your team, boss, work group) without forgetting to "think

199

like an outsider" (always attuned to external views). And you must "be independent" while also "recognizing your interdependence" (no one makes it alone).

12. BE KIND TO YOURSELF

- Do you remind yourself of your successes or do you beat yourself up for things that didn't work out?
- Can you live comfortably with "less than perfect" in some domains of your life, or are you constantly struggling for everything to be 100 percent?
- Do you have a "community" of people you go to – friends, colleagues, or family members, who *appreciate* you?
- Do you take time for yourself?
- Do you recognize, much less celebrate, your own successes?

Be gymnastically flexible. Be able to "multitask" five things simultaneously. Be ever vigilant for future trends which may impact your career. Be a great parent, staff member, manager. Be active in the community. Stay current. Be able to live with constant ambiguity . . .

With so many demands being made upon you, remember to make time for yourself. Otherwise, you cannot carry out any of the important roles in your life effectively.

Set realistic expectations of what's doable. Learn to live with the best you can do at this point, to live with less-than-perfect. Congratulate yourself on your successes. In a thankless work world, the only thanks you get may be from yourself. When you've done a good job, pat yourself on the back. Regularly keep track of your successes, no matter how apparently small, and take credit where it's due. Above all, be kind to yourself.

TEN

Career Intelligence for Managers and Organizations

> *"We understand our own lives less and less. We live in a postmodern world where everything is possible and nothing is certain . . . Our civilization has essentially globalized only the surface of our lives. But our inner self continues to have a life of its own."* — VÁCLAV HAVEL, PRESIDENT OF THE CZECH REPUBLIC

*A*t the beginning of this book, we looked at the growing gulf between the corporate agenda — an obsessive preoccupation with profits, productivity, and the bottom line — and the needs of individuals. In a lot of ways, many organizations are shaping a workplace antithetical to human needs and values.

We have also looked at what individuals can do to prepare themselves to chart a successful course in this turbo-charged and turbulent new marketplace, and, as we have seen, there is much that individuals *can* do to master the new work and life realities.

But the fact that individuals are capable of using career intelligence doesn't take organizations off the hook. Organizations need to use career intelligence, too. They need to understand that while in the short term they may be able to improve results by squeezing more out of people, their longer-term survival depends on how they treat their employees. The stresses people are experiencing in organizations today are simply untenable, from both the point of view of individual well-being and long-term organizational effectiveness.

For organizations, using career intelligence means providing a work environment that is more psychologically compatible with human needs for belonging and community, as well as learning and challenge – to create what I like to call a *life-friendly* organization.

Corporations and individuals alike need to ask: What kind of a workplace do we want? How can we better balance the needs of shareholders with the community good? How do we shape organizations that are both profitable and life-friendly? How can everyone – individual contributors, managers, senior executives – play a role in making organizations more in sync with our basic human needs to feel part of something, to feel we are doing important work that is valued, and to feel we are learning?

Wouldn't we all like to see a workplace where anxiety is not the norm, where people have time to think and reflect on what they are doing, where busyness and fatigue no longer rule the day, where "toughness" and the ability to "take it" are not the measure of a person's worth – in short, a workplace where you would be happy and proud to see your own child working?

A life-friendly workplace is supportive of, and meets the human needs of, individuals struggling in an often-thankless work world. In this chapter, we will look at how organizations can create such a workplace.

How Organizations Can Help People Deal with the New Work Realities

I have had the good fortune throughout my consulting career to work for some wonderful people. What I have seen over and over again is that, as a general rule, clients who treat outside suppliers of services (such as me) well, also treat staff well, enjoy high levels of customer satisfaction, and are well-respected for their contribution to the community. Unfortunately, I have also noticed in recent years that just as they have become insensitive to their staff's needs, many companies have also become mean and arrogant to their suppliers. While some clients treat their suppliers like the partners they are, others seem to take satisfaction in making people jump through hoops.

In recent years, it has become fashionable in business books to "name names," drawing lessons from the Microsofts and IBMs and Royal Banks of this world. For the most part, I have chosen not to follow this trend. First of all, many excellent managers work for not-so-excellent companies. And many of the organizations that have been touted for excellence over the years have since shifted course.

The challenge facing organizations is to help their people cope with the new work pressures by providing them with a renewed sense of purpose. Let's look at some ways they can do this.

Educate Staff About New Work Realities

As long as people believe other people in other careers in other organizations work less hard, have more fun, get paid more, get more recognition, and have more career advancement opportunities, they will believe their own organization is a lousy place to work and basically they are getting a lousy deal. As I have already emphasized, it's imperative that people understand that whatever they are experiencing, the "grass *isn't* greener" elsewhere (see "Dispelling the Myths" in Chapter 8).

In most industries and sectors, there is insecurity about the future, slower career growth, and pressure to produce more with less. Acknowledging these career/work/family pressures, and enabling staff to recognize that they are not alone, and not personally deficient, is an effective morale booster.

Foster Marketability

I have some clients who were hired into senior human resource roles by their organizations to promote a "learning culture," who then found themselves begging for every training dollar. Despite the new corporate mantra that everyone has to be a "continuous learner," it is becoming increasingly difficult for people to get either the time or the financial resources to pursue training and development.

In part, this lack of support for training is due to extreme productivity pressures. But it also reflects deep-rooted attitudes in at least some managers, who ask, "Why should I invest in developing a potential future competitor? Why can't they get their training on their own time?" They worry that if they spend money on their staff's development, their people will only leave and take their expertise elsewhere. Well, that has always been a risk, but it has never been a good excuse for not providing training and development. You *have* to train people if you want them to perform at a high level in your organization, not to mention if you want to meet individual needs for learning. And in the light of the new contract at work, such attitudes make even less sense:

"In exchange for your hard work and commitment, in lieu of job security we will provide you with skill-building, resume-enhancing experiences that will increase your marketability whether inside or outside the organization."

If you tell people this, follow through – allow people to determine their learning needs, and provide training and genuine learning experiences. (The same goes for that old chestnut, "You are our most important resource . . .")

Moreover, the value of these learning experiences needs to be benchmarked against *external* standards. For example, if a person spends a long time mastering a particular computer system that is only used by your organization, and that has no currency in the outside marketplace, it's not meaningful in terms of improving marketability.

Organizations have a number of strategies available to them, ranging from the "learn-on-the-job" training (especially characteristic of small to medium-sized businesses) to more extensive educational programs. Even when internal training resources are limited, smaller companies can take advantage of the rich educational resources available in the community, as well as electronic communications media.

Two simple examples I've come across:

- One midsize life insurance company gives every person a career development account (2.5 percent of a person's annual salary, which can be accumulated for three years) to use at their own discretion for career-related courses, conferences (including travel), association dues, PC hardware for home use, etc. The assumption is, "If we trust you to work in our organization, we trust you to make your own learning decisions. You are, after all, responsible for your own career development."
- Because of demanding work loads, many managers are reluctant to let people off the job to attend workshops. In response to this, some companies hold every manager responsible for ensuring every one of their people receives a minimum number of learning hours, and that these learning hours represent a good balance between the technical and the so-called "softer" skills.

In Chapters 7 and 8 we looked at how individuals can enhance their long-term marketability. Does your organization have the tools, resources, and training in place to enable people to career-proof themselves and ensure that their portfolio of skills is up to date? Does it provide educational experiences that meet the needs of different learners? Later in this chapter we will look at the manager's role in providing staff with portfolio-building experiences.

Change Focus

Changing focus means re-evaluating all the human resource systems and processes in your organizations, from small details to complex policies and processes. For example, one of my clients, a hotel chain, realized its long-service awards were communicating the wrong message about who they valued and why. Part-time staff were the backbone of their business, but many would never achieve full-time status, much less long-term employment status. To reflect this reality, the company dispensed with long-service awards.

Given the growing importance of the part-timer to the success of an enterprise, organizations should reconsider the training policies, benefits, and the career development opportunities available to these employees. Part-timers complain they are treated as if they are "at the bottom of the food chain" – and yet these are often the very same people who are front-line customer service providers.

Moreover, many full-time staff would actually prefer to work part time, but can't afford to give up the benefits attached to full-time employment status. Improving benefits for part-timers makes these roles more attractive and increases internal mobility by freeing up the work of full-timers who would prefer to work fewer hours.

The importance of accommodating part-timers' needs is now starting to be recognized. Some large Canadian banks, for example, have recently extended employee benefits to casual part-time workers, including the same cash performance bonuses available to full-time staff.

Foster Self-Knowledge/Restore Belief in Personal Competence

"Thinking about and recalling experiences and skills gained throughout my career restored my confidence and the belief in my abilities. Where the future used to frighten me, I now see it as exciting, something I can navigate and thrive in."

This statement, made by a forty-year-old engineer whose work had been radically changed by technology, is typical of the kind of comment people make after going through a self-assessment process. Self-assessment is a powerful tool in promoting an individual's confidence, sense of competence, and, ultimately, their employability.

At the same time, given the links among individual confidence, work satisfaction, morale, and organizational effectiveness, providing people buffeted by change with an opportunity for self-assessment also promotes organizational renewal. Reflecting on accomplishments reminds people they really are making a meaningful contribution – something all too easy to forget when they are drowning in relentless demands. People also understand that if the "worst" happens, and they lose their job, they have skills that can be used in other work.

Provide Career-Nurturing Support

Daphne J., a computer programmer, has been on a project for the past year and a half that will be winding up in the next six weeks. Already she has been offered the opportunity to work on another high-profile project. Her career manager is discouraging her, however, saying that she should take a few weeks "off" to think about what she really wants to do next – perhaps she should consider exposure to a new business area.

Most people's number one career fantasy is to have their own on-call personal counselor and agent, whose job would be to advise and counsel their clients and to promote their services to potential buyers.

I have a few clients (systems departments, R&D organizations, professional accounting and consulting firms) who are working on this model. Their work is largely project-driven; staff are typically drawn from a resource pool; and there is often intense competition for high-profile projects.

There are pros and cons to this approach. A client spent three hours explaining to me who was responsible for what, and I still didn't get it, so complex were the respective responsibilities of the project manager and the career manager. Apparently, a lot of the staff had similar problems. This confusion can also lead to conflicts between the project manager, who is responsible for the needs of the business, and the career manager, who needs to balance the needs of the business with the skills, interests, and developmental requirements of the individual.

Project manager John, for example, approaches Daphne and sells her on his project, which involves using a technology with which she is already highly skilled. He knows that she can deliver results without any learning curve. Meanwhile Daphne's career manager wants her to think about her long-term interests, and get some exposure to some new technologies.

Still, while career manager programs may not be perfect, having an internal champion is a wonderful asset to an individual's career development. Recently I was privileged to sit in on a meeting between a career manager and one of the people she was responsible for. Although this career manager is primarily a line manager – career managing occupies only 25 percent of her time – I was struck by the depth and helpfulness of her comments. If I had not known otherwise, I would have thought that I was listening to a professional counselor.

As a general rule, these formal "career manager" programs work best in large project-driven systems, in which there are a number of projects going on simultaneously at different stages of completion, and the needs of the individual can be easily lost due to the intensity of the work and the high degree of competition for high-profile assignments.

Mentoring programs, whether formal or informal, can provide an excellent alternative for organizations that want to provide some support, but feel that a full-fledged career manager program would be too cumbersome. The mentors in such a program typically have fewer formal responsibilities than a career manager, but they do perform similar functions in terms of advising and counseling their clients, and promoting their career interests.

Providing this kind of intervention, whether formal or informal, has two direct benefits:

- Most successful people have had or still enjoy a strong mentoring relationship, and by providing mentors, organizations develop long-term assets; and
- The coach/advice-giver/counselor is typically rejuvenated by the opportunity to make a difference in someone's life.

I am often asked what kind of people make good career managers or mentors. Although there are no hard-and-fast rules, in general they would possess some combination of the following qualities:

- They derive a genuine pleasure from promoting others' interests. They are proud of the accomplishments of their protégés rather than threatened by them — even when the protégés go on to surpass them.
- They are adept at reading people and situations. They understand how to manage complex interpersonal situations such as negotiating financial support for an M.B.A. or handling a conflict with a team member.
- They have an intuitive sense of what different types of work require in terms of personal characteristics, and where different work experiences can lead to.
- They understand the business, and can balance its needs against the needs of the individual. They are sensitive to individual differences in personality and values.

Develop a Life-Friendly Culture – Avoid the Politics of Overwork

To raise awareness of their new work/family policies, my client (a major Canadian financial institution) held a conference, kicked off by a senior woman who was supposed to model "having it all" — the perfectly balanced work and personal life. She got off to a good start, talking about how she had taken advantage of various flexible work arrangements the company offered. As she got into the meat of her presentation, however, she was so overcome by the *actual* realities of her life that before an audience of five hundred people, she started to cry.

Large organizations have, for the most part, done a good job of developing programs to address work and family issues, such as flexible work hours, telecommuting options, and so on. These are important, and organizations should be encouraged to extend them further (see "Support Staff in Balancing Work and Personal Life," below). Unfortunately, few people who would like to take advantage of these programs actually do so.

As long as organizations celebrate the working/doing/acting paradigm, and reward people for working seventy hours a week, it's hard to imagine the use of these programs – no matter how extensive and well-thought-out – becoming more widespread. There has to be a fundamental shift in attitudes and values first.

A recent study of telecommuting, for example, shows the gap between policy and uptake. The 1996 Olsen Forum on Information Management studied 305 American and Canadian companies. Its findings indicate that although there has been a significant increase in the number of firms offering telecommuting – from 33 percent to 42 percent in just one year – the number of actual telecommuters has remained steady at 7 percent for several years, showing how critical it is for organizations to identify the barriers to participation in their programs: What is interfering with people making full use of them? What are the internal myths about "the kind of people" who take advantage of them?

Potential telecommuters, for example, worry about lack of visibility – "out of sight, out of mind" – and being passed over for interesting assignments or promotional opportunities. Job sharers and part-timers are similarly concerned that they will be seen as not being fully committed to their work or, equally undesirable, that they will end up doing a full-time job for a part-time salary.

What does your organization reward people for? In one episode of TV's

Seinfeld, George leaves his car in the parking lot at work overnight. His bosses, assuming George has worked all night, reward his apparent obsessive work dedication by promoting him. The episode pointed to a well-known but previously nameless syndrome, one that organizational psychologists have now dubbed "the George Factor" – for example, programming your computer to send e-mail to the boss at midnight to demonstrate dedication.

Consider whether boundless stamina, and the ability to pull all-nighters and work one-hundred-hour weeks, should be the barometer of high performance. How many of your colleagues do you think are working at peak performance?

Are employees taking *all* vacation days? One telling indicator of contemporary work pressures is the number of people who do not use their full vacation entitlement. In the light of unforgiving work loads, they feel they can't afford to take time off, or worry that if they are away for an extended period of time, the company will decide that it can do without them (a syndrome that might be called the "Ted Baxter Factor," after an episode of the old *Mary Tyler Moore Show* in which newscaster Ted is forced to take a vacation, and discovers that he is all too replaceable).

Most people need two consecutive weeks to really benefit from a vacation. For some years now, many organizations have been concerned about people who never take a long enough break to be properly refreshed and rejuvenated. They have tried to communicate to their staff the importance of taking a vacation by limiting the number of vacation days staff can carry over from one year to the next. Some innovative organizations have gone even further, treating additional vacation days as a negotiable benefit staff can "buy" – reinforcing the value of vacation time in people's minds.

Recognize That People Are a Nonrenewable Resource

Some years ago I came across an article by a psychologist who suggested that people are designed to work at 60 percent efficiency so they would have available the wherewithal and additional resources to respond to life crises. When I look at people working at 110 percent all the time, I think it's small wonder that use of employee assistance programs is at a record high, as are absenteeism, sick days, and long-term disability claims.

People don't have endless resources to cope with the pressures placed on them at work and home. Ultimately, productivity declines — or as one person put it, "You start doing twenty hours of work in eighty-hour work weeks."

Support Staff in Balancing Work and Personal Life

Thirty-eight-year-old senior marketing analyst Gena K. works a four-day week. Free to design her own schedule, she often telecommutes from home. As a general rule, she keeps to an eight-to-nine-hour work day, but last month she "pulled two all-nighters . . . The project was at a critical point. You have to be flexible," she says. Of course, the company paid for home care.

On the days when Gena goes into the office, she has her three-year-old daughter and eighty-year-old mother in tow. She drops off her mother at an eldercare program in a community center supported in part by her employer, and takes her child to the company-supported, state-of-the-art, on-site daycare center.

At noon, Gena drops by the daycare to have lunch with her daughter, and then sometimes goes to work out at the company wellness center. Before she leaves work, she visits the company cafeteria to pick up a nutritionally balanced take-out dinner.

Recently, Gena took an unpaid leave to sail in the Bahamas with her family. In two years, when her daughter is older, Gena plans to go back to school and complete a master's degree in psychology. She will continue to work part time as a consultant for her organization.

Fantasy? No. This is, in fact, what some organizations are starting to provide their staff with, and ten years from now, it may well become a common feature of the workplace.

Recognizing work-family issues has key benefits as a business strategy. For example, Aetna Life and Casualty halved the rate of resignations among new mothers by extending its unpaid parental leave to six months, saving itself one million dollars a year in hiring and training costs. A University of Chicago associate professor found that workers in one company who took advantage of "family-friendly" programs were more likely to participate in team problem-solving, and nearly twice as likely to suggest product or process improvements. As Eli Lilly CEO Randall L. Tobia observed, "The impact we're having on morale and our ability to attract and retain the people we want is clearly going to give us an economic payback."

Some elements through which organizations can help create a more life-friendly culture include:

- Flexible work arrangements, including flexible work hours, "compressed" work weeks, part-time work, job sharing, and telecommuting (home to office, client's office to office, satellite office to office).
- Opportunities for personal or educational leave/sabbaticals.
- Tuition support/reimbursement of costs associated with continuing education.
- On-site daycare/eldercare centers or subsidy of off-site care; paid care for evening stints.
- Paid nursing care for sick dependants (this is usually cheaper than a missed day of work).
- Extended maternity/paternity leave – paid or unpaid.
- Schedules set by the work teams themselves, to match work demands with personal needs (some accounting departments, for example, have allowed their clerical staff to set their own work hours according to work flow, working fewer hours mid-month to balance overtime in peak periods).
- Job-sharing arrangements.

- Counseling programs on child care and elder care.
- Nutritionally balanced take-out meals from the cafeteria.
- Wellness centers, available for employees *and* their partners and dependants.
- Information sessions (lunchtime, evenings, weekends) for employees, and where appropriate their families, on life planning and wellness issues such as parenting, aging, and retirement planning.
- Training of managers and supervisors, and follow-up auditing, to ensure that managers support and promote these practices.

The promotion of work practices showing concern about work–family issues is a key business strategy. And, as I've said, people should feel comfortable taking advantage of these policies without fearing that their careers are at risk. One client organization of mine, for example, sent an important message to their employees by promoting a part-timer into a high-profile senior role, and then redesigning the role to support her schedule. Another client emphasized their "family-friendliness" by banning all early-morning and late-evening meetings except for genuine emergencies.

Senior management can also set a powerful example for staff. Imagine the message this CEO communicated to his senior management group, when in a workshop he said, "One of the things I've learned from this experience is that I need to spend more time with my family and look after myself more. It's 5:30. I'm leaving. Thank you for a very important insight."

PROVIDE OPPORTUNITIES FOR RESPITE AND REFLECTION

A *do it! do it! do it!* culture – with its accompanying siege mentality – is antithetical to contemplation and reflection. How can people *learn* if they don't have the opportunity to reflect on why their actions did or didn't work? This is the foundation of continuous learning.

Restore sanity into the workplace by valuing the reflective pause, the introspective musing about how something might have been handled differently. Encourage people between assignments to reflect on what they learned from their experiences, and provide them with enough time to do so. For example, instead of treating slower work periods or time between assignments as downtime, reaffirm the value of that time as an opportunity for reflection and rejuvenation.

Rethink the Distribution of Work

More and more, people are concerned about the kind of society we are creating, in which people either work too long and hard or not enough; in which people are either overchallenged or underchallenged by the professional content of their work. This maldistribution of work has profound implications for the cohesiveness of our society, and for the future of our children, who are deprived of spending time with us because of our long work hours, excessive work demands, and fatigue at the end of the day (an issue we will return to in Chapter 11).

In his book *The End of Work*, Jeremy Rifkin presents some compelling arguments in favor of the redistribution of work. As automation continues to lead to vanishing jobs and record unemployment, Rifkin suggests, the result will be soaring crime rates and political instability. He calls for a shortening of the work week to produce a "fair and equitable distribution of the productivity gains of the new industrial revolution."

The idea of a shorter work week is not new. According to American historian Benjamin Hunnicut, there was a live option to move toward a mandatory thirty-two-hour work week in 1932 during the depths of the Great Depression. As a result of pressure from industry, President Franklin Delano Roosevelt instead opted for a host of job creation measures.

There are some good reasons why industry is reluctant to embrace the shorter work week. There are fixed costs associated with recruiting and training, for example, which remain the same whether that employee works thirty-two or fifty hours. And it is cheaper to use existing employees for longer hours than to bring in new recruits to share the work load.

But one thing is clear in terms of people's physical and emotional well-being, and that of their children: organizations must *promote* options for shorter work weeks by encouraging senior managers, removing road blocks, and creating a culture that celebrates the entire human being. This means finding "success stories" and communicating them (for example, people who chose to work three days a week, or to go back to school).

Organizations have to be *sensitive to the entire life cycle*, and recognize that different people, at different stages of their lives, have different needs that may compete with work, whether it's time with family or opportunity to pursue a personal passion.

Organizations may discover that many people will willingly take a reduction in income for less work, using the freed-up time to spend time with family or to pursue a personal interest or passion – whether going back to school, writing a novel, or working in the garden. (This is borne out by surveys, as well as my own experience.)

Hire and Develop Young Workers

A senior marketing manager at a bank, on hearing that her employer was one of the first corporations to make a commitment to the Canadian "First Jobs" initiative to increase the percentage of payroll going to hiring young people, commented, "I'm proud that we're good corporate citizens."

Good corporate citizens? Perhaps so, in comparison to other organizations in a position to support this initiative who failed to do so. And yet, I wondered, if this bank did not hire young people now, who would design and market their financial products fifteen or twenty years from now? More importantly, who would be able to afford to *buy* their products if this bank, and other large organizations like it, failed to provide young people with opportunities to develop meaningful work experiences and skills?

I am reminded of the question posed by auto maker Henry Ford, when he boosted his employees' wages well above the prevailing standards: If he didn't pay his workers a decent wage, he asked, how would they be able to afford to buy his cars?

Organizations that don't provide young people with appropriate early career experiences are, in effect, mortgaging their own future as well as that of society. Ask yourself, *what will be the long-term effect of having a highly educated, technically savvy group of workers who are marginalized into a cycle of dead-end work, education, unemployment, and dead-end work?*

Moreover, in not hiring younger workers, organizations are depriving themselves of an extraordinary talent pool and fresh, non-tradition-bound ideas about business and business markets.

Organizations can foster the development of early career employees through formal and informal strategies. Formal vehicles include joint ventures with universities and colleges such as "co-op" educational programs. On an informal basis, many young people will happily do an internship — working for little or no money on a temporary basis in exchange for challenging, skill-building, and resume-enhancing experiences. Both the individual and the organization benefit — as long as the organization does not see this as a source of cheap labor, but rather takes responsibility for providing broad exposure and opportunities for meaningful work.

I started my own career this way. While working on my Ph.D., I approached a sympathetic organizational psychologist at a petrochemical company with a proposal that he hire me as an intern — a role that up to that time did not exist in the company. He and his line manager went out of their way to expose me to the work of their department.

Hire for potential, train on the job

In our hit-the-ground-running organizational culture, we have set the performance bar too high for young recruits. This is a recent blip in hiring practices, as traditionally, in hiring young people, organizations have followed two rules:

- Hire for potential (e.g., creativity, interpersonal skills, enterprise, initiative, and so on); and
- Buy skills that require several years of education to hone, whether it be computer programming or marketing.

Now, organizations have expectations of people having skills that could be quickly learned on the job or acquired in an evening course.

Provide skill-building, challenging work

It's not enough to simply hire younger workers. You also have to provide them with meaningful and challenging work. Do you have early career professionals in your organization who are being underutilized? Do you look for opportunities to stretch them to the limit? And are you prepared to support them if they don't succeed?

As we saw in Chapter 4, the best of this generation think unconventionally about work, are resourceful, are prepared to take risks, and want challenge and learning opportunities above all else. There are many ways of meeting these needs that do not require the kind of endless career promotions that previous generations enjoyed.

Cultivate a long-term resource for the organization by involving young hires in the "business of business." One of my clients, for example, routinely schedules exchanges between senior managers and twenty-something staff, with both groups profiting from the cross-fertilization of ideas.

Organizations can do some simple things to foster skill-building experiences. They can reward managers on their performance evaluations who actively mentor and develop early career staff (for example, by inviting twenty-something staff members to accompany them to an important customer presentation or to a critical negotiation with a supplier, or by assigning them to a high-profile project where they will be working with "the best and the brightest"). These developmental experiences should not be evaluated in terms of whether they are directly linked to present work requirements, but rather in the context of long-term development. In the short term, a company may not be able to provide twenty-four-year-old computer programmer Johnny G. with work and career opportunities commensurate with his skills, but it can provide him with opportunities to learn.

Respond to generational values/think creatively about rewards

"Salary is just one consideration. If I'm having fun, learning, and have a good quality of life, then money is much less important." The late boomer and post-boomer generations care a great deal about quality of work life, and see that work life as part of the larger landscape of their personal life. They are nonhierarchical in their thinking, and are looking for opportunities where they can learn, be stretched, and make a contribution.

Many of the best of this generation are most attracted to smaller, more entrepreneurial organizations where their risk-taking skills are valued, they can have an impact on the business, and they can get more flexibility in accommodating personal lifestyles.

This generation understands that they may not have the same kind of material goods or career opportunities that their parents did. At the same time, many are cynical about organizations that they perceive as having chewed up their parents (see Chapter 4 for more detail). Larger organizations are going to lose if they don't develop strategies that are supportive of twenty-something values, whether it be educational sabbaticals, exposure to new leading-edge technology, or personal leave. Organizations can think creatively about different reward systems. For example, in lieu of handsome salaries, they can offer more vacation time, or educational stipends. What's extremely important is that their boomer managers don't impose their own values.

TAKE A LESSON FROM THE PUBLIC ACCOUNTING FIRMS

The public accounting firms have to be very sensitive to the needs of early career professionals to attract and retain them. These young professionals are the lifeblood of the firm, its prime client servers – whether in the long term they become managers or partners, or leave.

Early career professionals, many saddled by student debt, have a common dilemma. Should they take a job in industry at what may initially be a higher salary? Or should they stay with the firm and focus on longer-term prospects by increasing their skills portfolio?

Some accounting firms have developed innovative approaches to career management for young professionals, designed to meet their early career needs and to encourage them to weigh up the value of training and development and longer-term financial gains versus immediate income. These firms:

• Routinely survey early career employees to find out about work interests and developmental desires.
• Provide career self-management/self-assessment experiences to look at personal attributes, skills, and desired work conditions so they can make the most effective short- and longer-term career decisions, and identify developmental interests.
• Provide flexible work options to respond to staff's family pressures and lifestyle concerns.
• Have highly skilled internal advisors who are savvy about the accounting profession and career opportunities inside and outside the firm, adept at providing meaningful counsel, and candid about the individual's prospects.
• Expose early career professionals to orientations from different practice areas to assist in their career decision-making – encouraging them to talk to people both inside the firm and out, including employees who have since left the firm.

Help Career-Proof the Next Generation: Extend Resources to the Community

"Our challenge as . . . business leaders is to consciously strive to help create the highest possible quality of life for the greatest number of people."

— J. E. NEWALL, VICE CHAIRMAN AND CHIEF EXECUTIVE OFFICER, NOVA CORPORATION

Many of my clients have extraordinary learning resources: talented educators, state-of-the-art learning technologies, and often a beautiful physical plant. Imagine what organizations could do to contribute to the employability of the next generation if they would extend these resources to the community.

I'm not talking here about buying computers for the schools, or visiting schools to talk about career prospects in the ABC Industry. These are important, but they are far from sufficient. Here are some ways in which organizations could do much more:

- **Community access to corporate resources:** Imagine if organizations could extend their state-of-the-art learning centers to the community. Imagine staff – whether human resource professionals or line managers – partnering with school teachers during the summer months to provide meaningful learning experiences in a camp experience: teaching children about work technology, how the world of business operates, and business methodologies such as marketing. Teachers would benefit also, both in terms of the rejuvenating effect on their own careers of working in another environment, and the new learning they would be able to incorporate into their school curriculum. At the same time, the industry professionals would benefit from being forced to *think through* what they actually do and translate it into generic applications that would be meaningful for young people. For example, instead of talking about selling Brand A to Customer Y, they need to talk about the whole sales and customer service process.

- **Educational partnerships:** As part of an "Employees For Tomorrow" program, Microsoft, Dell, and Manpower have a three-day training package for teachers, who then go back into the classroom and develop real-life work projects, such as improving the efficiency of housing or hosting a web site on local historical landmarks. Students use these projects as a vehicle for learning about teamwork, technology, problem-solving, customer service, and other important business skills.

- **Cooperative education programs:** Cooperative education is structured to provide work experience as part of an educational program. Students who participate in these programs typically get off to an earlier and more effective start on their careers, with graduates from the "hot" co-op programs in information technology and electrical engineering often finding themselves with multiple job offers (see Chapter 11).

- **Staff involvement in the community:** Until recently, many organizations promoted staff involvement in community activities by releasing employees to the community for a significant percentage of time while giving them full pay. Exchanges between the public and private sector were also more common, with senior managers on both sides benefiting from the cross-fertilization of ideas and the infusion of expertise from the other sector. Unfortunately, in our obsessive focus on the short-term bottom line, these practices have all but disappeared: individuals, organizations, and the community pay a price for the loss.

- **Focusing on the less-advantaged:** To help ensure the long-term health of our society, not to mention their own future, it's imperative that organizations nurture the development of skills in the next generation on a *broad* basis. Growing numbers of children are being excluded from participation in a techno-literate society, due to poverty, lack of role models, and lack of access to technology. Organizations should deploy their resources to support those who are most at risk of being marginalized, whether by establishing literacy skills programs or setting up inner city gardens or carpentry workshops to foster business management skills, teamwork, and self-management.

Rethink Retirement

With people living and working longer, for both psychological and financial reasons, organizations need to think about, and manage, the retirement process differently. Increasingly, people see "retirement" as a shift from one endeavor to another – whether part-time work, consulting, starting a business, or going back to school – rather than as the end of all work activity. This poses both challenges and opportunities for organizations.

Don't throw away wisdom

Organizations need to think more creatively about enabling older workers to pass down their organizational wisdom and know-how. They may do this by using older employees as a resource in formal mentoring systems, task force assignments, community liaison, or simply as valuable sources of advice and information about how to get things done. Unfortunately, in recent years, organizations have used early retirement unimaginatively as a workforce reduction tool, leaving many in their late forties/early fifties feeling "like used Kleenex" and remaining employees with an unappetizing message about their own value to the organization.

Phase retirement

In the late '70s, I was part of a research team that looked at, among other things, how people felt about moving from work to non-work life. Although the world has changed dramatically since then, the results we found at that time are consistent with what people in the current workforce tell me – most people prefer to make a gradual transition from the workforce, rather than the abrupt one more typical of current practices.

Gradual retirement has obvious advantages for individuals, providing them with a bridge until their retirement funds kick in. But it can also be a tremendous boon to organizations who can capitalize on the accumulated wisdom of this group while at the same time creating more mobility in their workforce.

Recognizing that most people don't want "all or nothing" but would prefer to phase out of full-time employment gradually allows organizations to increase the uptake on voluntary separation programs. Some people in their late forties and early fifties, for example, are interested in moving out of their current work to pursue other career options such as starting a business, becoming a consultant, or going back to school. But they won't do so unless they have sufficient retirement funds, or the ability to replace lost benefits. When offered the choice of phasing out, with income continuation to help bridge them to retirement, they may well elect to work part time while pursuing their other interests. But if they are asked to decide between full salary and no salary, they may reluctantly decide to continue on their full-time work status because they can't afford the alternative.

Provide decision-making support

The decision about whether to take early retirement – and when – carries potentially huge consequences, both financial and psychological. Some organizations have offered very little decision-making support, saying in effect: "Take this handsomely enriched voluntary severance now, or risk being asked to leave later with a bare bones package. Here's the phone number of someone you can talk to for two hours about your pension. You have four weeks to make a decision."

Many early retirees who took this sort of deal now regret their decision. They find that their financial projections were off-target and they have less money to live on than they expected. Or else, having failed to think through carefully what they would do next, they find it difficult to adapt to their new circumstances.

By the same token, other employees will turn down the offer, even though it actually makes a lot of sense: they *can* afford to "retire," and they *do* have interests they want to pursue after retirement, but they hold back because of fear and insecurity. They haven't taken the time to properly explore their financial situation, or to think through how they could take advantage of the company's offer. They made a knee-jerk reaction: "I can't afford it"; "I'm not ready yet." Not having done a thorough assessment of their skills, they have underestimated their opportunities elsewhere.

Other organizations offer a range of retirement incentives and support, such as retirement planning, financial planning, self-employment skills seminars, educational grants, and seed money for new business start-ups. These programs ensure that early retirees understand the *financial* consequences of their decision. Unfortunately, what is often missing even from these more sophisticated interventions is a proper consideration of the *psychological* consequences.

People need support in thinking through what it really means to lose their office, their colleagues, and their work role as they have known them. Whether they become "Jim Smith & Associates" surrounded by $2,000 worth of IKEA furniture, start a fly-fishing business, or head straight for the golf course, many early retirees find themselves missing the camaraderie and structure provided by organizational life.

To support people in making the right choices about retirement options, organizations should provide opportunities for meaningful self-assessment to look at individual psychological needs and preferences as well as skills. For example:

- "What do I want to do with the rest of my life? Is leisure enough for me? Or do I want to keep on working in some capacity?"

- "If I do start my own business, am I comfortable spending long hours by myself with little or no people interaction? Do I have the self-discipline to go downstairs every morning and start working?"

How Managers Can Help People Deal with New Work Realities

"How can I expect them to give me their best when I don't give them my best?"

— MARKETING MANAGER

The manager – whether team leader, project manager, or manager in the more traditional sense of the term – has a tremendous opportunity to promote individual well-being and career satisfaction. Unfortunately, managers themselves, beset by tremendous pressures, are often too distracted to notice staff and abrogate this responsibility – leading their staff to see them as spineless, "political," or simply uncaring.

It's important that managers understand what an integral role they play in people's working lives and that their most apparently insignificant gestures can have a major impact in determining how people feel about themselves and their work.

It has never been more challenging for managers to provide career support for their staff, given the diverse demographic landscape and the complexity of both the new work configurations and of people's lives. Managers must help staff navigate in a jobless, promotion-less, security-less environment – a challenge that becomes even harder when a significant percentage of the workforce may be temporary, contract, or part-time.

Still, managers have a number of opportunities to restore people's faith in the future, even when operating with scarce resources.

Make Change as Safe as You Can

"We're going through a dramatic transformation. Five years from now, this organization will be unrecognizable. The work as we currently know it will no longer exist . . . As a learning organization, this will create many exciting opportunities. But those who cling to the old ways of doing things will be toast." These are the words I heard recently from a senior manager talking to his assembled staff. His intention was to convey the excitement of change and his vision of the limitless opportunity this would create. Unfortunately, rather than motivating his people as intended, many reacted with anxiety.

Most people tend to overestimate the gap between the skills they have now and what will be required of them. "Will I be able to cope under this new regime?" they worry. Heightened levels of anxiety lead to low morale and lackluster performance.

Instead of concentrating on the dramatic nature of the changes, and possibly instilling panic, managers can make change safer by *emphasizing continuity*. Often, the forecasted change is not as dramatic and transformational as it appears – representing a shift in direction rather than an all-out revolution. Probably, no matter how apparently extensive the change, the organization will still be in the same core business, and will require many of the same skills. Emphasize how people will be *building* on underlying current skill sets. And where new skills are required, discuss what you and the organization will be doing to provide training and support in building these skills.

Think carefully about the words you use. Quite frankly, many people get turned off when they hear "consultant-speak" – terms like "dramatic transformation," "continual learning," "meet challenges of tomorrow," "limitless opportunities," "empowering technology," "virtual anything" . . .

Don't Make Promises You Can't Keep

Never, under any circumstances, tell someone that if they do something (take a particular assignment, work on a particular project, "just hang in there a while longer") it will lead to a predictable result ("you will be promoted/made partner"). Too many factors outside your own control as a manager will determine what will happen to someone in the longer term.

Be honest with staff about events that may affect their career prospects. Often, managers keep to themselves what might be bad or uncertain news for fear that it will have a negative impact on morale. In fact, nothing is worse for morale than the belief that "someone up there knows something but isn't telling." So don't hold back information. People will think you know what's going on, whether you do or not: if you really don't know what's going on, say so.

Inspire Loyalty: Provide Opportunities for Belonging

A client of mine, a senior marketing executive, seems to change jobs every three or four years. And he has inspired such loyalty among his team, that every time he moves, his team members look for opportunities to follow him. This client is by no means a "pushover." In fact, he is regarded as quite a tough manager. What does he do to inspire such loyalty? Basically, he has a unique appreciation of each individual's strengths and personal interests, and actively pursues assignments that play to his people's strengths as well as supporting their long-term developmental goals.

I am always surprised when people talk about the "death of loyalty." Loyalty continues to exist in very powerful ways. It's just that the package is wrapped differently. Although corporate loyalty may be a thing of the past, people still want – indeed, need – to feel that they are part of something and are contributing to something bigger than themselves. Managers who understand this basic human need, and are able to earn their people's trust, can *replace corporate loyalty with the natural trust and loyalty that people have for individuals.* Indeed, contemporary workplaces, with their teamwork environments, are predicated on relationships. Managers are uniquely positioned to build on the natural loyalties that emerge in these relationship-driven team environments.

Appreciate the Individual

When you ask people about their most memorable bosses, many will talk about a manager who took a genuine interest in them as people, rather than someone who played a significant role in advancing their career. For example, a boss who wished them good luck on an exam, or who was sensitive to a work/family conflict, or who went out of his or her way to thank them publicly for some work they had done.

In a louder, faster, quicker world, basic interpersonal courtesies such as giving compliments, or saying "thank you," have been lost. At the risk of stating the obvious, one extremely effective strategy for maintaining morale and productivity is simply to be considerate and sensitive with people reporting to you, and to be generous in giving feedback. Unfortunately, this apparently obvious strategy is widely overlooked in a work world that values toughness and being able to "take it" as a measure of an individual's worth.

Actions showing appreciation range from the simple, such as encouraging a day off after an intense project, to the more demanding, such as reorganizing work to accommodate an employee who is completing a graduate degree while working part time.

Another powerful yet simple strategy managers can use is in the repertoire of any socially and emotionally competent human being – *promoting people's self-esteem* by giving them opportunities to achieve and to feel that they are important, along with positive feedback for their efforts. Too often, managers worry "If I compliment them, won't they just get a swelled head?" or, equally stupid, "Why should I give them compliments – they're getting paid, aren't they?"

BE GENEROUS WITH YOUR FEEDBACK

A friend of mine who has an amazingly loyal and committed staff has occasionally been criticized by her senior managers for being "too complimentary" to her staff. They say she is too effusive, too expressive.

"What kind of work world are we living in," she asks, "when you're criticized for giving positive feedback to your colleagues?"

Under any circumstances, people want and need feedback from their managers — whether it's praise on doing a good job, advice on how to work smarter, or just simply being noticed. Given the ambiguity and complexity of modern work, and the shape-shifting nature of accountabilities, such feedback becomes all the more critical. Unfortunately, many people say that they are not getting that feedback, because their managers are themselves too busy and preoccupied to notice that their people are doing well, much less comment on it. Probably the most common complaint people have about their managers is, "If I do something wrong, they're down my back, but if I do something well no one notices."

"I don't have time to notice what people are doing" is an excuse that doesn't cut it. Maybe you can't offer people security or promotions. But by noticing people and giving them feedback, you can make a significant difference in their lives.

Provide Portfolio-Building Experiences

"I know I'm not going to be promoted, I'm not going to get a salary increase — at least let me feel like I'm learning something new or adding to my resume." People recognize that their value lies in what they know and the skills they have in their portfolio. When you think about each of your people in turn, to what extent are they involved in skill-building work that contributes to their personal portfolio and enhances their marketability?

Be sensitive to individual needs for stimulation and challenge. Because managers are held accountable for very demanding performance targets, and have such tight budgets, they may be reluctant to move someone into an area where they can't "hit the ground running." Instead, they keep that person doing work at which they are highly accomplished, even though they have been in that role so long that they experience it as mind-numbingly boring.

If people do the same thing for too long, often their performance suffers. Is there some way you can leverage people's skills into new areas?

Treat People as Individuals

In supporting career development, tailor strategies to individual needs. Look for individual rather than off-the-shelf solutions. People vary in what they want and need in their career development, according to their age, career stage, individual temperament, and specific work/family situation. For example, while some people may be looking for skill-building, resume-enhancing work, others may be looking for opportunities to spend more time with their families or to increase their community work. Hold regular career discussions with your people to highlight individual wants and needs.

Don't Impose Your Own Values

As noted earlier in this chapter ("Respond to Generational Values"), the twenty-something generation has its own distinctive aspirations and experiences that affect how they see the world. Nothing is more irritating for this group than to be told that "When I started my career I was prepared to (work long hours) (put in my time) (give up leisure time)."

Don't try to shape people in your own image. You may think someone has the potential to be an excellent manager, but they may prefer to be a specialist.

Be Creative in Thinking About Career Development

Jason P. had plateaued at a fairly senior level in human resources with a major financial institution, and had become bored and restless. In consultation with his manager, he opted to move back into a line function. Strictly speaking, this was a downward move, with Jason now reporting to someone who previously reported to him. But as a result of the move, he felt re-energized, and able to develop in new ways.

Motivating people in the face of limited career mobility means being aware of the full range of development options, and using them creatively. The solutions you arrive at with your staff will not usually be as sweeping as Jason P.'s. It's amazing how re-energizing even apparently very small changes in routine, or new learning experiences, can be for people, whether it be attending a conference that exposes them to new ideas, or networking with people in other work areas.

It's also important to *provide opportunities for meaningful work*. As Mihaly Csikszentmihalyi observed in *Flow*, all human experience lies on a continuum with "boring sameness on one end" and "anxiety-producing chaos" at the other. People are most engaged, confident, and focused in the "enjoyable middle regions."

Display Optimism, Model Enthusiasm

Employees at the pharmaceutical company knew they were the likely object of a merger. Senior management called people together and told them that they shouldn't be worried – it was likely that most would keep their jobs, and the synergies resulting from the merger would result in tremendous opportunities.

Or at least, this is what they *said*. What they *did*, unfortunately, was to huddle together on the executive floor in endless meetings among themselves and with other "suits"; avoid contact on the elevator; talk in hushed, funereal tones; and walk around looking like they'd lost their best friend. Needless to say, the pep talk didn't pep people up at all.

Do you show a positive, proactive, resilient attitude to your staff? Or do you walk around looking as if the world as you know it has ended?

Be a Career Promoter

Demonstrate that you understand the new work realities and their implications for how people look at careers by talking about your own career, including some of the unexpected turns it may have taken. Advance your staff's career interests by seeking out meaningful assignments for them, and by promoting their interests at higher organizational levels.

A Coach – Not a Therapist (and Certainly Not God)

Managers are dealing with exactly the same issues as their staff. As often as not, they don't have any greater understanding of new career realities, or how to navigate in the new work world, than their staff do. Neither are they trained career counselors.

It's not surprising, then, that some managers are reluctant to coach their staff on career issues. They worry that they will be called upon to "play therapist," to "mess about in people's heads," to "crystal-ball gaze" . . . even to "play God with people's lives." Actually, none of this is necessary, or desirable.

The role of the manager is not to draw out the individual the way that a counselor might do ("What do you want to be when you grow up?"), nor to make career plans for them. Instead, it is up to individuals to articulate their own career interests (ideally using career planning tools provided to them by the organization). Your role as a manager should be one of first listening to the individual's ideas about their strengths, skills, and developmental requirements; and then offering feedback on these ideas and plans, based on your understanding of both the individual and of current organizational realities.

ELEVEN

Preparing the Next Generation: Career-Proofing Your Kids

"*What can I do for my kids?*"

"*How can I better prepare my kids for an uncertain work world?*"

"*What should my kids study at school?*"

Everywhere, people ask me these same questions. Parents are deeply troubled about their children's future, and they feel at a loss on how to help them prepare for it. They no longer believe that they have a proper framework to understand their own careers, much less provide support and counsel for their children. At the same time, they realize that never before has it been more crucial to provide such guidance.

Parents understand that the career choices facing their children are very different from those that were available to them. At every level of society, people worry about "what side of the line" their children will end up on — fears exacerbated by futurists promising a brave new world of technology in which only the most skilled and nimble will thrive.

COMPUTER SKILLS – NO MAGIC BULLET

I recently asked a friend of mine, a new father, how he planned to prepare his daughter for the future. A management consultant in his early thirties, with a Ph.D. in information science, my friend is an excellent example of the best and brightest of the knowledge aristocracy, and typically has interesting insights to offer into the new work realities. But in this case he disappointed me. He pointed to a computer and said, "I'm going to get her bashing on that as soon as possible."

It is unlikely that keyboarding will be a valuable skill by the time today's youth enter the workplace. With the rapid development of voice recognition and smart devices of all kinds, computers will probably have changed out of all recognition by then. But more important, surely my friend could be more creative in identifying skills and opportunities he could provide his daughter over and above the everyday school curriculum.

The current fetish about computer technology in the classroom and "computer literacy" is a clear indication of the strength of anxiety about the future. Parents are frantic about getting more computers into the schools, and having their children learn keyboarding skills. And politicians are promising Internet access in every classroom by the year 2000.

Of course, computer literacy is important. But what is more important is how technology is used. *The challenge is not operating a machine, but understanding how to optimize its potential for manipulating ideas and images.* Later in this chapter we will examine in more depth the skills and education youth will need.

A New Paradox: Independent or Interdependent?

There are some other very difficult questions that parents are grappling with, questions for which there are no easy answers. After hearing a prominent futurist present a picture of a highly individualistic, competitive future world, one client asked me some interesting questions: "Are we making a mistake at home when we tell our children that they have to be kind, tolerant, and learn to share? Are they going to be lost in a future that is individualistic, ruthlessly competitive, and dog-eat-dog?"

On the one hand, we must prepare our children to work in the teams and networks that are so important to how business gets done. They need to be able to recognize their interdependence with other team members, and to cultivate relationships in never-ending alliances. Yet on the other hand, we must ensure that our children have the independence and resilience to survive in a free-for-all future where everyone is a free agent, and where competition comes from every direction.

Finding the "Right" School

Another powerful indication of parents' anxiety about their children's future is the widespread preoccupation with the type of schooling their children are receiving. Get any group of boomer parents together and what's the conversation about? Education in general, and the comparison of specific schools in particular. The discussion will range from curriculum to standardized testing to the availability of computer technology and instruction.

Parents believe that there is a direct connection between the quality of education their children receive and ending up on the "right side of the line." In an increasingly uncertain world, they think that the right diploma could be their children's only chance of success, a sentiment amusingly captured in a recent cover story in *New York* magazine: "Give me Harvard or give me death."

The result of this anxiety about the future is ever-escalating (if often unrealistic) expectations placed upon both children and their schools. Parents try to "micro-manage" their children's educational curriculum: Are they getting enough homework? Are they getting enough time management skills? Are they in a class with the "right kind" of kids? Every activity is evaluated in terms of longer-term usefulness in the workplace.

And what constitutes a high-quality education? Parents must wrestle with a plethora of choices. They must choose between public and private schools; schools that specialize in science and technology and those that favor the performing arts; schools that emphasize values and personal responsibility and those that emphasize tradition and structure; alternative schools and feminist schools; and on and on.

Research shows that parents have good reason to worry about educational decisions. In his recent book, *Learning About Schools: What Parents Need to Know and Where to Find Out*, Professor Peter Coleman argues that the choice of school as early as grades six, seven, and eight is critical to a student's future: the "dropout decision" and academic orientation gets shaped early in a student's career.

Interestingly, when young adolescents are asked about their educational aspirations, most indicate that they expect to go to university. But only about 28 percent actually do so. That leaves a large window of opportunity for disappointment in overachieving parents, who are often unable to cope with their kids' decisions.

Children Share Their Parents' Anxiety

Parents are transmitting their worries about education directly to their children. According to educational psychologist William Ford, children as early as grade six are displaying anxiety as a result of being micro-managed – lying about homework or projects or marks, for example. Parents obsessed with marks communicate this obsession to their children, who internalize it. If parents are anxious about the impact of the difference between a 77 and a 79 in a grade six history test, children become anxious and competitive about their marks, too — as if somehow getting a 77 as opposed to a 79 will affect their long-term success in life.

As early as grade six, many children are concerned about getting into the right junior high school, so they can get into the right high school, so they can get into the right university, so they can get into the right job. They see their very future as being on the line and feel they have to seize it *now* or it may pass them by. Even extracurricular activities are evaluated in terms of whether they look good on their resume.

By the time they are teenagers, an age when children should be at their most idealistic and hopeful, the grueling pressures and competition have left them *overprogrammed and exhausted, cynical and pessimistic, and chronically anxious about their future.* As one fourteen-year-old said, "The minute you get an average grade, you go: 'That's it. I'm not going to get into university.'"

Educational psychologist colleagues tell us that they are seeing record numbers of teenagers who are overwhelmed by the pressures and paralyzed by the tremendous number of choices available to them (which course? which school?) and the perceived consequences of making the "wrong" decision.

These kids also worry about what will happen after they graduate: "Am I going to have to spend five or six years at university at tremendous sacrifice to my parents and myself and still end up flipping hamburgers or working as a bicycle courier?"

Some develop a high level of performance and evaluation anxiety, fussing about every mark, competing intensely with their peers, evaluating their personal worthiness by their report card: "If I'm not getting 90 percent I'm a failure."

Other kids go to the opposite extreme and become apathetic: "What's the point of killing myself? It still won't make any difference." Or: "Since I need a 90 average to get anywhere and that's impossible, I might as well not bother." By the time they reach their early teens, many are already demotivated much like some of their twenty-something siblings. They have picked up their parents' and the general society's malaise and feelings of helplessness, and adopted a "why bother?" attitude.

Disturbingly, nationwide surveys of schoolchildren in the United States and Canada find *significant increases in children's stress levels.* One study reported that over half of Canadians between the ages of thirteen and eighteen routinely experience stress, with 65 percent naming school as the biggest cause. In the United States, data from a nation-wide random sample of children in the mid-1970s and late 1980s show a profound sea change in the nature of childhood. Children across the board have become more emotionally distressed – more anxious, depressed, impulsive, angry, self-centered, and less cooperative.

Finding the Right Balance – Overprogrammed, Undernurtured Children

When I look around at the lives of friends, family, and clients, I worry: In our rush to get our kids well-positioned for the future, *are we robbing them of those very things they will require to get them there safely?* Will they have the sense of security and belief in themselves that flow from childhood experiences of being well-nurtured? Will they have the emotional maturity to deal with what may be a very complex new social universe?

This has been trumpeted as an age of "lifelong learning." But we still seek to cram as much learning as possible into the early years. Unfortunately, in our zealous pursuit of ensuring our children's success, we risk turning learning into a commodity, stripped of all its pleasurable characteristics.

Parents are caught in a constant struggle to find the right balance between, as one woman put it, "not stealing their childhood" and making sure they have the necessary experiences to prepare them for the future.

Worried about a tougher economic future, many parents have involved their children in a whirlwind of extracurricular activities, such as language classes, music and computer camps, math, and other "great" learning experiences. Allowing children time to just play, on the other hand, creates guilt and fear — parents worry that they are allowing their kids to "fall behind," depriving them of some important early learning experience.

These fears are particularly acute amongst part-time parents who are concerned about spending "quality" time with their kids. One father whose children's crammed weekend agenda includes museum visits, the zoo, and tennis and ski lessons put it this way: "I only get them for two days, and when they're adults I don't want them to resent me, to say I never did anything to help them get a leg up . . ."

Across North America, parents and children participate in early-morning vigils to secure places in the schools they believe will provide an educational advantage. In New York and other major centers, parents' efforts to get their children into the "right" university starts with a mad scramble to get into the "right" nursery school — the one that will allow them to get into the elite private schools that will get them into the right universities. Similarly, in Japan children as young as three years old have days crammed with classes in music, physical education, and reading, with no time left for respite or play.

Parents don't want their children to be underequipped to face the future. But at the same time, they have a nagging sense that their children are being deprived of what it means to be a child. And they worry with good reason.

Are We Rewarding the Right Behaviors?

Everyone recognizes that early childhood learning experiences are important in fostering long-term cognitive and emotional development. But we also need to recognize the value of allowing free time for free play.

Children learn about how the world operates — its rules, roles, and expectations — and about their emotions and sense of self through free play.

Playing gives them time to imagine, time to assimilate information, time to learn. The current obsession with accelerating children's learning robs them of these vital opportunities.

We should be concerned, too, about the way in which we selectively reward children for academic performance at the expense of the qualities they will need to thrive in tomorrow's world — qualities such as creativity and the ability to identify and manage emotions (see "Promote Emotional Intelligence," below). *In a free-form world where little is predictable, how well will these overprogrammed children be able to manage ambiguity?* In a work world where people will increasingly be moving among different life spheres of education, work, leisure, volunteer work, and so on, how will they cope with periods of time that are "nonproductive" in terms of work participation?

RECOGNIZE THE IMPACT OF WORK DEMANDS ON YOUR CHILDREN'S DEVELOPMENT (OR, SPEND TIME WITH YOUR CHILDREN)

"[Many parents] do not think of children and youth as requiring a full helping of security, protection, firm limits, and clear values, and many of those who still believe in the goodness of those things no longer have faith in their ability as parents to provide them in today's complex world."

— HARVARD SCHOLAR DAVID ELKIND IN HIS BOOK
TIES THAT STRESS: THE NEW FAMILY IMBALANCE

"We are eating our young."   — OFF-THE-RECORD REMARK BY THE CEO OF ONE OF
NORTH AMERICA'S LARGEST CORPORATIONS

The time famine in North American society does not just affect working adults. Children are starved, too — starved of meaningful time spent with their parents.

As we saw in Chapter 5, the demands of our hyper-metabolic, work-intoxicated lifestyles are keeping us away from our children. We spend much more time with our coworkers than with our families. And when we are able to spend time with them, we are often tired and distracted, if not chronically anxious about the future.

Many parents cannot even name their children's teacher. The actual amount of time that parents spend with children is less than at any other time in the sixty years for which statistics have been kept.

But it is not only the amount of time we spend with our children that matters. It is also, to use an overworked cliché, the *quality* of that time. Children complain not only about their parents often being absent, but also about their being cranky and distracted when they are around. Parents are working longer, sleeping less, worrying more. This is not a recipe for mental wellness, and it is impacting directly on our children.

There are some significant ways in which the new work demands are affecting our children, including:

- **Nutrition:** There is an increased awareness today of the importance of good nutrition in childhood development in general, and academic achievement in particular. And yet children's nutrition is suffering. One study of a large Toronto school found that 50 percent of kids in junior school were coming to school without having eaten a proper breakfast – or, for the most part, any breakfast at all.

- **Homework:** According to author Ken Dryden, the amount of homework a child does is the best indicator of long-term success in school. But tired or absent parents don't have the time or energy to exercise the necessary involvement in overseeing their children's homework.

- **Reading Skills:** After analyzing hundreds of hours of eighty families' discussion over eight years, Harvard researchers concluded that the quality of dinner table discussions is the single best predictor of how well a child reads. Wide-ranging and stimulating conversations promote intellectual curiosity, which, in turn, inspires the child to read more. But today, with current time pressures and seventy-hour work weeks with unpredictable schedules, business travel, and meetings, few families are able to have dinner together on a regular basis. Indeed, according to a study by the Family and Work Institute, 12 percent of working parents say that they either never have dinner with their children, or that they do so once a week or less.

— **Overall Emotional Development:** University of Toronto Professor of Psychiatry Dr. Paul Steinhauer has labeled contemporary children and youth "The Needy Generation." Dr. Steinhauer has put together a compelling body of research summarizing the effects of the new work demands on children's development – and the report card is not good. He found that in a random sample of eight hundred mainstream youth (not "street kids" or children in group homes) 44 percent of girls and 18 percent of boys reported that at times they have trouble sleeping due to stress. Dr. Steinhauer warns that it is not just poor children who are in trouble these days: lots of children from mainstream, affluent families who should be making it are not. He estimates that one out of three of today's children will not achieve their developmental potential.

There is, however, one possible silver lining in the clouds of change still gathering over our heads. The future will see many more people working at home all or part of the time, whether on a flex-work basis, as independent contractors, or running home-based businesses. This will allow parents more flexibility in child care arrangements, and the option of spending more time with their kids. At the same time, children will benefit, too, from the opportunity to learn directly about work and careers from seeing their parents working.

If your job offers you the flexibility to work from home for part of the week, consider taking advantage. You won't work any less hard, but you will free up time (otherwise spent on commuting, lunches, and sometimes pointless meetings) to spend with your children.

CAREER CASUALTY

A few years ago, my son invited his friend David for a sleepover. That evening I created a special dinner to celebrate the weekend: with tablecloth, candles, and the like. When David arrived for dinner with a comic book in hand, he put his boot-clad feet on the table, tilted his chair back, and proceeded to read. The next morning, at breakfast, I made the boys toast. David looked at me passively until I realized he was waiting for me to butter it for him.

David is the son of a broadcaster and a lawyer, both extremely busy people. But I was astonished to hear that he *never* eats dinner with his parents, and at breakfast his nanny does everything from setting the table to buttering his bread.

TALKING ABOUT WORK AND CAREERS

A few years ago, I had a very sobering experience. After I finished a talk on work and careers to my son's Grade 6 class, I asked the students what they thought their parents felt about their work. These were middle-class kids whose parents were managers and professionals: I assumed that on the whole they would report positive work experiences to their kids. In fact, these kids competed about whose parents were more miserable:

"My mother hates her job."

"Oh yeah? Both my mother and my father hate their jobs."

"Well at least your parents have jobs to hate . . ."

Children develop many of their initial ideas and beliefs about work on the basis of what they hear from their parents, as well as what they observe for themselves. When children witness their parents' distress about work, they develop a negative view of work's impact on people's lives. This is often exacerbated by the fact that children resent the tremendous number of hours their parents work and the intrusion of work into their family's time together.

Parents worry about the results. Workshop participants routinely tell me that their children make such statements as, "I want to go into any field other than yours because you don't have a life," or "I don't ever want to work for a company because that means you don't have any personal life," or, most poignantly, "Why should I work when work makes you so miserable?"

Many parents are deeply hurt by this. *They feel their children are rejecting them, their values, and their lifestyle on the most personal level possible.* And yet they don't seem to realize that they are reaping what they have sowed. When they come home at the end of the day saying "I'm exhausted" or "My boss, the jerk . . ." or "Boy, today was brutal . . .," they are providing their children with important information about the world of work.

One friend told me recently that she can't understand why her daughter, who is in her late twenties, is so cynical about work. I pointed out that she had spent the last fifteen years telling her daughter that corporations were toxic places, run for the most part by abusive workaholics. What, I asked her, did she expect her daughter to say; "I just can't wait to get a job"? If you come home grim, angry, and upset, night after night, you are passing on a definite message to your children.

Which is not to suggest that you have to present them with a false, completely unblemished view of work. That can create problems, too. As an unemployed forty-one-year-old manager observed, "I was one of those people who always 'left my work at the office' and presented a Pollyanna-ish image of work. So when I lost my job, the kids were doubly devastated at both the loss of income and of something that had always appeared as an almost fairy tale–like way of spending my day." He had made the mistake of not communicating a more realistic view of work — even though he had actually been unhappy in his job for some time.

Some parents tell their children almost nothing about their work. Others tell them too much — much more than they need to know, or are capable of absorbing. Remember that children see the world much differently from the way we do.

For example, one self-employed friend of mine who was suffering business reversals spent his days pacing wildly back and forth, tearing his hair, wondering out loud about who would pay the bills, who would put food on the table. My friend was *catastrophizing* his business problems, even though his wife was working and there was some money in the bank. What his sixteen-year-old son heard was that "life as he knew it was over." The boy worried that he would have to leave school, get a job, and help support the family.

The goal is to strike a balance. Your children should understand the important role that work plays in your life. Try to present a well-rounded picture of your work — the good and bad, the rewards and problems. (A parent of a four-year-old said she realized she was giving the tearful kid the wrong message every morning when she said, "I *have* to go to work" as opposed to "I'm *going* to work.") Be honest about your feelings. If you have realistic worries about the future, share them. Children need to understand that the world is sometimes less than perfect. But try to present them with an attitude of guarded optimism that everything will work out all right in the end.

Avoid Early Career Decisions

Some parents, frantic about their children's future, push them to make career choices at an early age in the hope that it will give them an edge. Other parents worry that their eighteen- and nineteen-year-olds are poorly motivated and heading for failure because they still "don't know what they want to do when they grow up."

Actually, this latter group of children who have kept their options open may well be better positioned than their counterparts who were pushed to make lifelong career decisions at the age of fourteen. Once they have dealt with their uncertainty and confusion about their career choices, they may have greater skills and flexibility in managing change, coping with ambiguity and uncertainty, and dealing with shifting work requirements.

Anxiety causes some parents to fall back on the "tried and true" – they convince themselves that if only their kids could choose the right occupation they would be on the fast track to the good life. But even becoming a lawyer or doctor – traditionally an occupation that guaranteed a high income – is no longer a guarantee of success. As a parent, avoid "micro-managing" your children's career choices as a means of managing your own anxiety.

DON'T PREPARE FOR JOBS – PREPARE FOR AREAS OF COMPETENCE

As we saw in Chapter 9, the traditional approaches to career planning no longer apply. It no longer makes sense for children to think of their future in terms of a particular job title or occupation. All the indications are that they will have many different jobs, or work roles, in the course of their careers. Instead, try to get your children to focus on their key competencies – the things they are best at doing, and most enjoy.

- **Don't rely on vocational tests:** When I was twenty I was dispatched to a career counselor and given a battery of vocational tests. These tests attempted to match up my interests and tastes with those of people currently in the workforce in particular occupational groups. At the time, I (the aspiring flower child) thought that there was something profoundly silly about comparing my interests and tastes with those of people who belonged to my father's generation. In fact, it seemed to me that the only thing the tests got right was that I definitely should not become a home economics teacher!

  I did not like these tests when I was twenty. I did not like them ten years ago. And I particularly do not like them now. As we have seen, jobs are morphing beyond recognition. So there is little merit in identifying occupations as if they were stable and predictable; or in attempting to describe these occupations in terms of the skills and abilities one would need for long term success.

— **Avoid the "top ten" syndrome:** Every fall I get calls from magazines preparing their prophecies for the next year about where the "hot new jobs" are. I always decline to comment. Such predictions are always fun to read – but they can all too easily prove misleading. By the time someone has trained in a particular area they may find their skills rendered obsolete, or no longer necessary, by virtue of new technologies, changes in legislation, or competition from offshore labor markets.

Moreover, employment patterns change so rapidly that there can be pockets of unemployment even in so-called "hot" areas. For example, even though biotechnology is considered a growth area, many people with degrees and experience in the field have periods of unemployment as research interests shift, management philosophies change, companies move locations, or required skills alter.

Given the speed of change, most people treat these "hot new job" lists as pure entertainment, or, at the most, as well-intended speculation. But there are always some people who look on them as literal truth. They make significant academic and personal investments in pursuing a particular trade or profession only to find that the need for the work has evaporated. Recall, for example, the aspiring health and safety specialist we talked about in Chapter 9 who went into the field because "they" told him to, only to discover no work existed for him.

Similarly, twenty-five-year-old John P. completed a two-year college diploma in law enforcement, reasoning that it would be a growth area because of increasing anxiety about crime. He then spent the next year looking for work. He has since given up on the field, having exhausted opportunities with the police, private security firms, and internal company security.

The truth is that interpreting and following trends can certainly be helpful, but it will not guarantee success. Although we can make general statements about the growth areas in the economy, such as biotechnology, telecommunications, and geriatric care, we should be very careful about making specific predictions about jobs.

ENCOURAGE PURSUIT OF PERSONAL PASSIONS

Children, like adults, excel in areas where they have both interest and aptitude. Accept your children for who they are rather than trying to make them something they're not (not only can this be expensive in terms of psychiatric bills, it's not very practical). Encourage them to choose an academic path that personally engages them, rather than trying to second-guess the future market for jobs. In the longer term, this will lead to greater success and happiness.

Your children should by all means examine job market trends in weighing up the consequences of different career choices. They should, to the best of their ability, attempt to gauge the likely demand for their skills and training. But they should not allow the market alone to drive their decision-making, by pursuing work in a field that doesn't interest them or make use of their real strengths.

As we've seen, even if your children were prepared to slavishly follow supposed market trends, there would *still* be no guarantee that they would find work. If, on the other hand, they follow their true interests and strengths, they are much more likely to attain satisfying work in the end, although it may not be in an area that they can currently envisage. There are often creative ways of combining even an apparently impractical interest with a viable way of producing income.

For example, twenty-seven-year-old Dan, who had a longtime love of dinosaurs, completed his degree in paleontology, only to find that the only work available in his speciality was as a $10,000-a-year research assistant. He returned to school, completed courses in business and graphics, and is now in high demand designing and building exhibits in museums around the world.

PURSUE EDUCATION TO THE HIGHEST AND BROADEST LEVEL – GIVEN INTERESTS, SKILLS, AND APTITUDES

What is a university education worth? What *kind* of university education represents the surest ticket to success? Or, given the widespread unemployment among modern university graduates, would my children be better off going to a technical college instead? Many parents are wrestling with these questions.

When I went to university, a university education was perceived to be of value in and of itself. I never really thought about its practical value in terms of whether one course of study would better prepare me for future employment than another. It's true that implicit in going to university was the notion that it would have long-term economic benefit. As one friend observed, "A university education was the promise of a trip to success that knew no boundaries." But above all, it was an opportunity to understand how the world operated, to *enrich* my life.

Nonetheless, not all my friends had the same freedom of choice. Some were only allowed by their parents to go to university if they chose a "professional" program to study that would lead them to work in such fields as social work, engineering, or medicine. So the debate over the "practical" value of an education is not new. But the stakes are much higher now.

Today, many students and their parents do not feel they can afford the luxury of spending four or five years studying something if it will not be instrumental in securing employment. With rising tuition fees and living costs, a university education has become a more expensive commodity. That's particularly true in relative terms: after nearly two decades of sliding family incomes, parents are less able to pay for that education than they would have been ten or twenty years ago.

Many cash-squeezed parents may now reason that they can't afford to make such a significant investment only to see their children either unemployed or engaged in work whose intellectual content hardly requires a university education.

- **Liberal or technical:** Anxiety about future employment, concern about the rising cost of education, and the progressive devaluation of the traditional liberal arts education have taken their toll. Some students who would previously have elected to pursue a university education are enrolling in two-year vocational diploma programs in such areas as hospitality, law enforcement, marketing, hairdressing, graphics, and so on.

  Although in the short run this may prove to be a more effective strategy in terms of securing initial employment, in the long run it may prove to be counterproductive. These occupations could disappear, or the skills required for success could be radically transformed.

  Moreover, as we enter into a very complex world, the ability to think, abstract, and interpret information, and to understand that information in a broader social and economic context, will increasingly be at a premium. The much-maligned liberal arts education, at its best, enhances precisely those skills. But they are typically not cultivated in highly specialized training of a more practical nature.

- **University vs. college:** Many subjects such as marketing, social work, business, criminology, journalism, and so on are offered at both the college level and the university level (although they may have slightly different names at the different institutions, such as "criminology" at university as opposed to "law enforcement" at college).

  The college route may look more attractive (more practical, easier to get in, less expensive, less time-consuming and so on), but many people later discover that their college diploma is not seen to have the same value as a university degree. Correctly or not, many employers equate a university degree with higher-order cognitive skills, such as thinking, reasoning, and problem-solving.

Ideally, those who have the choice, and who qualify for the university program, should opt for the university qualification. Longer term, it will give them more flexibility because of the greater breadth and depth of the curriculum. Moreover, as noted above, a university education will provide a better generalist grounding that will enhance their skills portfolio, which employers typically favor.

This is not to suggest that colleges have no potential role to play. One route that is increasingly popular, and favored by employers, is to combine an undergraduate university degree with a specialist college diploma.

Some people, however, by reasons of either inclination or aptitude, are simply not suited to pursuing a university education. Their interests and talents may overwhelmingly predispose them toward a craft, a trade, or other more technical occupation, such as plumbing, computer graphics, or fashion design.

Take, for example, the child of one client who had almost completed an undergraduate degree. University had been a continuing struggle for her, even though she was extremely bright, and much to her well-educated parents' chagrin, she dropped out of university to enroll in a hairdressing program. She has since blossomed, combining her intelligence with her flair for fashion and design, and has moved rapidly through the ranks of apprentice to become a sought-after fashion stylist.

— **Specialist or generalist:** There is also a significant controversy as to the value of a liberal arts education as opposed to one specializing in one of the professions, such as engineering, law, or commerce. As we have already seen in Chapter 9, there is no simple answer to this question. While specialists appear to be in greater demand right now, they must still have generalist skills. And being a specialist is certainly no longer a guarantee of employment.

Universities are churning out thousands of graduates in law, medicine, social work, journalism, education, commerce, and engineering every year without any regard to the market demands for these skills. As a result, thousands of students who have been trained to pursue one occupation now find themselves either unemployed or underemployed — with their resource-rich education and time-consuming degrees put to no use.

The sheer number of people pursuing these degrees testifies to the continued fundamental belief in the value of specialization, despite the fact that in many professions unemployment is rampant. Take lawyers, for example: there are high levels of unemployment in the profession, and new entrants are scrambling to get a foothold.

A question I have posed to many CEOs and VPs of human resources concerning this issue is: "When you think about hiring young people into your organization, would you prefer them to have a liberal arts or more specialized education?" They are evenly divided in their responses. But there is broad agreement that a specialized degree, in the sciences, for example, is not sufficient, unless that scientist *understands his or her area of expertise in a broader social and economic context*; has the cognitive capacity to interpret complex information; and can communicate that information in nontechnical language to people from different specializations.

Kids should get the best possible education in the light of their skills, interests, and aptitudes. If they do specialize, they should ensure that they have the foundations (social sciences, writing, and thinking skills) to understand the broader context in which they are carrying out their work, interact with people from different disciplines, talk persuasively, write clearly and effectively, and be able to abstract important information from a situation.

They might also consider combining two areas of study to maximize their flexibility, such as business with history or art; information technology with English literature; and so on.

Get Work Experience

All work experience counts. It helps in determining future career paths, and in being positioned for long-term success.

This advice applies equally to cooperative education (see below) or to any part-time or summer job, be it baby-sitting, tutoring, or working as a veterinarian's assistant. Even an unskilled and apparently lowly job can provide a wealth of experience, as long as your child approaches it as a learning experience.

For example, one seventeen-year-old got a summer job selling postcards at a theme park. She took the job with the understanding that when her boss met with his regional manager, she could sit in on their meetings. At the end of her summer, not only had she developed confidence in approaching customers and making a sale, but she had also received a hands-on education in marketing, including projections, sales forecasts, and so on.

In evaluating work opportunities, your children should ask:

- What technical and nontechnical skills and competencies will I develop as a result of this job?
- How much supervision and mentoring will I receive?
- Will I have an opportunity to sit in on and observe meaningful business/client/customer interactions, for example, sales meetings, presentations, clinical rounds, team problem-solving sessions?

Cooperative Education

Cooperative education teaches "practical skills" through periods of work placement with organizations alternating with periods of academic study. It is becoming increasingly popular amongst students and educators, and has found growing favor amongst employers. Indeed, some companies now hire *only* graduates of cooperative programs in certain disciplines.

Recruiters say that graduates of these programs can "hit the ground running." Because they have had some work experience, organizations don't have to invest as much time and money in training and orienting them. Co-op graduates have a basic understanding of how organizations operate; they have reasonable expectations (for example, they know that they won't start their first job with four weeks vacation); and they understand the importance of good communication and team skills and have had practice in applying them.

The new buzz around cooperative education has led to the incorporation of its principles at the high school level, where students can get academic credits in exchange for unpaid work experiences. This holds tremendous appeal for young people.

One student, for example, was to spend six weeks in a local hotel, working two-week stints in three departments learning not just how each of these three departments worked but how they worked together. She would then go on to do the same in Japan. She said, "I feel that in school we live in a textbook world and don't get a chance to get a taste of the real world and to see how business operates."

In theory, co-op education should be of value not just from the point of view of developing "hard" job skills, but also for enriching an adolescent's opportunity to discover areas of interest, and — just as important — areas of no interest. For example, one high school student who had spent time at an oil company concluded that she did not like the bureaucracy associated with large organizations and realized that ultimately she would probably prefer to be her own boss.

Unfortunately, there is a potential downside to cooperative education, particularly at the high school level. Sometimes local businesses use co-op students as a source of unpaid labor doing non-skilled work in service jobs.

Similarly, there are instances where resource-strained teachers and business-people may not be appropriately trained to provide the supervision and mentoring students need in order to really benefit from the experience. In evaluating cooperative programs, look at what kind of training those in charge (teachers, businesspeople) have been given.

PROMOTE EMOTIONAL INTELLIGENCE

Whether as a worker, parent, or citizen, the challenges that will be facing young adults in the year 2000 and beyond will require a high level of *emotional* maturity and intelligence. As we have seen, these challenges will include managing ambiguity; quickly establishing effective relationships; operating in fluid environments with constantly shifting competing pressures and priorities; working in fast start-up teams; interacting with people from all over the world from significantly different cultures; and alternating between intense pressures to produce and periods of leisure, education, and volunteer work.

Daniel Goleman, in his bestselling book *Emotional Intelligence*, demonstrates the critical importance of being emotionally "smart" in determining long-term success. Emotional literacy includes social skills; sensitivity to your own and other's feelings; being able to read situations; empathy; optimism; managing conflict; and the ability to manage one's feelings.

Foster Independence

In what many of us see as an unsafe world, it is very difficult sometimes to give our children the independence they need. When I was eighteen, I traveled across Europe more or less by myself, an amazing experience that gave me a real sense of self-confidence and maturity. But I shudder when I think of my son doing some of the stupid things I did.

But it is only from age-appropriate experiences that stretch and challenge them that kids start to develop the self-management and problem-solving skills critical to long-term success. Some of these skills will come from learning they can handle challenging situations — just as a fair number of skills went into *my* personal portfolio as a result of my trip. So don't overprotect.

Encourage kids to take responsibility for their own decisions even if they don't turn out perfectly. Don't blame them when things go wrong: instead, praise them for having taken a risk and discuss what other strategies they might have used.

Talk the Language of Feelings

Encourage your children to expand their emotional vocabulary by helping them identify and articulate their feelings. Learning to deal with adversity and frustrating experiences will contribute to their ability to engage in impulse control and manage anger in the long term. You can also promote empathy by having your children look at an interpersonal conflict from many perspectives. ("How do you think Jill felt when . . .?")

Consider your child's interpersonal experiences (conflicts, relationships) as a *laboratory for real life*. For example, children who are intolerant of others need to recognize that they will often have to interact with people they might not like, and that this is part of life. We will have teachers we don't like, and we will have bosses and clients whom we don't like.

Similarly, we will have fellow students whom we don't like, just as we will have colleagues or team members we don't like. In the teamwork environments that characterize business, obviously it is critical to be able to manage conflict and to work with different types of people.

Teaching children to understand and stay connected with their feelings early on will not only promote their long-term career success — it should also help make our society more civilized and more humane.

ACADEMIC ACHIEVEMENT ONLY TELLS PART OF THE STORY

A client told me the following story about the importance of emotional maturity. He interviewed two people — one we will call Carol and the other, Mary — for an entry-level position in marketing.

Carol had an outstanding academic record and glowing references from her professors. During the summer Carol had held different kinds of service jobs, mostly of the order of flipping hamburgers.

Mary, in contrast, had an only slightly better than average academic record of accomplishment. Where Carol had completed her degree one half-year faster than average, it had taken Mary a year and a half longer than usual. The length of her education had been extended when she had switched her major from psychology to sociology halfway through her program. It had also been interrupted when she had spent six months traveling in Europe and when she had served as a volunteer leader in an international youth organization.

Despite Mary's relative academic weakness, the client decided to hire her. Here is how the client "decoded" Mary's experience as evidence of superior emotional maturity:

- Switching her major showed that she was open to experience and able to identify a passion and follow it.
- Taking time off for travel demonstrated that she was adventurous, open to new experiences and change, and intellectually and culturally curious.
- Her volunteer work proved that she was comfortable and skilled in dealing with people from different cultures; and that she had leadership skills in having developed a vision and successfully marketed a program to members.

Give Positive Feedback on Strengths

Just as it is important for adults to know themselves, so it is important for children. Your feedback can provide them with vital information on their strengths.

Some parents are reluctant to give children positive feedback on their strengths in the belief that they will give them a "swelled head" or somehow demotivate them (although they have little hesitation about offering criticism of their faults). But just as you value positive and concrete feedback from clients and bosses (as well as suggestions as to how you might improve), so too do children.

Moreover, when you praise your child for a positive behavior, you *reinforce* that behavior, making it more likely that your child will repeat it. If, on the other hand, you ignore it, your child will be less prone to do it again. And if you only seem to pay attention to your children when they do something wrong, you may be inadvertently reinforcing a pattern of *negative* behavior.

Try to give children feedback on strengths over and above those commented on in the school system, such as work habits and academic achievements. Focus on general behaviors they have exhibited. For example, your child has reorganized his cupboard without your asking. You might comment, "I really liked the *initiative* you showed in . . ."

And remember, for feedback to be useful to children (or anyone else), it must be concrete, specific, and behavioral, and avoid gender-typing. Instead of ascribing success to a *fixed personality or physical attribute*, such as "you did well at school because you are smart" or "people like you because you are handsome," focus on *behaviors and efforts*, such as "your friends really appreciate your listening skills . . ." or "you did well at school because you tried hard." (See *The Optimistic Child*, by psychologist Martin Seligman, for more on the kind of parental communication and life skills that promote feelings of mastery and self-esteem in children.)

PROMOTE INTELLECTUAL CURIOSITY AND VERSATILITY

Parents get annoyed when their kids make categorical statements and confuse opinion for fact. On the other hand, they themselves may be guilty of failing to make a distinction between a hypothesis and a fact: for example, "It's always hot in Europe in the summer" vs. "In my experience, it's usually hot in Europe in the summer." Similarly, the same parent who never reads, or only reads one type of publication, may complain about their kid's poor reading habits.

In an information society, it is obviously impossible to function effectively without the ability to think, understand, and interpret complex information. This is particularly true as we increasingly need to make decisions based on incomplete or ambiguous information. Kids need to know:

- how to learn
- how to question received wisdom
- how to develop hypotheses
- how to understand the difference between a hypothesis and a fact.

Perhaps most importantly, they need to be able to think creatively and to be curious about the world in which they are operating. They will be interacting with people who bring to the table diverse backgrounds, cultures, and disciplines; the capacity to understand and evaluate information in a broader social context will be at a premium.

LEARN A LANGUAGE

Thirty-year-old Laura speaks Japanese, holds a B.A. in English, and has worked for the past five years as an office manager. She says that whenever she looks for work she has found that because of her language proficiency she has been able to write her own ticket, even during periods of high unemployment.

Being able to speak a foreign language has always been an important and valuable skill. It provides access to another way of thinking, to another culture. It is a passport to a "richer life."

Today, in a globalized economy, fluency in a second language is becoming increasingly important to career success. A study of top senior managers conducted by executive search firm Cambridge Management Planning found that at the top of the list of important traits CEOs will need at the turn of the century and beyond were being prepared to travel extensively and to move to a foreign country.

With the liberalization and commercialization of Eastern Europe, professionals who speak Hungarian or Russian have significant opportunities that their unilingual counterparts do not. In the near-future, with the rising commercial prominence of the Pacific Rim nations, being able to speak Chinese and Japanese will be even more highly valued – Chinese because it is the language of the world's largest and fastest-growing population, Japanese because it is the language of one of the world's most prosperous and powerful countries. Fluency in Spanish will also be prized with the increasing importance of Mexico through the North American Free Trade Agreement, and with the growth in trade with other powerhouse economies such as Chile.

WHAT ARE YOUR CHILDREN LEARNING ABOUT WORK FROM YOU?

- Do your children know how you earn your living? (What you do, for whom, where.)
- Do your children know who your clients/customers are?
- Do they know what gives you the greatest sense of satisfaction at work?
- Do they know what your major headaches at work are?
- Do they know how you feel about your work overall? (Love it, don't like it, indifferent, etc.)
- Do they feel that you've neglected them in order to meet work demands?

- Do they think of your job and your income as guaranteed?
- Do they understand the importance of always being up to date with your skills and learning?

Promote Opportunities to Learn About Work (and Life)

There are a number of ways in which you can promote your kid's opportunities to learn about work and careers.

– **Use your own experience as a vehicle for discussing a wide arena of work issues:** It is amazing the number of people whose children don't know what they do for a living, or else only understand their work in the broadest outlines: "My mother works for Company X"; "My father's an executive"; "My mom is a lawyer." Look at your work experiences as a laboratory for providing your children with insight into how the world works. Talking about your work gives them critical information about different occupations, the skills you need to be successful, how teams work, how to manage clients and bosses, what it means to give something your best, and so on.

– **Model a balanced life:** Ask yourself: "What are my children learning about work from me? Have I worked so hard and so many hours that they feel work is something that takes you away from your family? Do they think the only way to earn a living is to be so consumed by work that you don't have a life? Do they have a concept of volunteer work or continuing education based on my behavior?" If you believe that there is more to life than work alone, then model a balanced life – well-balanced between education, work, family, leisure, and volunteer activities – or reap the consequences.

– **Foster "trade skills":** Success in business – whether as an entrepreneur running a small business, a consultant, or a manager with a large organization – is often rooted in earlier experiences of buying, selling, and exchanging. All things being equal, the child who runs a lemonade stand, sells baby-sitting services, or trades baseball cards to improve a collection will have more strongly developed trade skills in later life than one who does not engage in youthful commerce. They will have a better practical understanding of how business works; greater comfort in negotiation and deal-making; an understanding of profit margins; superior ability to assess opportunities; a concept of responsibility; and so on. Some ways in which you can help your children develop their trade skills:

- Provide/encourage meaningful entrepreneurial experiences (garage sale, lemonade stand, paper route). Don't underestimate what kids learn from collecting and trading cards, comics, etc. Gail Vaz-Oxlade in *The Money Tree Myth* has many practical examples of how to help children understand concepts of saving, making money, and growing money.
- Tell stories. Use the dinner table to discuss different aspects of business – for example, a relative starting a new venture, a friend having trouble because a bank is calling his loan.
- Participate in "take your child to work" opportunities.
- Encourage your children to read the business section of the newspaper/ business magazines.
- Encourage your children to follow a stock or invest their earnings/ allowances.
- Involve them in the day-to-day administration of your household budget.

RECOGNIZE THAT CHILDREN ARE NOT JUST TOMORROW'S WORKERS – THEY ARE TOMORROW'S CITIZENS

In writing this chapter, I was torn between writing about how to better equip children for the future in terms of work, and how to better equip them as human beings in an increasingly challenging social universe. Our children will be inheriting complex social, economic, and environmental problems – an increasingly divided society, a resource-depleted world, a fragile economy. We have to teach them values over and above those determined purely by the marketplace.

Are we simply raising a generation of effective producers to service the needs of the global economy, workers who can produce, compete, and consume? Or are we preparing future citizens who are capable of acting morally as well as productively – human beings capable of thinking, feeling, caring, and contributing?

There is one thing that is certain and predictable in an uncertain world: You – your capacity to manage ambiguity, to deploy intellectual curiosity, to demonstrate interpersonal savvy, and to show compassion, tolerance, and concern for community. If you use these qualities, you will thrive.

And if *you* nurture and model these qualities for the next generation, you will help to create a society in which you would be proud to live.

References

Introduction
p. xiii: Spence, Larry. "The soul of a corporation." *Utne Reader*, February 1989.

Chapter One
p. 7: Solow, Robert. "Dr. Divlin's diagnosis, Mr. Clinton's remedy." *New York Review of Books*, March 25, 1993.

p. 11: Goldsmith, Sir James. *The Trap*. New York: Carroll & Graf, 1994.

p. 12: Statistics of white collar job loss (Robert Topel): Pascale, Richard. "The false security of 'Employability.'" *Fast Company*, April/May 1996.

p. 12: Nohria study of company downsizing: "Cant anyone here play this game?" *Fast Company*, premier issue.

p. 13: Software Research Council: Crane, David, and David Israelson. "Victims of change." *The Toronto Star*, February 26, 1996.

p. 13: Increase in temp work in the United States: Aley, James. "The temp biz boom: why it's good." *Fortune*, October 16, 1995.

p. 13: Increase in temp work in Canada: Wells, Jennifer. "Jobs." *Maclean's*, March 11, 1996.

p. 14: Drucker, Peter. "The age of social transformation." *The Atlantic Monthly*, November 1994.

p. 14: Rifkin, Jeremy. *The End of Work: The Decline of the Global Labor Force and the Dawn of the Post-Market Era*. New York: G.P. Putnam's Sons, 1995.

p. 15: Ide, T. Ran, and Arthur Cordell. "The New Tools: Implications for the Future of Work." Occasional publication, Toronto: Between the Lines, 1994.

p. 15: Cassidy, John. "Who killed the middle class?" *The New Yorker*, October 16, 1996.

p. 15: Thurow, Lester. "Why their world might crumble." *The New York Times Magazine*, May 9, 1995.

p. 17: Bielski, Vince. "Our magnificent obsession." *The Family Therapy Networker*, March/April 1996.

p. 18: Home-Douglas, Pierre. "The examined life? Who has time?" *The Globe and Mail*, March 4, 1996.

p. 19: Hornstein, Harley. *Brutal Bosses and Their Prey*. New York: Riverhead Books, 1995.

References

Chapter Two

p. 22: Whyte, William. "The Organizational Man: a rejoinder." *The New York Times Magazine*, December 7, 1986.

p. 23: Kenneth Thomson: Saunders, John. "Timmins paper 'Roy's favourite.'" *The Globe and Mail*, May 1, 1996.

p. 27: Downsizing at CBC: Cuff, John Haslett. "Feel good bulletins add insult to injury at CBC." *The Globe and Mail*, November 29, 1995.

p. 28: The New York Times editorial board. "The downsizing of America." *The New York Times*, March 3–9, 1996.

p. 28: Davenport, Thomas H. "Why re-engineering failed." *Fast Company*, premier issue, 1996.

p. 31: Stevenson, Howard H., and Mihnea C. Moldoveanu. "The power of predictability." *Harvard Business Review*, July–August 1995.

Chapter Three

p. 37: Calvin Klein: *Elle*, September 1995.

p. 38: Foot, David, and Daniel Stoffman. *Boom, Bust & Echo: How to Profit from the Coming Demographic Shift.* Toronto: Macfarlane Walter & Ross, 1996.

p. 39: Strauss, William, and Neil Howe. *13th Generation: Abort, Retry, Ignore, Fail?* New York: Vintage Books, 1993.

p. 41: Whyte, William H. *The Organizational Man.* New York: Simon and Schuster, 1956.

p. 43: Marshall, Victor. "Issues of an Aging Workforce in a Changing Society." Special Report, Centre for Studies in Aging: University of Toronto, 1996.

p. 44: "NetWords." *Exec-U-Net Newsletter*, Vol. VI., no. 1.

Chapter Four

p. 58: Coupland, Douglas. *Generation X: Tales for an Accelerated Culture.* New York: St. Martin's Press, 1991.

p. 62: Brown, Robert. Personal Communication. May 1996.

p. 64: Rutherford, Cynthia. "Commitment and other fading customs." *The Globe and Mail*, November 1, 1995.

p. 65: Post-boomer employment statistics: Ratan, S. "On the trail of Generation X." *Fortune*, October 4, 1993.

p. 65: Employment of university graduates: Little, Bruce. "A tough lesson in jobs for high-schoolers." *The Globe and Mail*, October 2, 1995.

p. 68: Attitudes of American youth: Snyder, David Pearce. "The revolution in the workplace: what's happening to our jobs?" *The Futurist*, March/April 1996.

p. 68: Statistics Canada on Canadian university students' employment: Saunders, Doug. "Graduates facing postponed beginnings." *The Globe and Mail*, April 22, 1996.

p. 73: Labich, Kenneth. "Kissing off corporate America." *Fortune*, February 20, 1995.

Chapter Five

p. 76: Coupland, Douglas: "Douglas Coupland." Profile on CityTV, 1995.

p. 76: Smith, Lee. "Stamina." *Fortune*, November 28, 1994.

p. 79: Schor, Juliet. *The Overworked American*. New York: Basic Books, 1991.

p. 79: Earl Berger: Scrivener, Leslie. "Why we all spend more time at the office." *The Toronto Star*, December 13, 1995.

p. 79: Time working couples spend together: Ventura, Michael. "100 Visionaries." *Utne Reader*, January/February, 1995.

p. 79: Time father spends with child: Ventura, Michael. "100 Visionaries." *Utne Reader*, January/February, 1995.

p. 79: Time business people spend away from home: "Report on business travel." *The Globe and Mail*, September 10, 1996.

p. 79: Stress levels of working parents: MacDonald, Gayle. "Working world." *The Globe and Mail*, January 2, 1996.

p. 80: Nine more hours of work: Roberts, Paul. "Goofing off." *Psychology Today*, July/August 1995.

p. 80: Increased productivity, fewer rewards: Clark, Kim. "Do you really work more?" *Fortune*, April 29, 1996.

p. 81: Working at night: Fierman, Jaclyn. "It's 2 am: let's go to work." *Fortune*, August 21, 1995.

p. 81: Jim Sha: Steinert-Threlkeld, Tomm. "Can you work in Netscape time?" *Fast Company*, premier Issue, 1996.

p. 84: Ron Zambonini, president, Cognos Inc.: French, Carey. "Digital world brings out best and worst." *The Globe and Mail*, September 15, 1995.

p. 84: University of Washington sociologist Pepper Schwartz: Steinberg, Lynn. "Missing manners." *Seattle Post-Intelligencer*, January 26, 1996.

p. 86: Coren, Stanley. *Sleep Thieves*. New York: Free Press, 1996.

p. 86: Time spent with children: Bielski, Vince. "Our magnificent obsession." *The Family Therapy Networker*, March/April 1996.

p. 87: Quindlen, Anna. "Why I quit." *Working Woman*, December 1995.

p. 89: Michie, Susan, and Anne Cockcroft. "Overwork can kill." *British Medical Journal*, April 13, 1996.

p. 89: Heart attacks: Dossey, Larry. *Meaning and Medicine*. New York: Bantam, 1991.

p. 89: Cary Cooper: Carpenter, Rosemary. "Do we work too hard?" *International Express*, February 19, 1996.

Chapter Six

p. 102: Whyte, David. *The Heart Aroused*. New York: Doubleday, 1996.

p. 103: Dominguez, Joe, and Vicki Robin. *Your Money or Your Life: Transforming Your Relationship with Money and Achieving Financial Independence*. New York: Viking, 1992.

p. 104: Quindlen, Anna. "Why I quit." *Working Woman*, December 1995.

p. 104: Polls (Gallup and Merck Family Fund) on reducing income to free up leisure: Ehrenreich, Barbara. "In search of a simpler life." *Working Woman*, December 1995.

Chapter Seven

p. 110: Grove, Andrew. *Only the Paranoid Survive: How to Exploit the Crisis Points That Challenge Every Company and Career*. New York: Currency Doubleday, 1996 .

p. 112: Look first, buy later: Lewis, James. "Looking for a fast-moving temp with a proven track record?" *Canadian HR Reporter*, May 6, 1996.

p. 113: Largest single employer in the United States, and growth in temp. labor market: Watson, Paul. "Tempzines." *Utne Reader*, September/October 1995.

p. 113: Growth in professional and technical temping: Aley, James. "The temp biz boom: why it's good." *Fortune*, October 16, 1995.

p. 113: Contingent employment in Silicon Valley: Benner, C. Letter in *Wired*, April 6, 1996.

p. 113: Downward pressures on wages of contingent technical workers: Benner, C. Letter in *Wired*, April 6, 1996.

p. 114: Cost of lifetime employment: "Management briefs." *The Globe and Mail*, April 30, 1996.

p. 114: Part-time jobs amongst workers under twenty-four: Little, Bruce. "Patching jobs together to survive." *The Globe and Mail*, December 11, 1995.

p. 114: Number of part-timers who would prefer to work full-time: Greenspoon, Edward. "Economy changing far faster than people." *The Globe and Mail*, April 20, 1996.

p. 118: Handy, Charles. *The Age of Unreason*. Cambridge: Harvard Business School Press, 1989.

p. 120: Sir Leon Bagrit: Snyder, Daniel Pearce. "The revolution in the workplace: what's happening to our jobs?" *The Futurist*, March/April 1996.

p. 121: Pensionable age and life expectancy in Canada: Taylor, Peter Shawn. "The end of retirement," *Saturday Night Magazine*, June 1995.

p. 122: Pensionable age and life expectancy in the United States: McPollan, Stephen, and Mark Levine. "The rise and fall of retirement." *Worth Magazine*, December/January 1995.

p. 122: Workers covered by fixed payment pensions: Rothenberg, Randall. "What makes Sammy walk?" *Esquire*, May 1995.

p. 123: White, Keith. "Sweet, portable lifestyle." *The Baffler*, Number 7, 1996.

p. 124: Attali, Jacques. *Millennium: Winners and Losers in the Coming World Order*. New York: Time Books, 1991.

p. 124: Castleton, Edward. "Post-urban, post-industrial, but never post-elite." *The Baffler*, Number Seven, 1996.

p. 128: Bridges, William. *Job Shift*. Reading: Addison-Wesley Publishing Company, 1994.

p. 131: Kettle, John. "Zap you're stupid." From "John Kettle's FutureLetter," reprinted in *The Globe and Mail*, October 25, 1994.

Chapter Eight

p. 157: Csikszentmihalyi, Mihaly. *Flow: The Psychology of Optimal Experience*. New York: Harper & Row, 1990.

p. 159: Study on successful women executives: Mainiero, Lisa. "The Longest Climb." *Psychology Today*, November/December 1994.

p. 160: Baker, Russell. "The Market God." From *The New York Times,* reprinted in *The Globe and Mail,* March 26, 1996.

Chapter Nine

p. 178: Carey, Elaine. "Study links success to leaving home." *The Toronto Star*, April 22, 1996.

p. 182: Learn on your own time: Labich, Kenneth. "How to fire people." *Fortune*, June 10, 1996.

p. 191: Royal Bank survey on adult education: Gibb-Clark, Margot. "Workers still hitting books." *The Globe and Mail*, November 18, 1996.

p. 191: Plans of employed workers to start a business: Globe and Mail Staff. "Workers want to be owners." *The Globe and Mail*, October 24, 1996.

p. 193: Dominguez, Joe, and Vicki Robin. *Your Money or Your Life: Transforming Your Relationship with Money and Achieving Financial Independence.* Toronto: Penguin, 1992.

p. 193: Elgin, Duane. *Voluntary Simplicity: Toward a Way of Life That Is Outwardly Simple, Inwardly Rich.* New York: Morrow, 1993.

p. 193: Rubin, Bonnie M. *Time Out: How to Take a Year (or More or Less) Off Without Jeopardizing Your Job, Your Family, or Your Bank Account.* New York: Norton, 1987.

p. 193: Long, Charles. *How to Survive Without a Salary.* Toronto: Warwick, 1991.

p. 193: St. James, Elaine. *Simplify Your Life: 100 Ways to Slow Down and Enjoy the Things That Really Matter.* New York: Hyperion, 1994.

p. 193: Kirsch, M. M. *How to Get Off The Fast Track – and Live a Life Money Can't Buy.* Chicago: Contemporary Books, 1991.

Chapter Ten

p. 201: Václav, Havel. "The spiritual crisis of our age." Speech. Receiving the Philadelphia Liberty Medal. July 4, 1994.

p. 210: Olsen Forum on Information Management, 1996.

p. 213: Eli Lilly CEO, Randall L. Tobia: Hammonds, Keith H. "Balancing work and family." *Business Week*, September 9, 1996.

p. 215: Rifkin, Jeremy. *The End of Work: The Decline of the Global Labor Force and the Dawn of the Post-Market Era.* New York: G.P. Putnam's Sons, 1995.

p. 215: Hunnicut, Benjamin. *Work Without End.* Philadelphia: Temple University Press, 1988.

p. 221: Newall, J. E. "Sowing the seeds of a learning culture." Notes for remarks. 1996 Canadian Business Leader Award, March 4, 1996.

p. 232: Csikszentmihalyi, Mihaly. *Flow: The Psychology of Optimal Experiences.* New York: Harper & Row, 1990.

Chapter Eleven

p. 237: Gardner, Jr., Ralph. "Poor little smart kids." *New York,* March 18, 1996.

p. 238: Coleman, Peter. *Learning About Schools: What Parents Need to Know and How They Can Find Out.* Montreal: Institute for Research on Public Policy, 1994.

p. 238: Ford, William. Personal Interview. June 4, 1996.

p. 240: Stress levels in children and youth: Driedger, Sharon Doyle. "Growing pains." *Maclean's,* January 1996.

References

p. 242: Elkind, Daniel. *Ties That Stress: The New Family Imbalance.* Cambridge: Harvard University Press, 1995.

p. 243: Statistics on parent time with children: Fuchs, V. R. *Women's Quest for Economic Equality.* Cambridge: Harvard University Press, 1988.

p. 243: Kids not eating breakfast: Galt, Virginia. "Innovative approaches to hunger." *The Globe and Mail*, September 28, 1995.

p. 243: Reading skills: "Social studies." *The Globe and Mail*, January 22, 1996.

p. 244: Parents having dinner with children: Bielski, Vince. "Our magnificent obsession." *The Family Therapy Networker*, March/April 1996.

p. 244: Steinhauer, Paul. "Children and youth in the '90s: The needy generation and how to meet their needs." Address on Behalf of The Toronto Board of Health and The Metro Task Force on Services to Young Children & Families, November 21, 1995.

p. 257: Goleman, Daniel. *Emotional Intelligence.* New York: Bantam Books, 1995.

p. 260: Seligman, Martin. *The Optimistic Child.* New York: Houghton Mifflin Co., 1995.

p. 262: Cambridge Management Planning. *Executive Employment Trend Survey.* March 1996.

p. 264: Vaz-Oxlade, Gail. *The Money Tree Myth.* Toronto: Stoddart Publishing, 1996.

Index

absenteeism, 212
accounting firms, 184, 196, 220
Advocate Placement Limited, 112
Aetna Life and Casualty, 213
age discrimination, 43–44
Allen, Robert, 113
androgyny, definition of, 24
Atalli, Jacques, 124
AT&T, 113

baby boom generation, 38–39. *See also* early
    boomers
baby bust generation, 39. *See also* late
    boomers
Bagrit, Sir Leon, 120
Baker, Russell, 160
balancing work and personal life, 63, 96,
    198–99, 212–14, 263
banks, improving benefits for part-time
    workers in, 206
Berger, Earl, 79
biotechnology, careers in, 249
Boom, Bust & Echo, 38
boomers. *See* early boomers; late boomers;
    post-boomers; pre-boomers
boredom, 95
bosses. *See* managers
boundaries between home and work, 18–19,
    82, 198
Bridges, William, 128

Brown, Robert, 62
Brutal Bosses and Their Prey, 19
burnout, 94–95
business
    cards, 175
    travel, 79
    trends, 182–83, 187, 190, 250
busyness, 78, 80–81
    effect on people's work, 83
    and loss of civility in workplace, 84–85

Cambridge Management Planning, 262
Canadian Broadcasting Corporation, 27
Canadian Old Age Pension Act, 121–22
Canadian Professional Sales Association, 79
career
    advancement, 51
    angst, 93, 96–97
        career regret, 100–101
        career vertigo, 97–99
        crisis of meaning, 101–2
    counseling, 148
    dilemmas, 164, 167–68
        balancing financial needs against core
            values, 165–66
        geographical transfers, 166
        putting your own needs first, 167
        settling for lower professional stan-
            dards, 166–67
        staying in wrong job, 164–65

intelligence, definition of, xv–xvi
"ladder," 119, 193
malaise, 89–90, 93
　boredom, 95
　burnout, 94–95
　conflict between work and personal
　　life, 96
management, 136
　being who you are, 159–63
　becoming a career activist, 138,
　　143–45, 157, 163
　finding work, 125, 126, 130–31
　importance of self-knowledge, 145–55
　knowing what you love, 155–58
　reconfiguring yourself, 154
managers, 207–8, 209
myths, 139–42
paths, 9–10, 119, 141–42
plateau, 50
portfolio, 147–48, 230
progress, 194
success
　being kind to yourself, 200
　being more of a specialist or more of a
　　generalist, 194–96
　building financial independence,
　　190–93
　and communication skills, 179–80
　ensuring your marketability, 170–77,
　　178, 205
　and lifelong learning, 180–82
　looking to the future, 187
　preparing for areas of competence,
　　183–87
　thinking globally, 177–79
　thinking lattice, not ladders, 193–94
　and time management, 196–99
　understanding business trends, 182–83,
　　187, 190, 250
careers
　in future, 111–12, 120–21, 187–90, 249
　new vs. old, 110–11, 119, 125–26, 127,
　　135

Castleton, Edward, 124
change
　in society, 7, 14–15, 16, 102, 125, 159–60,
　　215
　in workforce, 13–14
　in workplace, 5–7, 17, 28, 30, 35, 81, 120,
　　133
Chase Manhattan Bank, 27–28
children
　career choices, 247–50
　computer skills, 236
　education, 16, 160, 221–23, 235–40, 241,
　　242, 243, 251–55
　emotional development, 244
　emotional intelligence, 257–60
　extracurricular activities, 241
　future standard of living, 7
　helping less-advantaged, 222–23
　homework, 243
　intellectual curiosity and versatility, 261
　learning a foreign language, importance of,
　　261–62
　nutrition, 243
　parents' lack of time to spend with, 79,
　　86–87, 241, 242–45
　personal passions, encouragement of,
　　250–51
　play, importance of, 241–42
　reading skills, 243–44
　stress in, 238–40
　values learned from parents, 265
　view of work from parents, 245–47, 262–64
　work experiences, 255–57, 264
Chrysler Corporation, 114
cobbling together a living, 115
Cockroft, Anne, 89
Coleman, Peter, 238
colleges. See universities and colleges
communication skills, 179–80
communities, walled and gated, 16–17
community, staff involvement in, 222
computer and software industries, 18
computer literacy, 236

contingent workforce, 13, 14, 112, 113–14, 116, 206
Cooper, Cary, 89
cooperative education programs, 222, 255–57
Cordell, Arthur, 15
Coren, Stanley, 86
corporate profits, 12
Coupland, Douglas, 58, 76
"credentialism," 68
Crompton, Susan, 65
Csikszentmihalyi, Mihaly, 157, 158, 232

de-jobbing, 128
depression, workplace, 104–5
discrimination, age, 43–44
distribution of wealth in society, 15
downsizing
    effect on employees, 10, 17, 30–31, 50
    in U.S., 11–12
downtime, 79, 119–20, 215
Drucker, Peter, 14
Dryden, Ken, 243
Dunberry, Linda, 80

early boomers, 39, 48
    career advancement, 50
    career options, 48, 49
    concern for their children, 54–55
    financial expectations, 52
    in today's workplace, 51, 52, 53
    values, 41–42, 53
economy
    changes in people's perception of, 159–60
    global, 11, 177, 178, 262
education
    of adults, 188
    careers in, 184, 188
    of children, 16, 160, 221–23, 235–40, 241, 242, 243, 251–55
    cooperative, 222, 255–57
    late boomers and, 59
    liberal arts, 253–55
    lifelong, 180–82, 188, 204

partnerships with business, 222
post-boomers and, 68
specialist vs. generalist, 253–55
university vs. college, 252–53
"edutainment," careers in, 188
emotional intelligence, 257–60
Emotional Intelligence, 257
employee assistance programs, use of, 212
"Employees For Tomorrow" program, 222
employment. See also unemployment; work
    contract, new, 22–23, 53
    nonstandard, 13–14, 111–12
    standard, 118
End of Work, The, 14, 215
environment, careers in preserving, 189
Exec-U-Net, 43, 44, 174

Family and Work Institute, 86, 244
feedback from managers, 229–30
finances, personal, 190–93
financial planners, 190
"First Jobs" initiative, 216
"5 Ws," the, 148–53
flow, state of, 157–58
Flow: The Psychology of Optimal Experience, 158, 232
Foot, David, 38
Ford, Henry, 217
Ford, William, 238
Freud, Sigmund, 161

Generation X, 39, 58. See also late boomers
"George Factor, the," 211
global economy, 11, 177, 178, 262
Goldsmith, Sir James, 11
Goleman, Daniel, 257
Grove, Andy, 110

Handy, Charles, 118
health care, careers in, 187–88
Heart Aroused, The, 102
Higgins, Chris, 80
home-based businesses, 190, 191, 244

Index

Home-Douglas, Pierre, 18
home offices, 82
homework, 243
Hornstein, Harley, 19
Howe, Neil, 39
Hunnicut, Benjamin, 215

Ide, T. Ran, 15
identity, challenges to, 29–35
income
    decline of, 113–14
    median household, 16
    median U.S., 15
    supplementing regular, 191
Industrial Revolution, 10
International Data Corp., 81
Internet, 179, 181, 236
internships, 217

Japan, 88
job(s), 127–28. *See also* careers; employment;
        work
    catalogs, 127
    location, 152–53
    market, 33, 183
    security, loss of, 6, 12, 30, 31, 183–84
    titles, 185
    training, 10
    transfers, 166
Job Shift, 128
just-in-time workers, 112

Karoshi, 88
Kettle, John, 131
knowledge workers, 14, 16, 82, 123–25

labor market projections, 183, 184
language, learning a foreign, 178–79, 261–62
late boomers, 39, 58
    career advancement, 59, 60, 62
    career expectations, 60, 61
    career options, 59, 62–63
    childhood, 58–59

education, 59
home ownership, 62
opinion of early boomers, 61–62
values, 63, 219
law, careers in, 67, 184–85, 254
learning, lifelong, 180–82, 204
*Learning About Schools: What Parents Need to
        Know and Where to Find Out*, 238
loyalty, 228

managers
    abuse of employees by, 19
    lack of positive feedback from, 83–84
    language of, 25, 27, 227
    loyalty to staff, 34, 228
    provision of career support to staff, 226–33
Manpower, 113
marketability, 170–77, 178, 205
medicine, careers in, 187–88
Medoff, James, 13
mentors, 196, 208, 209
Merck Family Fund, 104
Michie, Susan, 89
middle class, 16
Mills, C. Wright, 45
Money Tree Myth, The, 264
morale, maintaining, 229
multiple job holders, 115

Netscape, 82
networking, 172–75
"New Tools: Implications for the Future of
        Work, The," 15
Nohria, Nitin, 11

office organization, new approach to, 133–34
Olsen Forum on Information Management, 210
Only the Paranoid Survive, 110
Optimistic Child, The, 260
Organizational Man, The, 22, 41
organizations
    career intelligence used by, 202
    career support for staff, 207–9

development of life-friendly culture, 209–11, 213–14
distribution of work in, 215–16
education of staff about new work realities, 203–4
extending of resources to community, 221–23
hiring of young workers, 216–20
human resource systems and processes, 206
new employment contract and, 22, 23, 24, 31–32, 204
provision of opportunities for respite and reflection, 214–15
reduction of core workforce, 112–13, 116–17
re-engineering in, 28–29
retirement process, 223–26
self-assessment process, 206–7
succession plans, 142
support for training, 204–5
supporting staff in balancing work and personal life, 212–14
technological transformation and, 11
temporary staff, reliance on, 116
treatment of employees, 5–6, 12, 23, 31, 51, 83–84, 203
treatment of suppliers, 203
workplace depression in, 105
outsourcing, 13
overseas workers, 11
overwork, 86, 88, 95. *See also* busyness
effects of, 88–89, 198
in organizations, 209–11
Overworked American, The, 79

parental leave, 213
part-time work, 114, 115
drawbacks of, 114, 117
positive aspects of, 117
part-time workers
fears of, 210
improving benefits for, 206

Pascale, Richard, 12
pension plans, 122
personal life
balancing work and, 63, 96, 198–99, 212–14, 263
effect of new economy on, 85, 86–87
personal services, careers in, 189
portfolio, career, 147–48, 230
post-boomers, 39
balancing of work and personal life, 71
career advancement, 64
career expectations, 65, 66, 67–68, 69
childhood, 64, 72
and making the "right" career decision, 70–71
skills, importance of acquiring, 74
in today's workplace, 64, 69
values, 67, 70, 219
view of organizations, 72, 73, 219
view of work, 73, 218
pre-boomers, 39, 40
career options, 41
and self-promotion, 46
"status panic" among, 45
in today's workplace, 42–43, 45, 46, 47
unemployment among, 44, 45
values, 41, 42
"presenteeism," 89
private schools, 16
productivity, 212
project work, 128
finding the right, 130–31
managers, 208
teams, 128–29, 180

Quindlen, Anna, 87

recreation, careers in, 189
re-engineering, 28–29, 30, 50, 87–88
Reich, Robert, 14
relocating, 123–25, 166, 178
retirement, 13, 121–23, 223–26
Rifkin, Jeremy, 14, 215

Index

Robin, Vicki, 193
roles vs. job titles, 185–86
Royal Bank of Canada survey, 188
Rushwin, Shamel, 114
Ryan, Alan, 21

safety net of public sector social programs, 7
schools, 237–38, 241. *See also* universities and
    colleges
Schor, Juliet, 79
self-assessment process, 206–7
self-employment, 44, 146
self-knowledge, 145–58
self-promotion, 33–34, 46, 131, 175–77
Seligman, Martin, 260
Sha, Jim, 82
skill(s)
    communication, 179–80
    general, 150, 195
    knowledge work, 161–62
    marketability of, 171–72
    obsolescence of, 119, 131–32
    reconfiguring of, 121
    required to work in project environment,
        129–30
    self-management, 186–87
    technical, 150, 195
    upgrading of, 180–82
Social Security Act, 122
Solow, Robert, 7
speed, importance of in new economy,
    81–82, 197
Spence, Larry, xiii
stamina, importance of in new economy,
    76–77, 129
"State of Re-Engineering Report," 28–29
Steinhauer, Dr. Paul, 244
Stevenson, Howard H., 31
stock options, 183
Strauss, William, 39
stress
    levels in children, 238–40
    in workplace, 79, 92–93, 202, 212

succession planning, 142

teaching profession, careers in, 184, 188
teamwork, 35, 128–29, 133, 180, 228
technology
    and nature of work, 10–11
    new, 180
telecommuting, 210
temporary workers. *See* contingent workforce
TempWorld, 111, 142
    manifesto, 132
Thomson, Kenneth, 23
time management, 196–99
Tobia, Randall L., 213
Topel, Robert, 11
Trap, The, 11
travel, business, 79
trends, 182–83, 187, 190, 250
"Type A" behavior, 77

unemployment
    in legal profession, 184, 254
    among middle-aged workers, 12–13, 43, 44
    in teaching profession, 184
    among young workers, 13, 65
universities and colleges
    comparison of, 252–53
    "co-op" educational programs, 217
    failure to meet job market demands, 13,
        254
    value of degree from, 65, 68, 251
unpredictability of workplace, 30–31
U.S. Bureau of Labor Statistics, 65, 114

vacations, importance of taking, 211
values, 97, 103, 104, 151–52, 159–60, 165,
    167, 192, 231, 265
Vaz-Oxlade, Gail, 264
virtual office, 132–34
vocational tests, 248–49
"Voluntary Simplicity" movement, 191

wages. *See* income

wealth, distribution of, 15
weekends, 198
Whyte, David, 102
Whyte, William, 22, 41
work. *See also* careers; employment; job(s);
    project work
  and emotional well-being, 89, 102
  finding, 125, 126, 130–31
  full-time, 13, 118
  in the future, 79, 111–12, 120–21, 133
  human need to, 24
  pace of, 153
  part-time, 114, 115, 117
  redistribution of, 215–16
  round-the-clock, 82
  and self-worth, 26, 78, 120
  as source of social identity, 34, 78
  temporary, 111, 113, 114
workaholism, 77
workforce
  anxiety about future, 17, 28, 29, 30
  career advancement, 51
  "commodification" of self by, 33–34, 127

contingent, 13, 14, 112, 113–14, 116, 206
core, 112, 118
demands made of, 17–18, 20, 85, 197, 200
multiple job holders in, 115
and new employment contract, 22–23, 24
older workers in, 43–44
social interaction of, 35
working hours of, 18, 80, 81, 89, 104, 197
workloads of, 75, 76, 80
young workers in, 216–20
workplace
  changes in, 5–7, 17, 28, 35, 81, 120, 133
  competition in, 110, 126–27
  depression in, 104–5
  life-friendly, 202, 209–11, 213–14
  loss of civility in, 84–85, 229
  loss of sense of connection to, 35–36, 102
  stress in, 79, 88, 92–93, 202
  unpredictability of, 30–31
  unprotected, 31–32, 110
work week, shorter, 215–16

Your Money or Your Life, 193

About the Author

Dr. Barbara Moses, North America's leading expert in career self-management, is the author of the acclaimed *Career Planning Workbook* and *Manager's Career Coaching Guide*.

A sought-after keynote speaker for senior business and professional audiences, she is consistently praised for her insight into contemporary issues, her knowledge of the new work and personal realities, and her stimulating and compelling delivery. Her innovative approach to career self-management has been reported on extensively in numerous publications across North America and abroad. Her articles have appeared in the *Globe and Mail, Journal of the American Society for Training and Development, LOMA Magazine, HR Professional, The Human Resource, Canadian Banker, CA Magazine, Financial Post Magazine,* and elsewhere. She has appeared frequently on radio and TV.

Dr. Moses holds degrees in psychology from McGill University, The London School of Economics, and the University of Toronto. She lives in Toronto with her husband, writer Andrew Weiner, and her son.

Clients: More than 1,000 organizations worldwide in every sector of the economy, including Four Seasons Hotels, Northern Telecom, Coopers & Lybrand, Exxon, Ernst & Young, Rhone Poulenc, Occidental Petroleum, the St. Paul Companies, Fluor Daniel, Liberty Mutual, Bell-Northern Research, Stentor, Royal Bank, Merrill Lynch, CIBC, Dofasco, Delta Hotels, Consumers Gas, Zurich Insurance, Levi Strauss, Apple, Oryx Energy, Bell Canada, Crown Life, Sears, Harris Bank, Wal-Mart, Toronto Stock Exchange, the Globe and Mail, Toyota, Bank of Montreal and

Abbott Laboratories, along with numerous government agencies, hospitals, and school boards.

CAREER DEVELOPMENT PROGRAMS FROM BBM HUMAN RESOURCE CONSULTANTS

The most pressing issues facing individuals and organizations today are self-management, managing change, employability, and learning for the future. Dr. Moses' firm, BBM Human Resource Consultants, provides proven interventions to prepare staff at all levels to meet these challenges and thrive in the new knowledge economy.

BBM shows organizations and individuals buffeted by change how to respond to the new career and work realities – promoting self-reliance and adaptation to change, managing work and personal life, motivating different demographic groups, advancing continuous learning, mentoring, and fostering renewal and revitalization. Over the past decade, BBM has helped over 1,000 organizations worldwide deliver career development and career self-management programs. BBM is a full-service firm, providing career planning materials, workshops, and consulting support. With its head office in Toronto, BBM has representative offices in New York; Chicago; Kansas City; Montreal; Calgary; Ottawa; Vancouver; Auckland; New Zealand; and London, England.

Career Planning Workbook

A corporate bestseller, the *Career Planning Workbook* has helped close to a million people manage their careers in the light of the new work and personal realities. It is a highly user-friendly, innovative, and cost-effective approach to providing comprehensive and practical career planning guidance.

Completing the *Career Planning Workbook* is like having your own personal career coach and counselor. Through a series of easy-to-complete self-assessment instruments, people identify core strengths and competencies, their unique profile of personal work style and preferences, and how to balance work and personal life, among other issues.

A highly flexible tool, the Workbook can be used on a self-study basis or in workshops, and is available in two editions – managerial/professional and clerical/technical – to provide professional quality career planning support to all staff.

Manager's Career Coaching Guide

This companion piece to the *Career Planning Workbook* prepares managers for their crucial role in developing and counseling staff, providing information and how-to advice on the new employment contract at work, coaching concerns, burnout, plateauing, managing Generation X, and other common career issues.

Workshops

All BBM workshops are built around the *Career Planning Workbook*. We offer a range of workshops for different employee groups, including:

- Executive Overview
- Personal Career Self-Management Workshops
- Managers' Career Planning & Coaching Workshop
- Train-the-Trainer to Implement Career Self-Management

Keynote Speeches by Dr. Barbara Moses

Extraordinary changes in the workplace have transformed the fundamental relationship between the individual and the organization. How do we have a sense of career, when everything we have been socialized to believe to be true is no longer true? In her lucid, compelling speeches, Dr. Moses provides insight into the new work and personal realities, along with practical strategies for dealing with them. Speeches are tailored to meet the needs and interests of different audiences, including managers, individual contributors, early career professionals, women, and so on.

For more information on services from BBM Human Resource Consultants, visit our web site at:

http://www.BBMcareerdev.com

Berrett-Koehler Publishers

BERRETT-KOEHLER is an independent publisher of books, periodicals, and other publications at the leading edge of new thinking and innovative practice on work, business, management, leadership, stewardship, career development, human resources, entrepreneurship, and global sustainability.

Since the company's founding in 1992, we have been committed to supporting the movement toward a more enlightened world of work by publishing books, periodicals, and other publications that help us to integrate our values with our work and work lives, and to create more humane and effective organizations.

We have chosen to focus on the areas of work, business, and organizations, because these are central elements in many people's lives today. Furthermore, the work world is going through tumultuous changes, from the decline of job security to the rise of new structures for organizing people and work. We believe that change is needed at all levels— individual, organizational, community, and global—and our publications address each of these levels.

We seek to create new lenses for understanding organizations, to legitimize topics that people care deeply about but that current business orthodoxy censors or considers secondary to bottom-line concerns, and to uncover new meaning, means, and ends for our work and work lives.

See next page for other books from Berrett-Koehler Publishers

Other leading-edge business books from Berrett-Koehler Publishers

The Power of Purpose
Creating Meaning in Your Life and Work
Richard J. Leider

WE ALL POSSESS a unique ability to do the work we were made for. Concise and easy to read, and including numerous stories of people living on purpose, *The Power of Purpose* is a a remarkable tool to help you find your calling, an original guide to discovering the work you love to do.

Hardcover, 170 pages, 9/97 • ISBN 1-57675-021-3 CIP • **Item no. 50213-252 $20.00**

Repacking Your Bags
Lighten Your Load for the Rest of Your Life
Richard J. Leider and David A. Shapiro

LEARN HOW to climb out from under the many burdens you're carrying and find the fulfillment that's missing in your life. A simple yet elegant process teaches you to balance the demands of work, love, and place in order to create and live your own vision of success.

Paperback, 234 pages, 2/96 • ISBN 1-881052-87-7 CIP
Item no. 52877-252 $14.95

Hardcover, 1/95 • ISBN 1-881052-67-2 CIP • **Item no. 52672-252 $21.95**

How to Get Ideas
Jack Foster
Illustrated by Larry Corby

IN *HOW TO GET IDEAS*, Jack Foster draws on three decades of experience as an advertising writer and creative director to take the mystery and anxiety out of getting ideas. Describing eight ways to condition your mind to produce ideas and five subsequent steps for creating and implementing ideas on command, he makes it easy, fun, and understandable.

Paperback, 150 pages, 11/96 • ISBN 1-57675-006-X CIP
Item no. 5006X-252 $14.95

Available at your favorite bookstore, or call (800) 929-2929

Put the leading-edge business practices you read about to use in your work and in your organization

DO YOU EVER WISH there was a forum in your organization for discussing the newest trends and ideas in the business world? Do you wish you could explore the leading-edge business practices you read about with others in your company? Do you wish you could set aside a few hours every month to connect with like-minded coworkers or to get to know others in your business community?

If you answered yes to any of these questions, then the answer is simple: Start a business book reading group in your organization or business community. For step-by-step advice on how to do just that, visit the Berrett-Koehler website at <www.bkpub.com> and click on "Business Literacy 2000." There you'll find specific guidelines to help in all aspects of creating a successful reading group—from locating interested participants to selecting books, and facilitating discussions.

The website is part of the Business Literacy 2000 program launched by the Consortium for Business Literacy—a group of 19 business book publishers whose primary goal has been to promote the formation of business reading groups within corporations and business communities.

Business Literacy 2000 is dedicated to providing you with tools to help you build a dialog with others in your company or business community, share ideas, build lasting relationships, and bring new ideas and knowledge to bear in your work and organizations. On our website, you'll find guidelines for starting and running a reading group, suggested readings, study guides, and activities to help ensure lively and useful discussions.

For more information on Business Literacy 2000, guidelines for starting a business book reading group, or copies of any of our study guides, please visit our website at: <www.bkpub.com>.

If you do not have Internet access, you may request information by contacting us at:

Berrett-Koehler Publishers
450 Sansome St., Suite 1200
San Francisco, CA 94111
Fax: (415) 362-2512
Email: bkpub@bkpub.com

Please be sure to include your name, address, phone number, email address, and the information you would like to receive.

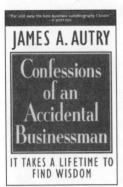

Confessions of an Accidental Businessman

It Takes a Lifetime to Find Wisdom

James A. Autry

I N *CONFESSIONS OF AN ACCIDENTAL BUSINESSMAN,* bestselling author James Autry blends candid and engaging autobiography with practical and realistic lessons in management and leadership. Reflecting on his thirty-two years in business, Autry shares a lifetime of hard-earned wisdom about the art of business leadership, as well as the art of living a balanced life.

Hardcover, 250 pages, 10/96 • ISBN 1-57675-003 CIP
Item no. 75003-252 $24.95

The 4 Routes to Entrepreneurial Success

John B. Miner

J OHN MINER details four personality types that characterize successful entrepreneurs—Personal Achievers, Super-salespeople, Real Managers, and Expert Idea Generators —then shows you how to use this information to map out your own path to success.

Paperback, 280 pages, 9/96 • ISBN 1-881052-82-6 CIP
Item no. 52826-252 $18.95

The Joy of Working from Home

Making a Life While Making a Living

Jeff Berner

D O YOU WORK AT HOME, or just dream about it? Jeff Berner shows the current or prospective home-office worker how to set up an efficient home office and provides the support for making this major life change. Both pragmatic and inspiring, *The Joy of Working from Home* tells how to make a living *and* a life.

Paperback, 240 pages, 7/94 • ISBN - 1-881052-46-X CIP
Item no. 5246X-252 $12.95

Available at your favorite bookstore, or call (800) 929-2929